CUSTODIANS

OF TRUTH

12⁵⁰

Tim Wallace-Murphy giving a talk on the Knights Templar
at Castello Visconti, Somma Lombardo, Varese
(with the Visconti Arms in the background).

CUSTODIANS OF TRUTH

THE CONTINUANCE OF REX DEUS

TIM WALLACE-MURPHY AND MARILYN HOPKINS

WEISER BOOKS
Boston, MA/York Beach, ME

First published in 2005 by
Red Wheel/Weiser, LLC
York Beach, ME
With offices at:
368 Congress Street
Boston, MA 02210
www.redwheelweiser.com

Library of Congress Cataloging-in-Publication Data

Wallace-Murphy, Tim.
    Custodians of truth : the continuance of Rex Deus / Tim Wallace-
Murphy and Marilyn Hopkins.
        p. cm.
    Includes bibliographical references and index.
    ISBN 1-57863-323-0
        1. Mysticism—Egypt. 2. Gnosticism 3. Pyramid texts. 4. Jesus
Christ—Miscellanea. I. Hopkins, Marilyn, 1950– II. Title.
    BL2443.W35 2005
    001.94—dc22   2005002432

Typeset in Bembo (text) and Caslon Antique, Exocet, and Mason Serif
(display).

Printed in Canada, TCP

12 11 10 09 08 07 06 05
8 7 6 5 4 3 2 1

This work is respectfully dedicated to
A warm and wonderful man
Whose support for our work
Has been crucial—
Our spiritual brother,
Pat Sibille, late of Louisiana,
Now of Aberdeen.

CONTENTS

ACKNOWLEDGMENTS

No work such as this is ever produced without the help, encouragement, and support of a large number of people. Responsibility for the book rests entirely with the authors, but we gratefully acknowledge the assistance received from: Stuart Beattie of the Rosslyn Chapel Trust; Richard Beaumont of Staverton, Devon; Laurence Bloom of London; Andy Boracci of Sag Harbor, New York; Robert Brydon of Edinburgh; Richard Buades of Marseilles; Nicole Dawe of Okehampton; Baroness Edni di Pauli of London; William and Heather Elmhirst of Dartington; Jean-Michel Garnier of Chartres; Michael Halsey of Auchterarder; Guy Jourdan of Bargemon; Patrick Keane of Paignton; Georges Keiss of the Centre d'Etudes et de Recherches Templière, Campagne-sur-Aude; Robert Lomas of Bradford; Michael Monkton of Buckingham; Dr. Hugh Montgomery of Somerset; James Mackay Munro of Penicuick; Andrew Pattison of Edinburgh; Stella Pates of Ottery St. Mary; Alan Pearson of Rennes-les-Bains; David Pykett of Burton-on-Trent; Amy Ralston of Staverton, Devon; Victor Rosati of Totnes; Pat Sibille of Aberdeen; Niven Sinclair of London; Prince Michael of Albany; and, last, but certainly not least, Michael Kerber, Michael Conlon, and Kate Hartke, and all at RedWheel/Weiser.

INTRODUCTION

In 1994, at the end of a talk on Rosslyn Chapel, a middle-aged Englishman approached Tim and introduced himself as Michael. The conversation turned to esoteric symbolism, a subject of which Michael displayed a deep understanding. When asked where he had gained this level of insight, he replied, "From the secret traditions of my family, which have been preserved for over two thousand years." Intrigued, Tim questioned him further. Michael claimed, and later was able to prove, that he was a direct descendant of the family of Hughes de Payen, a founder of the Knights Templar and the order's first Grand Master. Tim and Michael met again over the next several weeks and, during the course of their discussions, the following story emerged.

In 1982, Henry Lincoln, Michael Baigent, and Richard Leigh first published *The Holy Blood and the Holy Grail*,[1] a book that infuriated Christians of every stripe with its claim that Jesus married and founded a dynasty. While most readers accepted Lincoln's research without question, a small number subjected it to close scrutiny and analysis—with devastating results. One BBC television program, *The History of a Mystery*,[2] condemned the book as a mixture of fact, fantasy, and outright fabrication. Yet Margaret Starbird, an American theologian intent on refuting this heresy, courageously wrote a book confirming the marriage of Jesus.[3] Several others followed, tracing the dynasty down to our own times.[4]

When Michael first read *The Holy Blood and the Holy Grail,* he was relieved. The book, he felt, released him from a sacred oath of secrecy. Michael claimed he was a member of a widespread group of elect families whose traditions identify them as descendants of the Davidic and Hasmonean royal families of biblical Israel, and of the twenty-four families that were the hereditary high priests of the Temple of Jerusalem at the time of Jesus. This tradition was passed down within the families through either the eldest child or the one showing the highest level of spiritual awareness. The children chosen to receive and transmit this tradition were carefully instructed and made to swear the following, if they disclosed their secret to any outsider: "May my heart be torn out or my throat be cut." With the publication of *The Holy Blood and the Holy Grail,* however, Michael felt it was safe to share his secret.

The families in Michael's story, who came to be known as the *Rex Deus,* originally had their genealogies inscribed on the walls of certain rooms under the Temple of Jerusalem. After its destruction, the Rex Deus families fled to a variety of destinations, but were enjoined by sacred oath to keep the tradition alive. Each family was under obligation to keep an accurate genealogy from generation to generation. They were also bound by their sacred duty to restrict their marital alliances to other members of the family group, in the manner of the Cohenite priesthood of ancient Israel.

Michael's story was bizarre, but he seemed rational, well balanced, and completely sincere. Tim decided to investigate his claims in great depth, for, if the story were true, it would explain many of the enigmas of medieval history. It might even help explain certain puzzling episodes in the medieval era and provide an understanding of the links between outbreaks of heresy in different parts of Europe.

Michael recounted a fascinating tale. Prior to the time of Jesus, he claimed, the Temple of Jerusalem maintained two boarding schools staffed by high priests—one for boys and one for girls. Male graduates were destined to become high priests, rabbis, or leaders of Israel. All the pupils at both schools were drawn from the tribe of Levi, the hereditary priesthood of biblical times. The twenty-four *ma'-madot,* or high priests, who taught at the temple schools were the hereditary leaders of the Jewish religion. They were the only people permitted to enter the Holy of Holies in the temple and, on ceremonial occasions, to stand in ascending order of rank on the temple steps. They were ritually named according to their rank; for example, Melchizadek, Michael, and Gabriel.

These little-known schools had strange traditions. The high priests were not only responsible for administration and teaching, but for impregnating the female pupils when they reached puberty. Once the girls' pregnancies were established, they were married into the leading families of Israel. Children born of these ritual unions would, at the age of seven, be returned to the temple school for education. This further preserved the hereditary nature of the high priesthood and ensured that the sacred bloodlines remained pure and unsullied.

One pupil at the girls' school was Miriam, or Mary as she is known to history, the daughter of an earlier pupil named Anne. The high priest Gabriel impregnated Mary and, when her pregnancy was confirmed, arranged a marriage for her.

Mary rejected the first man chosen for her and finally accepted a young man of Davidic descent, Joseph of Tyre, whose ancestor was Hiram of Tyre, known to Masonic legend as Hiram Abif. This wealthy young man is known in Christian tradition as St. Joseph. The child of the union of Miriam and the priest Gabriel was Jesus who, after spending the years of his early childhood in Egypt, returned to Jerusalem and, in his turn, attended the temple school.

There are gaps in the historical record, however, and in Michael's story as well. In fact, Michael moved abruptly from his account of events at the time of Jesus to those occurring sometime in the 4th century c.e. It was only then that it was deemed safe enough for members of the Rex Deus families to return to Jerusalem and rebury the body of the Messiah in the one place no one would ever dream of looking for it—the Temple Mount, a place considered inviolable in Jewish custom and therefore forbidden as a place of burial. We can easily understand how this site ensured the safekeeping of the body of the Messiah. What is more difficult to understand is what would have impelled families who sprang from the most orthodox branch of Judaism to contravene the prohibition of burial on the Temple Mount.

After the 4th century, the Rex Deus families continued to live in Western Europe. Their traditions dictated that they outwardly

Statue of Mary and Jesus
(or perhaps the Magdalene and child), Rennes-le-Chateau.

Statue of Joseph and the baby Jesus
(or perhaps Jesus and child), Rennes-le-Chateau.

profess to follow the prevailing religion of the time and culture in which they lived, but that secretly they were bound by oath to follow the "true way."

Quietly and sincerely, Michael told Tim that he was a descendant of Hughes de Payen and that, as such and due to intermarriage, his family had, until recently, held a hereditary court appointment in England. Michael mentioned Rex Deus connections with certain important families in Byzantium, the eastern Roman Empire founded by Constantine the Great in 330 C.E. He also spoke at length of the symbolism employed by this secretive group and stressed that their heraldic colors were green and gold.

Based on these conversations, Tim constructed a "Rex Deus hypothesis," which he then began to test against the historical record of the medieval era. The new hypothesis worked well and provided a series of explanations for many otherwise insoluble puzzles. For example: Why were the Knights Templar founded only after King Baldwin II succeeded to the throne of Jerusalem? How did they know where to dig under the Temple Mount? Why did certain families seem to weave a web of tight-knit political and marital alliances right across Europe, which, if judged by any other criteria, defied logic and common sense? Not only did the Rex Deus tradition provide rational answers to some of these anomalies, it also pointed the way to documentary proof of otherwise misty episodes in the past.

After many years of research and several more interviews with Michael, we wrote the book *Rex Deus*, filling in the gaps in his story with our knowledge of European and biblical history. The part of the story that we believed would be hardest to substantiate—the existence of the schools attached to the Jerusalem Temple and Mary's attendance at the girl's school—proved, to our intense amazement, to be the easiest to corroborate. The book was completed and published in March 2000.

Some weeks after our book was published, we received a letter on impressively headed notepaper that contained the following, worrying phrase:

> . . . before you rushed so precipitately into print, it would have
> been better if you had contacted me first to verify some of your
> allegations. We should talk, or better yet, meet.

Rex Deus symbolism of the serpent of wisdom,
Castello Visconti, Somma Lombardo, Varese, northern Italy.

Tim phoned the author of the letter, introduced himself, and asked: Where did we get it wrong? The answer was surprising: You didn't, dear boy, it's just incomplete—do you want the rest?

We spent the next three years checking on the information our mysterious correspondent gave us. We studied the Pyramid Texts, Dead Sea Scrolls, the Nag-Hamadi scrolls, and much of European and Middle Eastern history from the time of Jesus to the Renaissance. The conclusions we reached will be profoundly upsetting to people of all Christian faiths. We found, quite simply, that the Christian church distorted the true teachings of Jesus and maintained its power by suppressing the truth, deliberately inculcating guilt and practicing repression, torture, and genocide. The real heroes of history, we found, are the Rex Deus families in both the Christian and Islamic worlds, whose message of true monotheism, tolerance, brotherhood, and respect for nature is as relevant today as it has ever been.

This book presents an extended account of the history of the Rex Deus families, reaching back to their earliest demonstrable roots and forward over millennia to the present day. It describes how these families were, from their earliest beginnings, regarded as heretics and unbelievers, as they still are by the Church. As the story unfolds, however, you will discover that the Rex Deus families deserve the far more accurate title of Custodians of Truth.

CHAPTER 1

Tep Zepi—The Origin of Egyptian Gnosis

The search for the true roots of the Rex Deus tradition begins in ancient Egypt, where we find the earliest demonstrable source of a sustained system of initiation preserved by a hereditary priesthood. This tradition passed its teachings down to the world's three major religions: Judaism, Christianity, and Islam.

The discovery and accurate translation of the Pyramid Texts was a major turning point in our understanding of ancient Egyptian history. These texts not only led to a deeper appreciation of the antiquity of Egyptian religious thought, but also cast doubt on the widely held theory that the pyramids were built solely as tombs celebrating the pomp and power of the pharaohs. In the Pyramid Texts, these previously silent tombs had at last spoken.

The Pyramid Texts

In the winter of 1879, a rumor began to circulate in Egyptian archaeological circles of an amazing new and seemingly accidental discovery of enormous importance—one apparently brought about by an earthly incarnation of the god Anubis. Among the ancient Egyptians, Anubis was a deified form of the jackal known as the Desert Fox; his other divine incarnation was as Upuaut, also known as the Opener of the Ways.

Standing near the pyramid of Unas at Saqqara, an Arab workman spotted a desert fox silhouetted against the light of the rising Sun.

The animal behaved rather strangely. It moved, stopped, and looked about as if inviting its silent observer to follow it. Then the animal moved again before disappearing into a large crevice in the north face of the pyramid. Scenting possible treasure, the workman followed and, after a difficult crawl, found himself in a large chamber within the pyramid.[1] Lighting his torch, he saw that the walls of the chamber were covered with hieroglyphic inscriptions superbly decorated with turquoise and gold.[2] Similar inscriptions were later found in other pyramids and, collectively, they are now known as the Pyramid Texts.[3] In total, over 4,000 lines of hymns and formulae have been found.

Professor Gaston Maspero, Director of the Egyptian Antiquities Service, was the first European to explore the interior of the pyramid of Unas[4] and view the texts *in situ*, on 28 February 1881. For him and the world of Egyptology, the modern four-legged incarnation of Upuaut had opened the way, both literally and figuratively. The discovery of the Pyramid Texts, in turn, played its part in opening the way to a more profound understanding of the spiritual beliefs at the time of Unas, as well as to an important understanding of the great depth that sacred knowledge or gnosis had attained in remote antiquity when the texts were actually composed.

Confusion, controversy, and dispute marred the first hurried interpretation of the texts by Gaston Maspero.[5] This, unfortunately, masked their true importance for decades—a situation compounded by a later translator, leading Egyptologist James Henry Breasted, who mistakenly described the texts as expressions of a solar cult.[6]

Gaston Maspero claimed that most of the texts were written versions of a far older tradition dating back to Egypt's prehistoric past,[7] arguing that they predated the events described in the Book of Exodus by at least two millennia, and the writing of the New Testament by nearly 3,400 years.[8] Professor I. E. S. Edwards of the British Museum confirmed this when he stated unequivocally: "The Pyramid Texts were certainly not inventions of the Vth or VIth dynasties, but had originated in extreme antiquity; it is hardly surprising, therefore, that they sometimes contain allusions to conditions which no longer prevailed at the time of Unas . . ."[9] Thus, in the opinion of two of Egyptology's greatest authorities, the Pyramid Texts are without doubt the oldest collection of religious writings ever discovered.

The world had to wait nearly ninety years for the first definitive translation of the texts. In 1969, Raymond Faulkner, professor of ancient Egyptian language at University College, London, published what is now accepted by most scholars as the authoritative version. In it, he concluded: "The Pyramid Texts constitute the oldest corpus of Egyptian religious and funerary literature now extant."[10] As a result of his translation, these texts are now accepted to be the earliest collection of sacred knowledge, or "esoteric wisdom," yet to be found.

The esoteric content of the texts only became apparent after the publication of Faulkner's translation, which clearly demonstrates that a highly complex and well-developed stellar cult is being described—one in which, after his death, the deceased pharaoh ascended to heaven and was ritually reunited with the stars.

TEP ZEPI—THE FIRST TIME

The Pyramid Texts make repeated reference to Tep Zepi, the so-called First Time, the legendary time of Osiris when Egypt was believed to have been ruled directly by the gods in human form. These gods, according to legend, gave the Egyptians the wondrous gift of sacred knowledge. The texts also disclose a complex, profound, and uncannily accurate knowledge of astronomy. How did this highly sophisticated level of astronomical knowledge arise in prehistoric Egypt when the texts were first composed without any evidence of a developmental period? And when was the First Time and where did it occur?

One noted modern author, John Anthony West, provides a possible answer to the first question:

> Every aspect of Egyptian knowledge seems to have been complete at the very beginning. The sciences, artistic and architectural techniques and the hieroglyphic system show virtually no signs of "development"; indeed many of the achievements of the earliest dynasties were never surpassed or even equalled later on. . . . The answer to the mystery is, of course, obvious, but because it is repellent to the prevailing cast of modern thinking, it is seldom seriously considered. Egyptian civilisation was not a development, it was a legacy.[11]

If these complex levels of knowledge were, in fact, a legacy, whose legacy were they? Nothing in nature or in history arises in a vacuum. As there is no extant evidence indicating any form of developmental period in Egyptian history, then the obvious conclusion is that this knowledge was either acquired and developed elsewhere or derived from a much earlier and as yet undiscovered civilization that flourished in Egypt itself. The latter idea is a viable possibility, as there are vast areas of Egypt yet to be excavated—areas buried by the sands of the desert or rendered inaccessible by the sprawling suburbs of Cairo and other cities. It is the first possibility, however, that has received the most scholarly and speculative attention and aroused the most controversy.

A variety of theories have been advanced to explain the origin of the highly sophisticated levels of knowledge disclosed by the texts. They range from suggestions that they originated with the survivors of Atlantis, from an earlier but undiscovered Egyptian civilization, or, more likely, as the result of an invasion by a vastly superior culture—the so-called "dynastic race theory" that was first seriously proposed by the father of modern Egyptology, William Matthew Flinders Petrie. While the idea of a dominant race is repugnant to modern adherents of political correctness, we should not allow this to blind us to the fact that there often were races that dominated others in many historical eras.

Pre-dynastic Clues

In the 1893–94 archaeological season, excavations by Flinders Petrie and James Quibell at Nakada uncovered over 2,000 graves of the pre-dynastic period. The pottery and artefacts discovered in these graves showed clearly that they were from two distinct periods, which Petrie designated as Nakada I and Nakada II.[12] In the Nakada II graves, pottery fragments were found that were distinctly Mesopotamian in character.[13] In excavations of Nile Valley sites prior to this era, however, artefacts of foreign manufacture are virtually nonexistent.[14] Petrie also recorded finding lapis lazuli in the Nakada II tombs, the only instance of this exotic stone in sites of the pre-dynastic period. The stone is not found again until the era of the Old Kingdom over 600 years later. It was, however, highly prized and sought after in Mesopotamia prior to the time of the Nakada II interments in the Nile Valley.

The sudden appearance of other signs of Mesopotamian culture in Egypt at this time may also indicate the Mesopotamian origins of the so-called dynastic race. Depictions of the pear-shaped mace, the cylinder seal, remarkable brick architecture, and hieroglyphic writing are all claimed as evidence of the true origin of this sudden cultural transformation.[15] One of Flinders Petrie's pupils, Douglas Derry, was specific about the origins of this great leap forward when he wrote in 1956:

> It is also very suggestive of the presence of a dominant race,
> perhaps relatively few in numbers but greatly exceeding the
> original inhabitants in intelligence; a race which brought into
> Egypt the knowledge of building in stone, of sculpture, paint-
> ing, reliefs and above all writing; hence the enormous jump
> from the primitive pre-dynastic Egyptian to the advanced civil-
> isation of the Old Empire (the Old Kingdom.)[16]

Another of Petrie's pupils and protégés, Dutch Egyptologist and orientalist Henry Frankfort, describes the appearance of the cylinder seal in pre-dynastic Egypt as "... the strongest evidence of contact between Mesopotamia and Egypt."[17] The sudden appearance of evidence of this type of cross-cultural contact within Egyptian records, however, fails to explain the route by which such influences and artefacts arrived in the Nile Valley. Discoveries made by Arthur Weighall, inspector of antiquities for the Egyptian government from 1905 until 1914, may help to clarify this problem.

Weighall explored the desert region of Wadi Abbad in the eastern desert during March 1908. The wadi leads from the Nile Valley at the town of Edfu toward the Red Sea port of Mersa Alam. It contains the Temple of Kanais built by Seti I, father of Ramses the Great, in honor of the god Amun-Re. Weighall recorded graffiti carved in the rocks of the wadi depicting strange high-prowed boats. His ink drawings of these maritime inscriptions found in the middle of the desert were published the following year.[18] In the spring of 1936, Hans Winkler explored the nearby Wadi Hammamat and found another series of rock drawings similar to those found eighteen years earlier by Weighall. When he published his findings,[19] Winkler suggested that these drawings were of seafarers who had landed on the west coast of the Red Sea and crossed the desert en route to the Nile Valley. He described these seafarers as a "military expedition."[20]

Intrigued by these discoveries, the English Egyptologist David Rohl reinvestigated both Wadi Abbad and Wadi Hammamat before extending the search into Wadi Barramiya in 1997. In Wadi Barramiya, Rohl found more drawings of the high-prowed boats and suggested that there was a direct connection between the people whose voyage was recorded in this manner and the Nakada II graves excavated by Petrie.[21] Rohl was seeking evidence for the *Shemsa-Hor*, the followers of Horus, who, he believed, were the immediate ancestors of the first pharaohs.[22] The earliest surviving references to the followers of Horus occur in the Pyramid Texts,[23] which refer to a succession of priestly initiates who transmitted an extraordinary body of knowledge from master to pupil down through the generations. The origin of this knowledge lay in the mysterious "time of the Neteru,"—when the gods supposedly ruled Egypt immediately prior to the time of the earliest pharaohs. These initiates were not necessarily kings, but immensely powerful and enlightened individuals carefully selected by an elite academy that established itself at the sacred site of Heliopolis-Giza in the era of Egyptian prehistory.[24] Georges Goyon, one-time Egyptologist to King Farouk, claimed: "Giza was chosen by the priest-astronomers because of certain religious and scientific factors."[25]

ANCIENT ASTRONOMERS

We know that the scholars of the classical world, who had firsthand experience of the knowledge of the ancient Egyptians, were awestruck by the levels of sacred knowledge and wisdom shown by the Heliopolitan and Memphite priests. The ancient Greeks especially revered the astronomical science of the Egyptians.[26] Aristotle wrote that the Egyptians were astronomers with advanced levels of knowledge, "whose observations have been kept for many years past, and from whom much of our evidence about particular stars is derived."[27] Later in the fifth century C.E., Proclus Diodachus wrote: "Let those, who believe in observations, cause the stars to move around the poles of the zodiac by one degree in one hundred years towards the east, as Ptolemy and Hipparchus did before him know . . . that the Egyptians had already taught Plato about the movement of the fixed stars . . . ."[28] The modern authors Robert Bauval and Graham Hancock conclude:"The Heliopolitan priests were high initiates in the mysteries of the heavens and their dominant occupation was the observation and recording of the various motions of the sun and the moon, the planets and the stars,"[29] a view endorsed by Professor Edwards of the British Museum.[30] John Anthony West paraphrased the views of one leading scholar, Schwaller de Lubicz, when he stated that Egyptian science, medicine, mathematics, and astronomy were all of an exponentially higher order of refinement and sophistication than modern scholars will acknowledge, and that the whole of Egyptian civilization was based upon a complete and precise understanding of universal laws.[31]

SACRED GNOSIS

The incredibly sophisticated levels of gnosis attained through initiation were not used for personal gain by the priestly and royal initiates of the Egyptian temple mysteries. While rank and royal birth undoubtedly had their privileges, the sacred knowledge of subjects such as astronomy, agriculture, architecture, building, medicine, mathematics, navigation, and metallurgy were used for the benefit of the entire community. Protected by the desert that surrounded it and sustained by this divinely inspired gnosis, Egyptian civilization developed a stability and complexity that has never been exceeded. This vast body of esoteric knowledge was recorded, in part, in the Pyramid Texts, the Edfu Texts, and the Books of the Dead, as well as being encoded on temple walls and elsewhere. Speaking of the dualism that lay at the heart of Egyptian sacred knowledge, Bauval and Hancock wrote:"The language of all these texts is exotic, laden with the dualistic thinking that lay at the heart of Egyptian society and that may have been the engine of its greatest achievements."[32] The Edfu Texts constantly refer to what they call the "wisdom of the Sages" and repeatedly emphasize that their most valued gift was knowledge.[33]

Schwaller de Lubicz came to the conclusion that the ancient Egyptians had their own unique and effective way of understanding

the universe and man's place within it—a knowledge system completely different from that revered by modern man.[34] They used a
manner of knowing that could not be clearly transmitted by normal
analytical language, but only through myth and symbolism.[35]
Schwaller began his own work on symbols and symbolism by restat-
ing that there are always two distinct ways of interpreting Egyptian
religious texts—the exoteric and the esoteric. The exoteric meaning forms the basis for the standard interpretation, which can be
arrived at by the study of the appropriate textbooks on religion and
history. It also serves as a vehicle for the hidden, or esoteric, meaning, which Schwaller described as the *symbolique* interpretation.[36]
He claimed that this form of esoteric knowledge had generally long
been forgotten, but its symbolic remnants were transmitted, in one
form or another, to all the great religions that sprang from Egyptian
roots.[37]

La Symbolique

Symbols and hieroglyphs evoke far more complex responses than
can ever be achieved by words, no matter how beautifully written.
Those familiar with the works of the modern initiate Rudolf Steiner,
or those who have studied the artefacts created by the medieval
craftmasons or immersed themselves in Egyptology will know the
truth of this from their own experience. The hardheaded, modern
writers Pauwels and Bergier commented insightfully on exactly this
aspect of ancient symbolism and the initiates who used it:

> They . . . wrote in stone their hermetic message. Signs, incom-
> prehensible to men whose consciousness had not undergone
> transmutations . . . These men were not secretive because they
> loved secrecy, but simply because their discoveries about the
> Laws of Energy, of matter and of the mind had been made in
> another state of consciousness and so could not be communi-
> cated directly.[38]

The ancient Egyptian initiates were not the only ones who used
symbols in this manner; this form of communication has been used
by the sages and initiates of all the world's great religious traditions,
from antiquity to the present. Nor did the ancient Egyptians restrict

their use of symbolism to matters of religion and knowledge, which at that time were synonymous or regarded as different aspects of the same reality. They also used it to reinforce the divine origin, power, and lineal descent of the pharaohs.

For millennia, depictions of the pharaohs showed them wearing the crown of both Upper and Lower Egypt. Clearly defined on the front of this formal headdress are the well-known twin symbols of the heads of a falcon and cobra. The falcon's head signified the pharaoh's incarnation as the living embodiment of Horus, while the cobra's head had two linked, but different, interpretations—one as the seat of wisdom and the other as a symbol of divine ancestry. Moreover, such symbolism was not restricted to use on the royal crown. Other religious symbols representing the descent of divine wisdom to the royal family and priestly initiates were transformed in later times to create a similar reinforcement of their claim to divine origin.

Egyptian temples, while they varied in design to a certain extent, were generally adorned with symbols and hieroglyphs celebrating the wisdom, power, and worldly achievements of the pharaohs who endowed them. Pairs of richly decorated obelisks flanked the avenue approaching most temples. The characteristic pyramidal top, or *benben* stone, found on each obelisk was traditionally believed to be the resting place of the phoenix, the legendary bird that arises from its own ashes in a ritually symbolic representation of spiritual death and rebirth.

By the time of Tuthmosis III (1476–1422 B.C.E.), this form of symbolism was transformed in a manner that was to reverberate in one form or another through Egyptian religion, emergent Judaism, and down to the present day. In an open courtyard before the main temple at Karnak, the traditional symbolism of the obelisks has been transformed into two freestanding pillars. These are purely symbolic, as they perform no architectural function whatsoever. David Rohl asserts that these pillars are representative of the two kingdoms of Egypt[39] and describes the carvings on them:

> The pillar on the south side has three tall stems ending in an elaborately stylised flower with partly pendant petioles. If one were to trace its outline and transfer the design to the coat of

arms of the French monarchy you would immediately recog-
nise the "Fleur-de-Lys."[40]

Lilies (*fleurs de lys*) are not native to Egypt and could only be
cultivated there at that time with considerable difficulty. They were
the sole property of the pharaohs and were used for their mood-
altering qualities. As sacred gnosis was gained during states of altered
consciousness, lilies became symbolic of wisdom, as did the pillars
themselves.

Over time, they also became inseparably associated with ancestral descent from the royal house of Egypt. From that time forward,
pillars came to represent the twin royal attributes of the divine gifts
of strength and wisdom.

Tim Wallace-Murphy

Ceiling painting of the Virgin Mary
with lilies, Sacre Monte, Varese, northern Italy.

CHAPTER 2

The Egyptian Origins of Judaism

The exploration of the monuments of the Nile Valley by the scholars who accompanied Napoleon to Egypt in the final years of the 18th century laid the foundations of the modern science of Egyptology. From these beginnings, it rapidly developed into a scientific analysis of the history and archaeology of this ancient land, initially under the guidance of French and British scholars mainly motivated by the desire to discover a historical basis for the events described in the Old Testament. This is still the stated objective of the Egypt Exploration Society in England.

Whether you view the Bible as a historical document or simply as a form of religious mythology based on real events, however, accurately dating any episode from it is incredibly difficult. The slipshod nature of scriptural accounts and their misleading chronologies have plagued every scholar trying to find any corroborative evidence in the Egyptian annals, for the Scriptures give no dates, name no specific pharaohs or dynasties, and demonstrably fail to cite any identifiable happening recorded in Egyptian history.

Abraham and Sarah

Egyptian civilization had been established for over 3,000 years when, according to the Bible, the patriarch Abraham arrived in Egypt from Canaan somewhere between 1500–1460 b.c.e. The Scriptures inform us that Abraham was warmly welcomed by the pharaoh, allegedly because of the beauty of his wife, Sarah (Genesis 13:16). They claim that Abraham originated from the city of Ur, which may simply be a calculated and successful attempt by Israeli scribes writing many centuries later to disguise the patriarch's true origins. In fact, the account in Genesis reveals several facts about Abraham and his family that clearly indicate he was a highborn Egyptian. Abraham says of his wife, ". . . and yet indeed she is my sister; she is the daughter of my father, but not the daughter of my mother; and she became my wife" (Genesis 20:12). The incestuous habit of marrying one's sister was characteristic of members of the Egyptian royal family and this account demonstrates that Abraham was most probably a member this family. This explains why the leading early medieval rabbinical scholar, Rabbi Solomon Isaacs, or Rachi, said, "You should know that the family of Abraham was of a high line,"[1] thereby contradicting the notion that Abraham was a nomadic shepherd and confirming his true social status.

The name by which the patriarch was originally known, Abram, translates as "exalted father," one of the many ritual names regularly used by the kings of Egypt (Genesis 11:27). This may be accurately construed as *Ab-ra-'am*, which in Egyptian means "the father of the House of Ra." The strange change of names for both Abram and Sarai, his wife, reinforces the concept of his Egyptian origin (Genesis 17:5,15). The patriarch's new name, Abraham, is usually held to mean "a father of many nations" in most Judaic, Christian, and Moslem traditions. His wife's new name, Sarah, also indicates their true ethnic and social origins, for it is the Egyptian term for princess. In addition, Genesis records that Sarah's handmaiden, Hagar, was not merely an Egyptian, but also the daughter of the pharaoh by one of his concubines,[2] and that the patriarch's son, Ishmael, took an Egyptian wife (Genesis 21:21).

The strange liaison between Sarah and the unnamed pharaoh gave rise to much scholarly speculation in both the Jewish and Moslem religions. The Babylonian *Talmud*[3] and the *Koran*[4] raise grave doubts as to the true paternity of Abraham's son, Isaac. Both imply that the pharaoh was the boy's real father, not the patriarch. So, in the accepted account of the foundation of the Jewish people, there are two controversial questions: Was Abraham from Ur of the Chaldees,

or was he an Egyptian? And whose descendents are the people of
Israel, the patriarch's or the pharaoh's?

> There certainly must have been a compelling reason for
> Abraham's close relationship with the pharaoh and it was, most
> probably, because he was a near relative whose status, wisdom
> and sacred knowledge commanded immediate and profound
> respect in Egyptian court circles. This theory seems to contra-
> dict holy Scripture, but is suggested by facts recorded in the
> Bible and apparently confirmed by the words of Melchizedek,
> the King of Righteousness: "Blessed be Abram, the most high
> of God, possessor of heaven and earth."[5] Melchizedek, accord-
> ing to ancient Judaic tradition, was Shem, the son of Noah.[6]
> Which then gives rise to an intriguing, but unanswerable ques-
> tion, Was Noah also an Egyptian?

This meeting between Abraham and pharaoh certainly signals
the beginning of an ongoing cross-fertilization of spiritual ideas and
experiences that took place between the people of Israel and the
land of Egypt—an exchange that led ultimately to the foundation
of the Jewish religion.

Leading scholars of international repute such as Sigmund Freud[7]
and Ernst Sellin[8] have written about the overwhelming significance
of Egyptian thought for early Judaism. For example, both Abraham
and Melchizedek, the priest-king of Jerusalem, use a telling phrase
to describe the deity—the Most High God. This is one of the
common terms used in Egypt for the supreme god of the pantheon.
Abraham also adopted for himself and all his children the Egyptian
custom of circumcision, ostensibly at God's command. Circumcision,
while an unusual practice elsewhere, had been mandatory among
Egyptian royalty, the hereditary priesthood, and the nobility since
4000 B.C.E.

The story of the infant Moses being found in the bulrushes by
pharaoh's daughter and his subsequent adoption by the Egyptian
royal family is the first major event of a sequence that leads to the
Exodus of the people of Israel from Egypt (Exodus 2:1–10). This
fascinating fable rests on the highly questionable assumption that,
by the time of Moses, the people of Israel were an identifiable,
monotheistic nation that had entered into a covenant, or *berit*, with

the God of Abraham. This deeply entrenched belief is the basic foundation, not only of Judaism, but also of Christianity and Islam.

Nothing could be further from the truth. To gain an appreciation of the true historical basis of these startling events, we must
examine the roots of religious practice and then carefully reexplore
the reality that underpins the scriptural account of the Exodus. The
Islamic scholar Ahmed Osman names the pharaoh who welcomed
Abraham as Tuthmosis III (1476–1422 B.C.E.),[9] while the English
historian Robert Feather opts for Amenhotep I (1517–1496 B.C.E.).

THE PATRIARCH JOSEPH

Ahmed Osman made the first crucial and definitive identification
of the patriarch Joseph with an individual documented in the
Egyptian records.[10] The Bible records that, when Joseph revealed his
true identity to his brothers, he said:

> . . . it was not you that sent me hither, but God: and he hath
> made me a father to Pharaoh, and lord of all his house, and a
> ruler throughout the land of Egypt (Genesis 45:8).

The phrasing of this passage enabled Osman to identify Joseph
with Yuya, a powerful man whose tomb was discovered in the Valley
of the Kings by Quibell and Weighall in 1905. Arthur Weighall
described his mummified features:

> He was a person of commanding presence, whose powerful
> character showed in his face. One must picture him now as a
> tall man, with a fine shock of white hair; a great hooked nose
> like that of a Syrian; full strong lips; and a prominent determined
> jaw. He has the face of an ecclesiastic, and there is something
> about his mouth which reminds one of the late Pope Leo
> XIII. One feels on looking at his well-preserved features that
> there may be found the originator of the great religious
> movement, which his daughter and grandson carried into
> execution.[11]

The telling phrase, "a father to pharaoh," recorded in the Old
Testament (Genesis 45:87) is repeated exactly in Yuya's book of the

dead.[12] His funeral regalia and citations also carry the title uniquely associated with Joseph in the Bible: The Holy Father of the Lord of the Two Lands—Father of the Pharaoh.

The identification of Yuya as the patriarch Joseph is the first credible correlation between the account in Genesis and Egyptian history yet made. Pharaoh Tuthmosis IV appointed Yuya to ministerial rank; a later pharaoh, Amenhotep III, married Yuya's daughter, Tiye, and celebrated this union by issuing two commemorative scarabs. These clearly demonstrate that the bloodline of the Jewish patriarch Joseph, a great-grandson of the prophet Abraham, again became inseparably entwined with that of the Royal House of Egypt.

THE IDENTIFICATION OF MOSES

In the early part of the 20th century, a Jewish scholar, Dr. Karl Abraham, published an article suggesting that the Pharaoh Akenhaten may have been the biblical character known as Moses.[13]

This received some confirmation when the father of modern psychology, Sigmund Freud, published his final work, *Moses and Monotheism*, just before the outbreak of the World War II. Freud showed that the story of Moses' birth recounted in the Old Testament was clearly based upon the mythology of Sargon (2800 B.C.E.) and Egyptian stories of the birth of Horus, both of whom were hidden in a reed bed. Freud claimed that the story of Moses' humble origins was a later fabrication to disguise the fact that this great Jewish prophet was a full member of the Egyptian royal family. He also demonstrated that the name Moses was a derivative of the common Egyptian name, *Mos*, or "child."

Karl Abraham and Freud were certainly not alone in claiming that Moses was born an Egyptian. This assertion had been made repeatedly by much earlier writers like Manetho, the Egyptian historian and high priest of the 3rd century B.C.E., the 1st-century B.C.E. Jewish historian Philo Judaeus of Alexandria, Flavius Josephus, a Jewish historian of the 1st century C.E., and Justin Martyr, an early father of the Christian Church who lived in the 2nd century C.E. Robert Feather, the modern English writer, claimed that:

> Detailed analysis of the Torah, the Talmud and Midrash led me
> to the conclusion that Moses was not only born and raised as

an Egyptian, but was, in fact, a Prince of Egypt—a son of the Royal House of Pharaoh.[14]

THE EXODUS

A major problem in establishing an accurate date for the Exodus—the expulsion of the people of Israel from Egypt—is finding an acceptable estimate of the time the people supposedly spent in Egypt. This has been in dispute for decades; some claim that it was 400 years, while other scholars have arrived at a consensus of four generations, or about 100 years.[15] Of course, both sides claim scriptural authority for their viewpoint. Ahmed Osman's four-generation hypothesis, taken in conjunction with his identification of Yuya as the patriarch Joseph, leads to the conclusion that "the pharaoh who knew not Joseph" was Horemheb (Exodus 1:8).[16] From this, it follows that his successor, Ramses I, was ruling at the time of the Exodus.

By the time of the Exodus, civilization in Egypt had reached a level of sophistication and economic, cultural, and military refinement that was never exceeded in later times. Religion had evolved from the stellar cults described in the Pyramid Texts to a mainly solar cult whose panoply of gods was headed by Amun. Temples to Amun, such as the one at Karnak, derived enormous benefit from both royal patronage and national prosperity. Despite this seemingly sound foundation, however, the stability of this theocratic system was more apparent than real. The unlikely agent of revolutionary change that transformed the religious face of Egypt and brought monotheism center-stage was the pharaoh Akenhaten, the grandson of Yuya, who abolished the pantheon of Egyptian gods and replaced them with the "heresy" of monotheism. His establishment of the worship of the Sun god, Aten, brutally consigned the worship of Amun to the past, bringing economic and religious chaos in its train. These traumatic circumstances provoked prolonged civil unrest and the deposing of Akenhaten, who seems to have disappeared from history without a trace.

In the controversy over the dating of the Exodus, a number of scholars, such as Dr. Karl Abraham and the popular writer Maurice Cotterell,[17] have concluded that it occurred in the era of Akenhaten.

Full-size figure of the horned Moses, Toulouse.

Sigmund Freud claimed that the historical character portrayed as the biblical Moses was an official in the entourage of Akenhaten—Tuthmosis, who some authorities claim was the pharaoh's older brother.[18] Certain other Jewish scholars who chose to attack the Pharaoh Akenhaten and the religion he founded rather than their illustrious colleague and fellow Jew, Freud, vehemently resented this thesis. The irony of this approach was thrown into stark relief when Osman's persuasive conclusions indicated that the most likely candidate for the historical Moses was not Freud's choice, Tuthmosis, but Dr. Abraham's original suggestion, the pharaoh Akenhaten himself.

ATENISM AND/OR JUDAISM

Freud described in detail many of the startling similarities between the religion of Akenhaten and that of the Jews. In fact, he claimed that, as an Egyptian, Moses had simply transmitted his own religion of Atenism virtually unchanged to the Jews. According to Freud, the prayer so beloved of the Jews, *Schema Yisrael Adonai Elohenu Adonai Echod* (Hear, O Israel, the Lord thy God is One God), far from being a new and unique, post-Exodus Jewish invocation, was almost an exact copy of an Atenist prayer. He postulated that, in translation, the Hebrew letter "d" is a transliteration of the Egyptian "t," while the Egyptian "e" becomes "o." Hence, this prayer, when transcribed into Egyptian, reads: Hear, O Israel, our god Aten is the only god.[19] More than two millennia before Freud published *Moses and Monotheism*, the priest and chronicler Manetho wrote that Moses discharged priestly duties in Egypt.[20] Akenhaten most certainly did just that in his newly built temple to the Aten at Amarna.

When we read the scriptural accounts of the religion followed by the Jews during the Exodus, we find more direct links between it and Atenism. First, there is the creation of the hereditary priesthood based upon the tribe of Levi. As we mentioned earlier, Egyptian priests were a hereditary caste who acted as guardians of sacred knowledge. The Levitic hereditary priestly clan was created by extending the rank, rights, and privileges of the Atenist priesthood to their Levitic successors in exile who, as we shall see, continued the transmission of sacred wisdom among their number in the traditional manner.

THE TEN COMMANDMENTS

The main foundation of Judaic belief, the Law of Moses, is founded firmly on the Ten Commandments. But did Moses receive the Commandments from God on Mount Sinai, or did they come from somewhere else?

There are two different renderings of the Commandments in the Bible. Deuteronomy reads as follows:

> I am the Lord thy God, which brought thee out of the land of Egypt, from the house of bondage.
>
> Thou shalt have no other gods before me.
>
> Thou shalt not make thee any graven image, or any likeness of any thing that is in heaven above, or that is in the earth beneath, or that is in the waters beneath the earth. Thou shalt not bow down thyself unto them, nor serve them: for I the Lord thy God am a jealous God, visiting the iniquity of the fathers upon the children unto the third and fourth generation of them that hate me (Deut 5:6–9).

Professor Flinders Petrie remarked that there is a major difference between Aten and all other Egyptian gods, for the Aten was not the supreme god in a pantheon, but the one and only god. He also noted: "The Aten was the only instance of a jealous God in Egypt, and this worship was exclusive of all others, and claims universality."[21] Messod and Roger Sabbah emphasized that Atenism abolished images and idols of the multiple gods and moved to a new and revolutionary concept of one god—abstract, invisible, transcendental, omnipotent, and all-knowing. This unique god was deemed to be the creator of the Universe in a manner that was in complete accord with ancient Egyptian wisdom.[22] The strictures against graven images given in Deuteronomy's recital of the Ten Commandments replicate those in the Atenist code.

The Ten Commandments listed in Exodus again display distinct Egyptian origins. Suspiciously, they mirror passages in the Egyptian *Book of the Dead*, which lists the principles attested to by souls being assessed by the court of Osiris[23] after death:

Carving of the horned Moses with the
tablets of the law, south aisle, Rosslyn Chapel.

I have done no falsehood against men,
I have not impoverished (robbed) my associates,
I have not killed.[24]

In Exodus, we can read the equivalent:

Thou shalt not kill.
Thou shalt not steal.
Thou shalt not bear witness against thy neighbor.
(Exodus 20:13,15,16)

As Judaism has traditionally claimed that the Ten Commandments, while universal in application, were a divine revelation made uniquely to the chosen people, this strange comparison certainly strengthens the hypothesis that Judaism is a direct evolution from the religion of Akenhaten.

A comparison between Psalm 104 in the Old Testament and Akenhaten's *Hymn to the Aten* lends considerable weight to this disturbing concept. Verse 24 of the psalm reads:

O Lord, how manifold are thy works!
in wisdom hast thou made them all:
the earth is full of thy riches (Psalms 104:24).

Allowing for problems in translation, almost identical phrasing and construction is found in the *Hymn to the Aten*:

How manifold are all your works,
They are hidden from before us,
O sole god, whose powers no other possesses
You did create the earth
According to your desire.[25]

THE ARK OF THE COVENANT

The word for ark or casket is the same in both Egyptian and Hebrew. Indeed, the word *ark* is described in Hebrew as a "loan word" of Egyptian origin. Nineteenth-century specialist in Semitic languages Antoine Fabre d'Olivet wrote: "I regard the idiom of Hebrew sensed in the Sepher (the scriptural rolls of the Torah) as a transplanted branch of the Egyptian language."[26] Both the veneration accorded to

the Ark and its ritual usage merits comparison in the Judaic and
Egyptian religious systems. The Ark was ritually employed as a symbolic form of transport for the god Aten in ceremonies held in the
temple at Amarna. The account in Exodus informs us that Moses
used the Ark of the Covenant to carry items associated with divine
revelation, such as the tablets of stone inscribed with the Ten
Commandments. When the people of Israel occupied the Promised
Land, the Ark was housed in Shiloh within a sanctuary staffed by
priests of the House of Eli. It will come as no surprise that these
priests traced their consecration back to Egypt. It was only after
King Solomon had built his temple in Jerusalem that the Ark of the
Covenant was moved from Shiloh and placed in the newly built
Holy of Holies within Solomon's Temple.

Egyptian practices that can be found within Judaism are not
restricted to the Ark or the Commandments; they also include the
ten *sephirot*, or attributes of God, found in the Kabbala, or mystical
wisdom tradition. These attributes include the terms *crown, wisdom,
intelligence, mercy, power, beauty, victory, glory, foundation*, and *royalty*.
According to Messod and Roger Sabbah, these were also listed as
attributes of the pharaohs.[27] Furthermore, at Amarna, Akenhaten
sacrificed animals traditionally regarded as sacred, as did Moses.
Armana was described as the Holy City, and it is written that
Akenhaten abandoned the sacred land of Karnak for "the Holy
Land" of Aketaten (Amarna), a telling phrase for both Jews and
Christians.[28] The Egyptians ritually inscribed sacred texts above the
entrances of their temples—a habit that was adopted by the Jews.
Such texts, known as *mezzuzot*, can still be found high up near the
doors of orthodox homes.[29]

Osman's identification of Moses with Akenhaten, plausible though
it may be, is still a matter of considerable debate. David Rohl, for
example, suggests that the Exodus took place during the reign of
the pharaoh Dudimose, the thirty-sixth ruler of the 13th dynasty.[30]
Yet despite these minor differences of detail, the majority of scholars originating from different religious backgrounds agree that Judaism
derived from Egyptian religious traditions. The similarities within
both systems are so numerous that the case for the purely Egyptian
origin and nature of early Judaism is proven beyond doubt. Moreover,
despite their differences as to the identification of Moses, Dr.

Abraham, Sigmund Freud, Ahmed Osman, and Robert Feather are all in total agreement that the central core of those who led and took part in the Exodus originated among Akenhaten's entourage and believed in his distinct form of monotheism.

> The strange desertion of Amarna and the sudden disappearance of all who lived in it imparts a high degree of plausibility to this new vision of the Exodus. Not only did the nobility and priest-hood vanish but also so did all the artisans, craftsmen, workers and servants. Akenhaten's Egyptian priests, scribes and nota-bles—the national elite—were the first true monotheists in humanity and believed in one god, Aten. Capable of unity like so many persecuted people, they were chased from their town and country of origin, bringing with them not only material riches but also the greater part of their culture, spirituality, and written and oral traditions.[31]

Other dissatisfied Egyptians, as well as various foreign residents described in the Bible as a "mixed multitude," augmented Akenhaten's followers (Exodus 12:38). The medieval Jewish scholar Rachi wrote that they were a mixture of nations newly converted to monothe-ism.[32] Arriving in the Promised Land of Canaan, then under Egyptian protection, they brought their own ancestral traditions and soon adapted Phoenician writing, creating a new alphabet in the process—Hebraic-hieroglyphic.[33]

THE ORIGINS OF THE PEOPLE OF ISRAEL

One important issue has puzzled the dedicated scholars who have tried to correlate Egyptian records with the biblical account of the Exodus. How could such a vast migration of people take place under such bizarre circumstances and yet fail to be recorded in Egyptian history? Trying to solve this conundrum has led a variety of schol-ars to suggest, among other theories, that the Hebrew people were either the Hebiru or the Hyskos. The problem is that there is no convincing archaeological evidence that links the Hebiru with the people of Israel at that time, and, while Egyptian records disclose that the Hyskos had a profound influence on Egypt, there is no trace whatsoever of the pre-Exodus Jews in early Egyptian records. Many other historians, Egyptologists, and biblical scholars, including modern Israelis, have voiced the unpopular belief that there are such grave doubts about the historicity of the Exodus that the entire account may simply be a matter of myth and legend.

Freud wrote that he found no trace of the term Hebrew prior to the Babylonian exile,[34] when the Scriptures were first transcribed from oral tradition into written form. In the case of the events described in Exodus and Kings, this occurred over seven centuries after the events took place. Messod and Roger Sabbah claim that there is no proof of the Hebrew's existence as a nation or tribe at the time of Moses as described in the Scriptures.[35] They pose the following question:

> How could a people so impregnated with such a major part of the wisdom of Egypt disappear from the (Egyptian) historical record so mysteriously? More than 200 years of research in the deserts, tombs and temples have shown nothing![36]

AFTER THE EXODUS

The fulsome Egyptian official records, just like official records elsewhere, document the power and knowledge of the pharaohs and priests. The might and invincibility of the Two Kingdoms and their rulers receive due and proper attention. Defeats and reverses, however, are largely ignored. If the pharaoh's actions brought the state into disrepute, they were never mentioned. In the matter of Akenhaten's heresy, this deliberate neglect went even further. During the reign of Horemheb, the name of the heretical pharaoh was deleted from statues and temple walls in an attempt to remove all trace of him. In Soviet parlance, Akenhaten became a nonperson. Thus the emigration of the "fallen one of Akehetaten" would not merely pass unrecorded, but would be quietly and completely expunged.

Another anomaly in the Scriptures is that the supposedly recently freed slaves, the people of Israel, carried vast amounts of treasure with them as they fled—including "jewels of silver, and jewels of gold"—which was a strange and inexplicable burden for newly emancipated slaves (Exodus 3:21–22). Robert Feather claims that this treasure was composed of Moses' personal wealth and the treasure of Amarna.[37] It is also possible that the new pharaoh may have contributed to it as compensation for Akenhaten's claim to the throne. The Sabbahs believe that the right to settle in Canaan went along with the right to export the Atenist treasures of Amarna.[38] As the land of Canaan was one of Egypt's provinces, the right to settle there without hindrance from Egypt was essential for the success of the Exodus.

While the fact that early post-Exodus Judaism was, both ethnically and spiritually, Egyptian in origin has been recognized by scholars for years, this salient fact has, sadly, had little impact on the public consciousness due to the theological blinkers that limit the perceptions of Jewish, Christian, and Islamic fundamentalists. It is time, therefore, for the devout in all three great faiths to recognize the essentially Egyptian nature of the foundation of their religious beliefs. Furthermore, the history of the Jews from the time of Moses until the time of Jesus discloses that the beliefs of the "chosen people" were constantly evolving and owe many more of their developments to polytheism and paganism and the transmission of sacred wisdom than most modern theologians would care to admit.

CHAPTER 3

From the Exodus to the Babylonian Exile

Both scriptural commentators and historians have assessed the dramatic account of the Exodus of the Jews from Egypt and their forty years in the wilderness with very mixed results. Many devoted followers in all three religions simply accept the biblical story as "the inerrant word of God"; some historians of the three faiths take it as more or less straight history. Modern historians read this episode in an altogether different light, however, and remind us that the Book of Exodus was written more than seven centuries after the events it purports to describe and under political circumstances that skewed the account beyond all recognition. Indeed, 20th-century scholars tend to view its contents with either extreme caution or outright skepticism. Freud described the era of the implantation of the people of Israel in Canaan as one "particularly impenetrable to investigation."[1] The Dead Sea Scrolls scholar John Allegro was even more blunt:

> We are in a shadowy half-world, where the hard facts of history fade off into mythology, and where the clear dividing line we like to draw between fact and fiction has no place . . .[2]

Several leading Israeli scholars suggest that the Exodus is pure mythology.

The American historian, Norman Cantor wrote:

... perhaps the whole Egyptian sojourn was fabricated in later centuries for some ideologically conditioned or socially advantageous purpose.[3]

Later in the same work, he carried this to a conclusion considered outrageous, or even blasphemous, by many devout Jews, Christians, and Muslims:

> Such is the biblical story whose verification defies the course of historical and archaeological science. It is a romantic fantasy.[4]

One devout Roman Catholic historian, Paul Johnson, who generally accepts the Scriptures as a true historical record, wrote:

> Some other sites mentioned in Exodus have been tentatively identified. But plotting these wanderings on a map, though often attempted, and undoubtedly entertaining, can produce nothing more than conjecture.[5]

However, despite his doubts about the story of the Exodus, John Allegro clearly recognized the essentially spiritual truth that lies behind this fascinating story when he said:

> During the desert wandering under Moses, following their providential escape from Egypt, the Israelites were welded into a nation, allowed to know the secret name of God, and given the inestimable gift of the *Torah*, or Law.[6]

Within this part of the Scriptures, we not only find clear indications that stress the Egyptian and gnostic roots of Judaism, but also discern a vague historical framework that is only verified by archaeology to a very small degree.

Pillar Symbolism

Just as man himself changes as an integral part of the evolutionary process, mankind's belief systems also evolve, change, and develop. The widespread assumption that Judaism today has hardly changed from the time of Moses certainly does not bear close examination. The monotheistic belief system that supposedly prompted the Exodus from Egypt has developed in ways that would horrify both Moses and many modern-day monotheists.

Early in the story, we encounter symbolism of plainly Egyptian origin that, in one form or another, has influenced mystical Judaism from that day to this. The symbolism of the freestanding twin pillars uniting mankind and God that marked the entrance to the temple at Karnak are vibrantly transformed and used to dramatize the sacred nature of the Exodus. As Moses led his people out of Egypt, we are told that:

> The Lord went before them by day in a pillar of cloud to lead them along the way, and by night in a pillar of fire to give them light, that they might travel by day and night; the pillar of cloud by day and the pillar of fire by night did not depart from the people (Exodus 13:21–22).

This vivid symbolism was repeated and used to signify the presence of God in the tabernacle:

> When Moses entered the tent, the pillar of cloud would descend and stand at the door of the tent, and the Lord would speak with Moses. And when all the people saw the pillar of cloud standing at the door of the tent, all the people would rise up and worship, every man at his tent door. Thus the Lord used to speak to Moses face to face, as a man speaks to his friend (Exodus 33:9–11).

Later in the Bible, the psalmists record that God spoke to them in a pillar of cloud (Pslams 99:7), which was later interpreted to mean the fount of revelation or the very seat of Wisdom herself.[7] This interpretation stressed the importance of the wisdom tradition, as though Wisdom were a separate divine entity from the Lord God of Israel. In the *Apocrypha*, we find this said of God: "In the high places did I fix my abode, and my throne was in a pillar of cloud (Eccles. 24:4)." Gnosis, or sacred wisdom, was at least as important to the "new" hereditary priesthood instituted by Moses as it was to its Egyptian predecessor. John Allegro claims that the author of *The Wisdom of Solomon* identified Wisdom with the pillars:[8] "She became unto them a covering in the daytime and a flame of stars through the night."[9] Proverbs 9:1 describes Wisdom as God's helper in the act of creation:"She built her house, she has set up her seven pillars (of Wisdom)," and she has been described in this context as "the consort of God," a rather strange term that poses immense problems for those who wish to describe early Judaism as truly monotheistic.

When, after many centuries, Judaic beliefs were codified and regularized, the understanding of this term changed and Wisdom became a creation of God. The author Karen Armstrong states that the understanding of Wisdom in this context evolved into the concept of an attribute of God, similar to the "glory" of God.[10]

Conquest in Canaan

The biblical account of the invasion and settlement of the Promised Land begins with Joshua and the battle of Jericho. According to the historian Josephus, writing in the 1st century C.E., Joshua was:

> A man of extreme courage, valiant in endurance of toil, highly
> gifted in intellect and speech, and withal one who worshipped
> God with a singular piety which he had learned from Moses
> and who was held in esteem by the Hebrews.[11]

However, as archaeological investigation was soon to prove, Joshua's supposed victory at the battle of Jericho is clearly based on knowledge of an earlier siege of the city.

A series of archaeological excavations conducted at Jericho between 1935 and 1965 by Albright at first seemed to confirm the biblical story. He found evidence for the collapse of the city walls and, understandably, claimed this as proof of the historical accuracy of the Bible. This news was received with unbridled delight by fundamentalists of all three faiths.[12] The euphoria did not last long, however, for further excavations made by Kathleen Kenyon disclosed that the ruins excavated by Albright had their origin in a much earlier period and, therefore, could not be ascribed to Joshua's conquest of the city.[13]

Modern Israel must rank foremost among the most heavily excavated countries in the world, yet archaeologists have discovered little evidence of destruction in Canaanite city sites. From the biblical perspective, therefore, there is absolutely nothing that can be described with any degree of conviction as evidence of conquest by the people of Israel at the time of their occupation of that land. Unpalatable as this may be to fundamentalists, it has nonetheless been widely accepted by most scholars. Robin Lane Fox, the biblical historian, wrote, "There is no sign of foreign invasion in the highlands, which would become the Israelite heartland."[14]

The scribes who wrote the Book of Joshua admit that Joshua's "conquest" was only partial (Joshua 17:11–18; Judges 1:27–36). The modern scholarly consensus is that, instead of being created by force of arms, Israel emerged peacefully and gradually from elements that arose from within Canaanite society.[15] Paul Johnson claims: "Much of the settlement was a process of infiltration, or reinforcement of affiliated tribes who, as we have already seen, held towns such as Sechem."[16] The fact that a nation or tribe called Israel had clearly been established by 1207 B.C.E. is confirmed by a stele recording the conquest by Pharaoh Mernephtah that reads: "Israel is laid waste, his seed is not . . ."

The present consensus suggests that there were three main waves of early Hebrew settlement in the land of Canaan. The first, led by Abraham, is recorded in Genesis; the second involved Abraham's grandson, Jacob or Israel, who settled in Sechem. Jacob's sons are named as the founders of the twelve tribes of Israel. The arrival of Moses/Akenhaten's people following the Exodus was the foundation of the third wave of immigration. This mixed multitude amalgamated with and began to dominate the Semitic tribes in Canaan. Uniting around their belief in Yahweh, they were eventually all called the people of Israel. Karen Armstrong claims:

> The Bible makes it clear that the people we know as the
> ancient Israelites were a confederation of various ethnic groups,
> bound principally together by their loyalty to Yahweh, the God
> of Moses.[17]

This clearly echoes the views of Rachi quoted earlier.[18]

THE ERA OF THE JUDGES

The Book of Judges appears to contain a certain degree of historicity. Indeed, some scholars have tried to construct a chronology for the development of the people of Israel from it. However, this approach, like so many other attempts at making sense of the chronology of the Bible, is highly flawed for a variety of reasons. First, the assumption that the individual judges ruled over all of Israel is incorrect, for each ruled over one of the twelve tribes. Many described within Judges ruled at the same time as others, and we have no possible way of clarifying this highly complex situation. This era is so confused that Paul Johnson was moved to write:

> The Book of Judges, though undoubted history and full of fascinating information about Canaan in the late Bronze Age, is flavoured with mythical material and fantasy and presented in a confused fashion, so that it is difficult to work out a consecutive history of the period.[19]

Therefore, any chronology that is based entirely on Judges can only be educated guesswork founded on highly questionable evidence. When we come to the religious beliefs of the people of that era, however, we are on safer ground and can support our conclusions with evidence from independent sources and archaeology. The Bible is most probably accurate when it describes the backsliding and lapses from true monotheism that continually plagued the chosen people of Israel from the time of the settlement to their exile in Babylon seven centuries later. This religious self-criticism, which could easily have been excluded or glossed over by biblical scribes, is almost certainly based on truth, especially when it accords with the archaeological evidence of Canaanite beliefs unearthed in the last century.

In the era covered by Judges and Kings, it is obvious that the ancient Israelites were not monotheistic as we now understand the term. Yahweh, the God of Akenhaten/Moses, was described as their one true God. Yet, while some Israelites knew that they should worship him and him alone, many believed that other gods existed and continued to worship these deities as their Egyptian ancestors had done. It was not until the period of the Babylonian exile (597–539 B.C.E.), when the Scriptures first took definitive written form, that the Israelites finally and clearly decided that Yahweh was their sole God and that there were no others.[20] Prior to that time, the issue is somewhat confused for a people claiming to be exclusively and uniquely monotheistic.

Polytheism and the Early Israelites

One of the earliest references to the God of Israel is as Melchizedek's god, El Elyon, "God Most High,"[21] on whose behalf Abraham gave Melchizedek tithes. El Elyon, or El, the title of the Canaanite god Baal of Mount Zaphon, was the generic West Semitic name for God. Similarly, Elot, the term for *goddess* with the feminine plural Elohim, is often used in the Scriptures as well. Israelites also participated in the fertility rites of Ba'al, worshipped many Syrian deities, and venerated the goddess of fertility, Asherah, who was El's consort in the Jerusalem Temple.[22] They described Asherah, who was known variously as She who walks in the Sea, Holiness, and Elath the Goddess, as the wife of Yahweh as he assimilated to himself the father god imagery of El.[23] When referred to as the consort of Baal, she was called Baalat. A later king of Israel, King Manasseh, erected an altar to Asherah in the temple,[24] an altar later broken up by Josiah (II Kings 23:12).

Further evidence for the polytheistic nature of early Israelite beliefs is found in reference to the pre-Exodus Jewish temple at Elephantine. Excavations have not yet revealed its precise location, but documents in Aramaic have been recovered that confirm its existence and show that its cult was highly irregular,[25] at least when judged by the standards of the Deuteronomists who wrote the Scriptures during the Babylonian exile. Several gods besides Yahweh were worshipped, while Yahweh is described as having much in common with other gods of the Middle East. Yet, when this temple was destroyed in the 5th century B.C.E., the Jews of Elephantine wrote to the governors of Judea and Samaria asking for help to rebuild it. That they wrote at all not only proves there was communication between the various Jewish communities, but also implies they did not believe that their manner of worship would be deemed deviant or blasphemous. Furthermore, the fact that they wrote to Judea and Samaria is a strong indication that, at this time at least, Jerusalem was not perceived as the central authority of the people of Israel.[26] An intriguing sidelight on their beliefs comes from the historian A. E. Cowley who wrote: "The Pentateuch, both in its historical and legal aspects, was unknown in the 5th century (B.C.E.) to the Jews of Elephantine."[27]

The Lord God of Israel

Prior to the building of Solomon's Temple, there is no real mention of Yahweh as the creator god, for Israelite tradition describes him as choosing a people, not creating the cosmos. Once ritually enthroned on Mount Zion, however, Yahweh took on aspects of the worship of the Canaanite god Baal or Melchizedek's El Elyon.[28] When King David took Jerusalem from the Jebusites and brought the Ark of the Covenant there in order to make his new capital the religious center of his kingdom, he appointed Zadok, a Jebusite, as high priest. Zadok was almost certainly a priest in the tradition of Melchizedek, who had previously served the god El Elyon. Probably to assuage discontent among the Israelites at this move, David also appointed Abiathar, who had guarded the Ark at Shiloh, as joint high priest (Samuel 8:17). While this joint appointment may have brought political unity, it had a bizarre long-term effect, for later, as we shall see, all high priests in Judaism had to prove their legitimacy by showing descent from Zadok and not Abiathar.[29] To justify this, a genealogy was constructed for Zadok that far exceeds in length any credible parallel lineage (Exodus 6:14–25).

King Solomon

Even Solomon's Temple carried within it overtones of polytheism. Its design conformed closely to earlier Egyptian, Canaanite, and Syrian models.[30] The entire edifice consisted of three square areas leading to a relatively small cube-shaped room known as the Most Holy Place or the Holy of Holies. This small space housed the Ark of the Covenant (I Kings 6:19). Despite the proscription against graven images, the temple contained carved cherubim ten cubits high (I Kings 6:26), as well as depictions of palms and flowers. True to the ancient Egyptian wisdom tradition, before the temple were two freestanding pillars, each thirty-five cubits high, called Joachin and Boaz (II Chron. 3:15–17). It also contained a bronze altar, a huge bronze basin supported by bulls cast in bronze that represented Yam, the primal sea of Canaanite myth (II Chron. 4:2), and two forty-foot-high freestanding pillars that symbolized the fertility of Asherah.[31]

Under the reign of Solomon, the people of Israel continued to worship Yahweh in the high places they had inherited from the Canaanites at Beth-El, Shiloh, Hebron, Bethlehem, and Dan, where there were frequent pagan ceremonies. Indeed, Solomon himself was known to have venerated pagan deities and is credited with the building of a high place to Chemosh, the Moabite god, and Moelch, the god of the Ammonites (I Kings 11:7). Even the worship of Astarte of the Sidonians was allowed in Israel. So, despite building the first temple to Yahweh in Jerusalem, even King Solomon can hardly be extolled as a true monotheist.

The various biblical reports of the building of the temple disclose further strange anomalies. The account in Kings makes no mention of priests (I Kings 8), yet Chronicles spends an inordinate amount of time detailing their precise duties—albeit at the time of David, but with the strong implication that this tradition continued from that time onward (I Chron. 23, 24). The biblical historian Sanmell gives the most valid explanation for this apparent contradiction when he states that:

> The ordinary view of modern scholars is that in Chronicles the ecclesiastical organisation which arose in the latter part of the post-exilic period was anachronistically read back into the times of David and Solomon, thereby giving the sanction of antiquity to the ecclesiastical system of the post-exilic period. This ecclesiastical organisation provided for twenty-four *ma'-madot*, priestly teams who took turns in serving in the Temple in Jerusalem.[32]

As Sanmell has indicated, the scriptural accounts of the reigns of David and his son, Solomon, were written four centuries or more after the events they purport to describe. The Old Testament as we know it began to take its present form during the Babylonian Exile and the process continued for several centuries after that. By that time, of course, Judaism had changed and developed into a rigidly and exclusively monotheistic system that had at its core a priestly caste that served a legalistic religion based upon the 613 strictures of the law.

The intellectual and spiritual honesty of the scribes was such that they not only recorded the history of backsliding and polytheistic influences on the people of Israel, but also continued to stress the importance of the principles of sacred wisdom. Nowhere is this tendency more obvious than in the account of the reign of King Solomon. One later father of the early Christian Church, Eusebius, cited Aristobulus in support of the biblical accounts of the importance of wisdom to King Solomon:

> One of our ancestors, Solomon [the reputed author of the biblical book of Proverbs], said more clearly and better that wisdom existed before heaven and earth, which agrees with what has been said [by Greek philosophers].[33]

The Scriptures record that:

> God gave Solomon wisdom and very great insight and a breadth of understanding as measureless as the sand on the seashore. Solomon's wisdom was greater than the wisdom of all the men of the East, and greater than all the wisdom of Egypt (I Kings 4:29–30).

Thus the Bible itself relates Solomon's wisdom to that of Egypt and also recounts that Solomon prayed for wisdom II Chron. 1:10). This divine gift of sacred wisdom and insight is further elaborated in the apocryphal book *The Wisdom of Solomon* and is advanced as the prime motivation for the visit to King Solomon's court by the Queen of Sheba (II Chron. 9:1).

THE QUEEN OF SHEBA

In the opinion of modern archaeologists, the ancient kingdom of Sheba, now known to be in the region of modern Yemen, was, in those days, a land of considerable culture based upon a lucrative trade in myrrh and frankincense.[34] As Solomon had recently built the temple, it is probable that the Queen of Sheba's visit was for economic purposes at least as much as it may have been a meeting of mutual admiration as suggested in the Bible.[35] While we can only speculate about the real reason for her visit, another highly venerated work of considerable antiquity, the Ethiopic *Kebra Nagast*, records the most significant result of the Queen's visit to Jerusalem—the fact that the Queen of Sheba bore Solomon a son. The *Kebra Nagast* is not merely a literary work; it is the repository of Ethiopian national and religious feelings in a manner similar to the Tanakh for Jews, the New Testament for Christians, or the Qur'an for Muslims.[36] According to the great Egyptologist Wallis Budge, the Jewish faith was introduced into Ethiopia around 950 B.C.E. with Menelik, the son of Solomon and the Queen of Sheba. He also claims that the Queen of Sheba became a Jew.[37] Thus the Royal House of David, through Menelik, gained a branch in Ethiopia and Judaism began to spread far beyond the borders of Israel and Egypt. Many centuries later, Jews fleeing from Elephantine in Egypt augmented this new Ethiopian Jewish community.[38]

The story of King Solomon in the Bible is perhaps the most fascinating, frustrating, and contradictory account in the entire Old Testament. This king of such legendary wisdom and power, so important to Jews, Christians, and Muslims alike, seems almost beyond belief in the range and importance of his attributes. Despite the detailed scriptural descriptions of his wealth, military might, and powerful empire, and the importance of the temple that he built, no archaeological trace of his work has ever been irrefutably located. The modern English author Graham Phillips described this puzzle succinctly when he wrote:

> There is not a single contemporary reference to Solomon in the many neighbouring countries that were keeping written records during the tenth century B.C.E. At the time when the Bible tells us that Solomon created a major empire in the Middle East, none of his contemporaries seem to have noticed it, not even the Phoenicians, with whom he apparently traded, worked closely and forged an alliance. The Egyptian pharaoh was supposedly his father-in-law, yet no Egyptian records of the period, of which many survive, make any reference to him. . . . Without the biblical accounts we would be unaware of Solomon's existence.[39]

Yet despite this complete dearth of external evidence confirming his existence, Solomon and all his works were of supreme importance to the scribes who wrote the Bible, even though dubious, polytheistic attitudes prevailed in Israel during his reign. At the time of Solomon, it is apparent that Yahweh was not regarded as the only god, but simply as a national god. Thus the way was open to a variety of cults and the veneration of strange gods of all sorts, as political expediency, foreign alliances, marriages, and economic relations dictated. This led to a shattering of religious unity, which had an inevitable effect on national unity. Advance warning of the consequences could be discerned before Solomon's death and, when he died, there was nothing to save the kingdom from disintegration.[40]

CHAPTER 4

The Exile and the Rebuilding of the Temple

The death of King Solomon marked the end of the ancient kingdom of Israel. The burden of taxes Solomon had instituted to fund his building program and maintain his power brought political tensions in the country to near boiling point. Matters came to a head with the accession of his son, Reheboam, who announced more of the same with the immortal phrase, "My father has chastised you with whips, but I will chastise you with scorpions" (I Kings 12:11; II Chron. 10:11). The country split in two, with each of its parts named after their principal tribes. To the south was the kingdom of Judah, with Jerusalem as its capital; to the north was the kingdom of Ephraim, called Israel in the Bible, which later became Samaria.

In the year 722 B.C.E., the Assyrians captured Samaria and the kingdom of Ephraim ceased to exist. The conquest of Samaria and the deportation of its people is one of the few important events described in the Bible during the First Temple period that can be verified in external contemporaneous sources. The annals of Sargon II, King of Assyria, record that, "In the beginning of my royal rule, I have besieged and conquered the city of the Samarians . . . I have led away 27,290 of its inhabitants as captives."[1] This event was of traumatic significance to Jews everywhere, for the specter of the "lost ten tribes of Israel" has haunted the collective memory of the Jewish people ever since. Twenty years later, the Assyrians besieged Jerusalem, but the city did not fall. Its freedom was comparatively short-lived however, for in 598 B.C.E., a new conqueror, Nebuchadnezzar, King of Babylon, entered the land. In 597, Jerusalem fell and 10,000 of its leading citizens, including the heir to the throne, were led away into captivity (II Kings 24:14). The exile was only one, albeit an important, episode in a catalog of disasters that befell the Jews between 734 and 581 B.C.E., for there were six distinct enforced deportations of the Israelites, and many others fled to safety in Egypt and other neighboring lands.[2]

The Diaspora had begun in earnest and, from this time forward, the majority of Jews would always live outside the Promised Land. They knew that, without a temple or a country of their own, they faced imminent extinction as a people through absorption by the heathen among whom they found themselves. They turned toward God. They had the Torah and their other sacred writings, and around these spiritual possessions they built up a new form of Judaism, stripped of all territorial limitations and political loyalties and founded upon piety and learning, religion and study.[3]

Thus the adversity of enforced exile in Babylon was turned to advantage in a manner that not only transformed the Jewish religion and ensured the survival of the people of Israel for all time, but also transformed the world. Out of their sacred writings, the priests and scribes created the literary and spiritual masterpiece that we call the Old Testament. The exiles had their laws, some records of their past, the Book of Deuteronomy (which had been discovered fortuitously just before the fall of Jerusalem), their oral traditions, the sayings of the prophets, and a passionate sense of purpose that projected their vision not only into the future, but retrospectively into the newly created and carefully embroidered accounts of their own past. They were continuing a process that had begun 200 years earlier, at a time when at least five centuries had elapsed since the Exodus. In consequence, it is apparent that many of the pivotal figures of biblical history—Saul, David, Solomon,[4] Elijah, and even Joshua—had lived and died without the benefit of the Scriptures to guide them. What guided these spiritual giants of the past was the mystical and initiatory heritage of their Egyptian origins, now incorporated in the emerging Scriptures taking written form in Babylon.

THE WRITING OF THE OLD TESTAMENT

Modern biblical scholarship has established a broad consensus on the manner in which the Scriptures were written. Contributions from the earlier sources and traditions enumerated above can now be identified according to either the terminology with which they describe God, or the bias or emphasis that discloses their probable origins. The scribes in Babylon and other later scribes blended them all into one viable, if sometimes contradictory, whole and used their understanding of Jewish history and mythology to give them a compelling narrative style. The modern scholarly documentary hypothesis claims that at least four major sources can be discerned. They are identified as J, who refers to God as Yahweh or Jehovah; E, who refers to God as the Elohim; D, the author of Deuteronomy; and P, the Priestly source.[5] Beyond the world of academia, most Christians and non-Orthodox Jews now accept this hypothesis or one of its variants instead of the traditional idea that the Pentateuch was written by Moses. Completed by the 2nd century B.C.E., the Hebrew Bible consists of three major parts: The Torah or Pentateuch, The Neviim or Prophets, and The Ketuvim or Sayings. While parts of Daniel, Ezra, and Jeremiah are written in Aramaic, the rest are written in Hebrew.[6]

The gifted priests, scribes, and scholars who compiled the Scriptures were not merely spiritually inspired in what they wrote, but had their own personal axes to grind. The new writings stressed the role and importance of the hereditary priestly caste and especially those among it who were members of twenty-four *ma'madot,* or priestly teams, who took turns serving in the temple in Jerusalem. They also reinforced the necessity of descent from Zadok as an absolute prerequisite for the high priesthood at the temple in Jerusalem.

Once again projecting their own spiritual understanding retrospectively, the priests came up with an apparently valid explanation for the travails of the present. The recurrent national apostasy detailed so often in the new scriptural accounts of their history was used to explain God's anger with his chosen people, the disaster of conquest, and the exile. The people of Israel were suffering, not because of the sins and shortcomings of its leaders, but because the citizenry had individually and collectively, signally and repeatedly, failed to keep the covenant with God. They had brought ruin on themselves, for the disaster of exile was the direct result of a sinful past that stretched from the time of Joshua to the fall of Jerusalem.

This explanation not only allowed the majority of Jews to keep their self-respect, but also, given due repentance and a return to righteousness, allowed for the renewal of God's blessing and protection.[7] Now Jews were encouraged to come closer to Yahweh by observing the Torah of Moses. Deuteronomy listed a number of obligatory laws, including the Ten Commandments, and these were now elaborated into the complex and scripturally sanctioned legislation of the 613 Commandments or *mitzvoth* of the Pentateuch.[8] Thus Judaism was transformed into a highly legalistic code that impinged on every aspect of its adherents' behavior.

In Babylon, the Jews were bereft of their central cultic shrine of the Jerusalem Temple and needed a focal point for activities that would bind them together in religious observance, serve as a center of dissemination for the new Scriptures, and reinforce their national and cultural identity. The development and use of the synagogue can be traced back to these meetings of the Jewish community in exile. With no temple, they had to forsake ritual sacrifice and rely on prayer and reading of the new religious texts.

While in Babylon, the Jews began to speak Aramaic, the language of the country, a Semitic language that closely resembles, but is still distinct from, Hebrew.[9] After the return to Jerusalem and Judea, Aramaic became the commonly spoken language of the Jewish people for many centuries; the same language was later used by Jesus. Even today, the Jewish prayer for the dead is recited in Aramaic. Hebrew was reserved for the sacred texts and ceremonial occasions and, although it is now commonly held to be the language of the people of Israel, it was not known by that name before its use in the prologue to Ecclesiasticus (circa 130 B.C.E.). It is called "the language of Canaan" in Isaiah (19:18), while later in the same book, Jerusalemite speech is referred to as Judean (Isaiah 36:12–13). The term *Hebrew* as an indication of race is not found prior to the exile and, before that, apart from the stele of Pharaoh Mernephtah mentioned previously, there is not much independent proof of the existence of the people of Israel as described in Genesis and Exodus.[10]

JEWISH INITIATORY TRADITION

The historian Norman Cantor records that some modern scholars, such as John Allegro and Professor Morton Smith, claim that the Jews learned more than Aramaic and synagogue worship while in exile in Babylon. They believe that this is where the Jews refined their monotheism. The fact that the Scriptures were written there, they point out, hints at this by placing the homeland of the patriarch Abraham close by in Ur instead of Egypt, his true country of origin. Post-exilic Judaism may well have been influenced by Mesopotamian religious culture, and both Allegro and Smith contend that Jews brought back with them from Babylon a volatile brand of esoteric religion to complement the more sedate biblical religion we recognize today.[11]

Whatever the truth of that assertion, however, one thing is clear from reading the Scriptures: the Jews treasured their own mystical and initiatory religious traditions and stressed their importance in the inspired writings composed during the exile. The mystical vision of the prophets was extolled time and time again, the role of the priest-kings David and Solomon was revered, and the initiatory concept of ascending degrees of holiness pervaded Jewish life and the very precincts of the temple. The prophet Ezekiel, who described the ideal temple in Jerusalem after a mystical vision in Babylon, made this very clear.

Ezekiel envisaged a special area surrounding the city and temple occupied by the spiritual elite, the king, high priests, and Levites. This district is holier than the remainder of the Promised Land occupied by the rest of the twelve tribes of Israel. Far beyond this sacred land lies the rest of the world, occupied by the other nations, the Goyim. As God is radically separate from all of creation, so his chosen people must share his holy segregation. In order to live in exile with God in their midst, the exiles had to make themselves into a sacred zone. There was to be no fraternizing with the Goyim or flirting with false gods. The people of Israel must make themselves into a house holy enough so that Yahweh would choose to dwell among them, a consolation for the exiles in Babylon who knew, in consequence, that they were closer to the divine than their pagan neighbors.[12]

THE EARLY SCRIPTURES

The required holy lifestyle described in the Priestly writings is made particularly apparent in the books of Leviticus and Numbers. P rewrote the history of Israel from the priestly perspective and described the wanderings of the Israelites in the desert. When he codified the laws that God allegedly gave them on Mount Sinai, he described a similar series of ascending, graded zones of holiness. In the heart of this sacred space was the tabernacle, or Holy of Holies, housing the Ark and the "glory" of Yahweh. Only Aaron, the high priest, was permitted to enter this place. The camp itself was holy because of the presence of God; outside the camp was the godless realm of the desert. Like Ezekiel, P described Yahweh as a mobile god with no fixed abode, continually on the move with his people, whose holy place is with the community.

For P, Israel only became a people when and because Yahweh decided to live among them. He "knew" that the presence of God was just as important as the Law and, in his account, Yahweh revealed the plan of the portable tabernacle to Moses on Mount Sinai at the same time that he revealed the Law, or Torah. Thus the Jews in Babylon were assured that Yahweh could be with his people wherever they were, even in the chaos of exile, for he had already moved about with them during the forty years wandering in the wilderness.[13]

The cumulative result of the composition of the sacred Scriptures, the absolute and exclusive monotheism, the codifying of the 613 strictures of the Law, the dietary laws, the institution of the synagogues, and the new religious vision of the priests and scribes was summed up superbly by Karen Armstrong:

> Yaweh had finally absorbed his rivals in the religious imagination of Israel; in exile the lure of paganism lost its attraction and the religion of Judaism had been born.[14]

The heart of this new Judaism was the blending of a legalistic with a prophetic and initiatory tradition, creating a religion of command and moral commitment. This was manifest in the difference of approach in worship. That of the First Temple period had been noisy, joyful, and tumultuous; in contrast, worship in the Second Temple period tended to be quiet and sober. In exile, the people of

Israel had become aware that their own sins were responsible for the destruction of Jerusalem, and the new forms that the cult created tended to reflect the broken and crushed heart of the people. This was marked by the new festival of Yom Kippur, the Day of Atonement, the one day in the year when the chief priest entered the *Devir* as the people's representative, pleading on his knees for forgiveness for the sins of the entire nation.[15]

THE TORAH

A pivotal development was that the Torah was no longer the exclusive monopoly of the priestly class and became accessible to all who desired to know it. Over time, it became the ultimate source of every Jewish practice, rule, and custom—not just in religious and moral matters, but also in the political, social, economic, and domestic aspects of life. This enthronement of the Torah in the very heart of life saved Judaism from becoming just another priestly religion, concerned only with matters of ritual and religious practice, and, instead, transformed it into one embracing every aspect of life. Isadore Epstein claims that this was the real origin of the ideal theocratic state of the people of Israel.[16] However, the old idea of the nation was no longer linked solely to territory: God's rule extended to the Diaspora, despite the fact that his special home was in the temple in Jerusalem.

God's message to his chosen people was contained in the ever-developing Scriptures that, formidable in bulk and often almost impenetrable in their obscurity, gave rise to an increasing army of scribes, priests, and commentators whose commentaries filled libraries and gave rise to endless debates and arguments. As a result, the entire Jewish world was luxuriant with internal conflicts that brought in their train a welter of sects and divisions that coexisted under the broad spiritual umbrella of Judaism. Under Persian rule, these developments proceeded without outside interference, as the Persian Empire was tolerant of its subjects' religious beliefs. When, in 333 B.C.E., Alexander the Great's army conquered the region, Judea was again granted considerable autonomy. The high priest remained both the religious and political leader of his people, and the only extra burden, which was considerable, was the high level of taxation imposed by the conquerors.

Later, under the rule of the Selucid king Antiochus IV, these high taxes were doubled. This pagan king appointed his own nominee as high priest, having deposed the last true Zadokite high priest in 175 B.C.E. The deposed high priests' son built a rival temple at Leontopolis in Egypt. The more zealous of the Zadokite priests of the ma'madot withdrew and formed their own sect in the wilderness near Qumran, basing their form of worship on strict rules of purity and observation of the Torah under the leadership of the man they called the Teacher of Righteousness.

The tendency toward religious division in Judaism was now becoming ever more apparent. Worse was to come. Antiochus IV resolved to extirpate Judaism in its entirety. Jewish religious practices were banned; the keeping of the Sabbath, circumcision, and the observation of all Jewish festivals were now subject to the death penalty. The Torah was banned and possession of a copy of it made a capital offence. The temple was dedicated to the worship of Zeus, swine's flesh was offered on the altar, prostitutes were brought into its precincts, and pagan altars were set up in towns and villages.[17] The result was predictable.

THE MACCABEAN REVOLT

The country rose in revolt under the leadership of the priest Mathias and, later, under his son, Judas Maccabeus. The war was fought on two fronts: the first against the Jews who were willing to obey the new Greek laws, the second against the Greeks themselves. The Maccabean family eventually led their forces to victory; the temple was purified and rededicated at the first celebration of Hanukkah. In 143 B.C.E., a great assembly in Jerusalem named Simon Maccabeus as the hereditary high priest and ethnarch. The Hasmonean Era had begun and, for the first time in centuries, the people of Israel had their own priest-kings.

At first, the country prospered and, as a result of a series of wars, grew considerably in size until, under Alexander Jananeus, it became comparable to that ruled by the legendary King Solomon of old. Sadly, this was not to last, as the Hasmonean dynasty was riven by internecine strife. In the ensuing civil war, the empire of Rome was sought as an ally by one of the warring factions. This eventually led to the rule of a man described as "a friend of Rome," a complex, politically gifted, and brutal man known to history as Herod the Great.

CHAPTER 5

BIBLICAL ISRAEL, JOHN THE BAPTIST, AND JESUS

Most Christians and those of other creeds living in the developed world feel that they have a reasonable understanding of conditions in biblical Israel. This understanding, however, is derived from 2,000 years of belief based on documents of great spiritual import, but little historical validity. These documents disclose no real understanding of either the social customs or religious obligations of the Jews in that crucial era. The New Testament view is that there were only two major factions within Judaism at that time—the Sadducees and the Pharisees—with a passing mention of the Samaritans. Apart from that, the implication is that Judaism was a fairly unified religion. Contemporary documents tell a very different story.

The Jewish historian Flavius Josephus describes four main sects within Judaism in the 1st century of the Common Era: the Essens, the Sadducees, the Pharisees, and the "fourth philosophy."[1] The Essens, now more commonly called the Essenes, were the spiritual and lineal descendants of those Zadokite priests of the ma'madot who withdrew into the wilderness as a protest against the defilement of the temple by Antiochus and the appointment of non-Zadokite high priests by the Maccabeans.[2] They held their goods in common, lived austere lives, maintained ritual purity, believed that the soul was immortal, and held as a major aspect of their belief an almost fanatical insistence on "doing Torah"—that is, living life in strict accordance with the law of God. Josephus wrote of them:

"They exceed all other men that addict themselves to virtue, and this in righteousness."[3]

THE SADDUCEES AND PHARISEES

The Sadducees did not believe in the immortality of the soul, but thought that the law of the Torah, as written, had to be followed without the slightest deviation.[4] They were deeply influenced by Hellenistic culture and, being mainly of the property-owning class, they preached cooperation with Rome. Isadore Epstein summed up the major differences between the Sadducees and Pharisees thus:

> The Pharisees desired that all the affairs of the State should be governed on strict Torah lines, with no concern for any other consideration. The Sadducees, on the other hand, maintained that whilst it was well to recognize the Torah as the basic constitution of the State, it was impossible to carry on a Government, which, under changed conditions, necessarily demanded close relations with heathen powers without making political expediency and economic interest the final arbiter of things.[5]

He claimed that the Pharisees were the only party truly suitable to deal with the needs of the times. Their principal doctrine was that oral law had been revealed in spiritual teaching to Moses when he received the Ten Commandments. They were liberal in their attempt to interpret this body of oral law and tradition, trying to modify its meaning and observance in order to make it relevant to the lives of the people, an attitude that gained them considerable support. In all these beliefs, especially those concerning the oral law, the Sadducees vehemently opposed them. Thus in some respects, the rise of the Pharisees can be seen as an inspired response to the demanding, anachronistic legalism of the Sadducees; in others, it can be seen as a reaction to the more profound Hellenization this ultra-conservative, powerful, priestly, and propertied class represented.[6]

The god of the Pharisees was not limited to the people of Israel; he was the god of every individual, Gentile or Jew. Indeed, he was the god of the entire world, of all mankind.[7] However, scholars of the Dead Sea Scrolls have recently found another, less flattering, description of the Pharisees—one that portrays them as "seekers after smooth things" who were only too ready to make accommodation with foreigners, which made them look like collaborators to their more extremist "Zealot" opponents.[8] From the time of the Maccabeans, the Sadducees and Pharisees became active rivals and competitors for control of the state.[9] Josephus also mentions a fourth sect among the Jews that he describes as having "an inviolable attachment to liberty which causes the nation to go mad with this distemper and makes them revolt against the Romans."[10]

OTHER JEWISH SECTS

These were far from the only important groups who made up the varied tapestry of the religious beliefs of biblical Israel during the last centuries of the Second Temple period. There was also a distinctive trend of charismatic Judaism that had Galilean roots,[11] as well as a many-faceted mystical trend of truly Egyptian/Hebraic roots. For example, from the 2nd century B.C.E., the Devir, or Holy of Holies, that had once held the Ark of the Covenant, God's throne on Earth, became the focus for visionaries who imagined ascending directly to God's heavenly palace and approaching his celestial throne. We read of Jewish mystics preparing for this mystical ascent by special disciplines.[12] Other mystical speculations in the Talmud focus on the *maaseh bereshith* (the work of creation) described in the first chapter of Genesis, and the *maaseh merkabah*, (the divine chariot) in the account of Ezekiel's vision. In Talmudic times, these mystical doctrines were carefully guarded and it was forbidden to expound them except to a few chosen disciples in the traditional Egyptian manner.

There are also "the Psalms of ascents" in the Bible and the Ascents tradition in the Kabbala—that is, the ascent through the various degrees of Neoplatonic enlightenment or gnosis, or—ascents to the higher heavens, another variation of the Merkabah tradition, also known as Hekaloth.[13] The Kabbala itself, or the tradition that was received from Aaron, is the major Jewish mystical tradition. One of its better-known tenets is the idea of the Zaddik, or the Righteous One.[14] The Righteous Man, as Ezekiel puts it, will not suffer for someone else's sin. He will not die. "The man who has sinned who is the one who must die. A son is not to suffer for the sins of his father, nor a father for the sins of his son" (Ezekiel 18:17–21) In the *Sepher-al Zohar*, it is written that Noah was a righteous one who was called the Foundation of the World, "and the Earth is established thereon, for this is the Pillar that upholds the world. So Noah was called 'Righteous . . . and the embodiment of the world's Covenant of Peace.'"[15]

APOCALYPTIC BELIEFS

In the Essene tradition, though not necessarily belonging to that sect, was a group of visionaries whose ideas are enshrined in the body of literature known as the Apocalypse.[16] In apparent contrast to the Essenes and the Apocalyptists, who embodied a seemingly negative reaction against the misery and oppression of the times, were the Zealots, who were out to fight against the oppressor and make an end to tyranny. They were deeply ardent patriots who combined a devotion to the Torah with an intense love of their country and were ready to fight and die for both.[17] In fact, despite what is written or implied in New Testament sources, Judaism at that time embraced at least twenty-four parties and sects that were not regarded as heretical, but as an integral part of mainstream Judaism.[18] Furthermore, a devout Jew could sit at the feet of a teacher in any one or several of these groups at various times in pursuit of spiritual knowledge and righteousness, without apparent contradiction.

HEROD THE GREAT

In 63 B.C.E., the Jewish state of Judea became a puppet state of Rome as a result of Pompey's intervention in the civil war between the Pharisees and the Jewish rulers Hyrcanus and Aristobulus.[19] At first, Rome was unsure how to handle these difficult people, but soon placed Judea under the rule of the Roman Governor of Syria. Herod the Great seized the throne of Judea in 43 B.C.E. and, four years later, was confirmed as King of the Jews by Rome. According to Strabo, Herod was, "so superior to his predecessors, particularly in intercourse with Romans and in his administration of the affairs of state, that he received the title of King."[20]

Contrary to general belief, Herod was, at first, a brave and resourceful king—a builder, an administrator, and a supremely able politician who brought order and stability to the area. He completely rebuilt the temple in Jerusalem, which became a source of wonder for Jew and Gentile alike, founded the port of Caesarea, and built fortresses as far south as the Jordan and in Damascus to the north. An Idumean who wore his Judaism lightly, he not only rebuilt the Jerusalem Temple, but also built temples to pagan gods: three were built to Roma and Augustus—one at Caesarea, another in Sebaste, and the third in Panias.[21] He also built a temple to Ba'al at Sia and gave help to temple building at Berytus and Tyre.[22] He helped restore the temple of Pythian Apollo in Rhodes.[23] A friend of both Pompey and Julius Caesar, he built the Antonia for Marc Antony, which later became the permanent residence of the Roman proconsuls and was eventually occupied by Pontius Pilate.

Herod is one of the best-documented characters in that period of history and it is well recorded that he behaved ruthlessly and murderously toward members of his own family whom he perceived as a threat to his power.[24] Indeed, the Roman Emperor Augustus said of this incident, "I would rather be Herod's pig than his son,"[25] which sums up the views of a powerful ruler on the actions of one of his most trusted subordinates. Toward the end of his life, Herod developed an even more cruel and violent streak that destroyed his reputation for all time, culminating in the execution of Rabbi Mathias and his students for pulling down the sacrilegious Roman eagle from the temple.[26] One well-known story that maligns him unjustly, however, is the New Testament account of his "slaughter of the innocents" (Matthew 1:22ff). The startling differences between the various Gospel accounts of the birth of Jesus, taken in the light of Josephus's failure to mention this event in his exhaustive litany of Herod's cruelty, gives us cause to question it. Furthermore, as there is no mention of it whatsoever in the Talmudic literature of the period, we are led to conclude that it simply did not happen.

In the early decades of Herod's reign, Rome's relationship with the Jews, both in Palestine and the Diaspora, was fruitful.[27] The Romans, who interfered as little as possible with the internal affairs of conquered provinces, granted the Jews a large measure of autonomy and the people were allowed full freedom of religious worship.

This, along with Herod's skillful political administration, managed to keep the lid on the seething hotbed of nationalist discontent fuelled by the activities of the Zealots and Hassidim. This unrest had been the constant backdrop to the affairs of state since the time of Antiochus IV (169 B.C.E.), long before the arrival of the Romans.

As before the occupation, the Sanhedrin continued to exercise its jurisdiction in all cases, whether religious or civil, involving an infraction of Jewish law. There was also the political Sanhedrin, constituted at the will of the high priest, with membership drawn from the politically minded Sadducees, who acted as intermediaries between the Roman administration and the people. They were charged with policing cases of sedition and insurrection and handing over the accused to the Roman procurators. Unfortunately, however, the procurators who governed Judea abused their power and did everything to render the lot of their Jewish subjects miserable and bitter.[28]

THE ROMAN OCCUPATION

With the death of Herod, the division of the kingdom between his sons, and the intermittent rule by Roman procurators, Jewish nationalistic and religious fervor bubbled to the surface repeatedly in violent confrontations with the hated Roman occupiers, the *Kittim*. The first major rebellion was called Varus' War in the Talmud. Varus, the Roman governor of Syria, reported a major revolt at the feast of Pentecost that spread from Jerusalem into Judea, Galilee, Perea, and Idumea. Acting with typical Roman efficiency, Varus put his legions into the field, burned Emmaus and Sephoris, and enslaved the survivors of those cities.[29] He then exercised the standard Roman punishment for sedition and ruthlessly crucified 2,000 Jews for rebellion.[30] Varus' War was merely the first in a series of violent episodes signaling Jewish discontent with the Romans. As the Herodian kings and their Roman masters steadily increased taxation, the heady mix of religious fervor and political agitation gathered momentum.

Biblical Israel was a theocracy, in that the Torah was the law of the land and Roman law an additional imposition. In this context, it was impossible to make a religious statement without it also being a political statement, and it was just as difficult for the Romans to impose any political constraints upon the people without them having overtones of religious infringement. This was the turbulent reality that formed the backdrop for the life and ministry of Jesus—not the gentle, rural atmosphere of peace implied by the Gospels.

The biblical scholar Robert Eisenman, director of the Center for the Study of Judaeo-Christian Origins at California State University, suggests that the apparently peaceful, Hellenized country where the Galilean fishermen cast their nets, the New Testament scenes depicting Roman officials and soldiers as "near saints," and the vindictiveness of the Jewish mob described in the Gospels have to be understood in the light of the fact that these allegedly "divinely inspired" accounts were written in complete subservience to the ever-present realities of Roman power.[31] Josephus made the same point over 2,000 years ago, when he wrote that all historical accounts of that period suffered from two major defects—"Flattery of the Romans and vilification of the Jews, adulation and abuse being substituted for real historical record."[32]

Furthermore, by the time the Gospels were written, in the decades following the destruction of Jerusalem by the Romans in 70 C.E., Christian doctrine and mythology were already well-developed. Therefore the Jesus described in the Gospels must be distinguished from the very different Jesus of history.[33] Using a mixture of non-canonical sources—contemporary histories, apocryphal materials, the Dead Sea Scrolls, noncanonical acts such as the Pseudo-Clementine Recognitions, the Nag-Hammadi Scrolls, early church literature, and modern scholarship—it is possible to reconstruct a valid picture of John the Baptist, Jesus, and James, and, more important, some realistic indications of the nature of their real teaching.

Josephus makes specific mention of the frequent acts of rebellion against Roman occupation inspired by leaders or prophets of the apocalyptic tradition of Judaism, a visionary train of thought that spoke of God's intervention in the ultimate battle of the righteous against the forces of evil. This was an important facet of messianic teaching within Judaism. Both the Zadokite/Essene and the Pharisaic traditions expected two messiahs, not one: a priestly messiah and a kingly messiah. Both schools believed that, until the elect of Israel adhered strictly to the covenant with God, the final redemption and the triumph of good over evil could not take place.[34] The priestly messiah was to purify the elect and the kingly messiah was to lead them to victory in a war against the evildoers. The Old Testament foretold the coming of the messenger of the covenant who would "purify the sons of Levi" (Malachi 3:1–4). It also spoke of the return of Elijah as reconciler (Malachi 4:5–6).

John the Baptist

The historian Paul Johnson describes how, in these troubled times, the example of the Essenes led to the creation of a number of Baptist movements in the Jordan valley, where the whole area between the Lake of Genasseret and the Dead Sea was alive with holy eccentrics, many of whom had been to Qumran where they were imbued with Essene teaching. He and most other scholars specializing in that era are convinced that John the Baptist was an Essene who saw as his mission the creation of an elite within an elite to hasten the purification that was the necessary prelude to the coming apocalypse.[35]

John's position within the prophetic tradition is indicated by the fact that his own people believed that he was Elijah come again (John 1:21). Josephus describes his mission and execution in the following terms:

> Herod had put him [John surnamed the Baptist] to death, though he was a good man and had exhorted the Jews to lead righteous lives, to practice justice towards their fellows and piety towards God, and so doing to join in baptism. In his view this was a necessary preliminary if baptism was to be acceptable to God. They must not employ it to gain pardon for whatever sins they had committed, but as a consecration of the body implying that the soul was already cleansed by right behaviour. While others too joined the crowds about him, because they were aroused to the highest degree by his sermons, Herod became alarmed. Eloquence that had so great an effect on mankind might lead to some sort of sedition . . . John, because of Herod's suspicions, was brought in chains to Machareus . . . and there put to death.[36]

In the context of the times already described, Josephus' reason for John's execution is entirely credible. However, that should not blind us to the fact that the version given in the New Testament is

Carving of John the Baptist at the Cathedral of Orleans.

also highly plausible in the light of John's connection with the Essenes, who fulminated furiously against what they called "fornication." The two accounts are different, but not mutually exclusive, and both may accurately reflect different and concurrent aspects of Herod's motivation.

What Josephus tells us of John's beliefs and his view of baptism is more important. The biblical scholar John Dominic Crossan states that Josephus' view means that John's baptism was not a ritual act that removed sin, but rather a physical and external cleansing symbolizing that spiritual and internal purification had already taken place among his followers.[37] One modern historian, using precisely the issues raised above, wrote:

> People placed themselves in the position of disciples of John
> [the Baptist] in order to learn how to be purified effectively
> both inwardly and outwardly. Once they felt fairly confident of
> their righteousness, by John's definition, then they came for
> immersion. . . . Not all the people became his disciples. Once
> people were immersed, however, they would already have
> accepted John's teaching and therefore become his disciples
> before this.[38]

The Church has always denied any teaching role of John the Baptist in his relationship with Jesus, yet modern scholarship tends to support the "heretical" view that Jesus was his pupil, a tradition that has been kept alive for 2,000 years among the hidden streams of spirituality preserved by the descendants of the ma'madot, namely the Rex Deus families and their spiritual heirs, the Templars and the Freemasons.

JESUS THE NAZOREAN

The teacher-pupil relationship between John and Jesus poses multiple problems for the Church. In the first instance, the Church is seen to have been a trifle "economical" with the truth in their accounts of the relationship between these two inspired figures. Second, as Jesus was a disciple of John, he must have been a sinner who was restored to righteousness in order to qualify for baptism— an impossible concept for those who believe he was divine. Knowing that Jesus was a devout Jew so committed to "doing Torah" that he became a pupil of John the Baptist, then underwent purification from sin and baptism, it is impossible to accept that he ever thought of himself as divine. For him and for all other Jews, that would have been the ultimate blasphemy. The modern author A. N. Wilson, after researching the period thoroughly, reached the same conclusion. He concluded that Jesus was a Galilean *hasid*, or holy man, a healer in the prophetic tradition. Wilson states categorically that:

> I had to admit that I found it impossible to believe that a first-century Galilean holy man had at any time of his life believed himself to be the Second Person of the Trinity. It was such an inherently improbable thing for a monotheistic Jew to believe.[39]

Apart from a plethora of so-called relics of extremely dubious provenance, there is only one archaeological artefact that makes any reference to Jesus, and that was only discovered in 2001. This is the ossuary inscribed in Aramaic with words that translate as "James son of Joseph and the brother of Jesus." Not surprisingly, this discovery was viewed with considerable scepticism when it first came to light. Sadly, it was later proven to be a clever modern fake, manufactured and sold for mere profit. This type of falsehood is nothing new; the manufacture of "holy relics" was big business during the medieval era. Unfortunately, fakes, ancient or modern, do nothing to attest to the historical reality of Jesus. Indeed, trying to arrive at any realistic understanding of the full extent and nature of his teachings is extremely difficult, for outside the canonical Gospels he made little impact. Therefore, we have to reconstruct a framework of his true teachings from the Apocryphal Gospels and Acts, fleshed out and supported by relevant documentation found among more recent discoveries at Qumran and Nag-Hammadi.

THE TEACHINGS OF JESUS

New Testament sources, with one or two notable exceptions, tell us more about the viewpoint of the authors than they do about Jesus himself. However, these exceptions are interesting, especially when they contradict Church teaching. For example, Karen Armstrong highlights one episode when she remarks: "Certainly Jesus' disciples

did not think that they had founded a new religion: they continued to live as fully observant Jews and went every day in a body to
worship at the Temple,"[40] Her comment is based upon a passage
from the Acts of the Apostles (Acts 2:46). According to Aristides,
one of the earliest apologists for Christianity, the worship of the first
Jerusalem "Christians" was fundamentally more monotheistic than
even that of the Jews. The teachings of Jesus, therefore, were plainly
not regarded by his disciples and apostles as either the foundation
of a new form of religion or as an indictment of Judaism. The only
difference between them and their Jewish neighbors was their fanatical adherence to Jesus' interpretation of the Torah, underpinned and
strengthened by their faith in the messianic nature of his role.

The title Jesus of Nazareth is a complete misnomer, as Nazareth
simply did not exist at that time. His true description is, more accurately, Jesus the Nazorean, a sect that was an offshoot of the Essenes.
The initiatory, gnostic nature of Jesus' teaching is made abundantly
clear in a passage from the Gospel of Thomas discovered among the
Nag-Hammadi Scrolls in Egypt in 1945, which records him as saying:
"He who will drink from my mouth will become like me. I myself
shall become he, and things that are hidden will be revealed to him."[41]
Jesus, in his role of supreme teacher of righteousness, initiated the elite
among his followers into the Nazoreans by a form of baptism. Proof
of this was discovered by Professor Morton Smith in his studies into
the *Secret Gospel of Mark*, to which he found reference in the
monastery of Mar Saba in Israel.[42] This document was, most probably, the one originally known as the *Gospel of the Hebrews*.

We can only safely accept the reported sayings of Jesus in the
canonical Gospels when they are authenticated in apocryphal works,
or can be validated by the material covering the beliefs of Jesus'
brother, James the Just. Others are plausible when they are obviously
uncontaminated by pro-Roman bias or are consistent with mainstream Jewish belief. For example, Jesus is quoted as saying: "Go not
into the way of the Gentiles and into any city of the Samaritans
enter ye not: but go rather to the lost sheep of Israel (Matthew 1:5–6),"
which is entirely in line with Essene teaching and can be taken to
be an authentic reflection of what he actually might have said.

By contrast, another saying attributed to him, "Go ye therefore
and make disciples of all nations, baptizing them in the name of the

Father and of the Son and of the Holy Spirit," should be rejected as an impossible idea to be held by anyone of the Essene tradition (Matthew 29:19), not only because of its instruction to preach to the Gentiles but, more important, because the use of the phrase, "In the name of the Father and of the Son and of the Holy Spirit," would be anathema to any Jew. The Jews, be they Nazoreans, Essenes, Zealots, or any of the other sects, only recognized one God, the Lord God of Israel. The phrase, "Father, Son, and Holy Spirit," does not occur in any authentic Jewish document and did not come into general use among Christians until long after the destruction of Jerusalem.

The crucial period to understand is the one that begins with Jesus' triumphal entry into Jerusalem and his crucifixion less than a week later. The deliberate staging of his entry into the holy city the week before Passover, as recounted in the Gospels,[43] gave advance warning to the Romans that serious trouble was brewing. Moreover, one Gospel records that he was hailed with the words "Blessed is the King of Israel" (John 12:13), which would be construed by the Romans as an open call to rebellion. There were also uncomfortable echoes of a similar event two centuries earlier—the entry into Jerusalem of the triumphant Simon Maccabeus, who purified the temple after he was greeted with popular acclaim, "with praise and palm branches" (Maccabees 13:50–51), a warning to the Romans that was amplified when Jesus upset the tables of the money-changers in the temple soon after he entered the city.[44]

All this, occurring just before Judaism's most important feast when the city was bursting at the seams with a full complement of Sadducees, Pharisees, Zealots, Hassidim, and assorted apocalyptic fundamentalists imbued with nationalistic and religious fervor, constituted a religious and political powder keg, with Jesus' entry acting as the fuse.

PONTIUS PILATE

The Roman man in charge was hardly the ideal choice to deal with these delicate and explosive circumstances. Pontius Pilate had a well-earned reputation for corruption, violence, robbery, and numerous executions without even the formality of a trial.[45] He had already weakened the power and influence of the Sanhedrin by depriving them of their jurisdiction in religious matters and had saddled the political Sanhedrin with the responsibility of arresting anyone suspected of plotting against Rome and handing them over to the Romans for judgment.

The temple guards, acting under the instructions of the political Sanhedrin, arrested Jesus and handed him over to Pilate.[46] There was no night-time Sanhedrin trial of Jesus for blasphemy; that would have been illegal in that era. There was no appearance before Herod; there was no prevarication on Pilate's part, for why should he concern himself with the life of one man when his predecessor, Varus, had crucified 2,000 Jews for sedition? The inescapable fact is that Jesus was crucified by the Romans for sedition and not arraigned by the Jews for blasphemy, for, by their standards, his message was in accord with Judaic tradition. He was tried and executed by the Roman procurator, Pontius Pilate,[47] a man renowned for his cruelty, in order to nip any potential insurrection in the bud. Crucifixion was the Romans' standard punishment for sedition, rebellion, and mutiny; the penalty for blasphemy was death by stoning, as we shall see later.

In order to discover who led the Nazoreans after the death of Jesus, how Jerusalem came to be destroyed by the Romans, and, most important, how, after that traumatic event, Judaism and the teachings of Jesus came to be transformed into two distinctly different religions, we must study the life and teachings of the brother of Jesus, James the Just, high priest of the temple and the so-called "first bishop of Jerusalem."

CHAPTER 6

JAMES THE JUST, ST. PAUL, AND THE DESTRUCTION OF THE TEMPLE

The long-standing tradition that Jesus appointed Peter to lead the disciples after the crucifixion was created by the Church over forty years later to proclaim the supremacy of Rome over all other centers of Christianity. The truth about the leadership of the original disciples can be found in the New Testament, the works of early fathers of the Church, and in a passage in one of the Apocryphal Gospels. Suppressed by the Church, the Gospel of Thomas vanished from sight for over 1,500 years, until a copy was rediscovered among other long-lost documents at Nag-Hammadi in 1945. In it, we find the following passage:

> The disciples said to Jesus:
> We know that you will depart from us.
> Who is to be our leader?
> Jesus said to them:
> Wherever you are, you are to go to
> James the righteous,
> For whose sake heaven and earth came into being.[1]

The phrase, "For whose sake the heaven and earth came into being," has distinct and deliberate overtones of the traditional Kabbalistic description of Noah, of whom it was said, "The Righteous One is the Foundation of the World." Another reference to Jesus' direct appointment of James as his successor occurs in the Pseudo-Clementine Recognitions,[2] and, according to another early Church father and historian of Christianity, Epiphanius, James was described as "The first to whom the Lord entrusted his Throne upon Earth."[3]

Clement of Alexandria, however, speaks of the election of James by the Apostles and not of a direct appointment by Jesus. Therefore, whether by appointment or election, it is established that it was James, and not Peter, who was the true successor of Jesus. The New Testament acknowledges this when it delineates James as "the first bishop of Jerusalem" (Acts 12:17). Robert Eisenman takes this to its logical conclusion when he states that:

> James was the true heir and successor of his more famous
> brother Jesus and the leader at that time of whatever the move-
> ment was we now call "Christianity," not the more Hellenized
> character we know through his Greek cognomen Peter, the
> "Rock" of, in any event the Roman Church.[4]

It was the deliberate creation of the Petrine foundation myth that forced the Church to marginalize the role of James. The Gospels make it clear that Jesus was a member of a large family that included James, Joses, Simon, and Judas Thomas, plus several unnamed sisters (Matthew 13:55), which tends to explain Jesus' choice of successor. Who would have known Jesus' teaching best and been deemed sufficiently trustworthy to carry it forward unaltered? One of his own brothers, of course, and James had already acquired a well-earned reputation for righteousness. Another important cause for an embarrassed reaction to James on the part of the Christian theologians began in the 2nd century when, in its divinely guided wisdom, the Church decided that Mary, the mother of Jesus, was a virgin, that Jesus was her only child, and that he was celibate.

The fact that the Gospels record Jesus as a member of a large family was not the only awkward problem that Church theologians had to overcome. There was another: the question of Jesus' marital status. Jewish custom at that time demanded that all males, especially rabbis, marry and produce a family. The few exceptions to this rule are clearly delineated in sacred literature, one being his brother James, for example, who was described by the early Church fathers and theologians as a Nazorite who was "dedicated to Holiness from his mother's womb"[5] and, as such, would have been celibate. As a rabbi, Jesus was subject to the 613 strictures of the Law and was bound to marry. Moreover, as he was of the direct line of David, it was incumbent upon him to produce an heir.

THE MARRIAGE OF JESUS

Father Jerome Murphy-O'Connor, Professor of New Testament Theology at the Ecole Biblique in Jerusalem, stated, in a BBC radio broadcast, that:

> Paul was certainly married . . . Marriage is not a matter of choice for Jews, that's why you have so few in the early centuries who weren't married and that's why . . . Paul . . . must have been married because this was a social obligation whose social fulfilment was obvious.[6]

The Church has signally failed to apply the same reasoning used by Fr. Murphy-O'Connor in respect of Paul to the case of Jesus, even though there is no mention in the New Testament that Jesus was unmarried, a situation that would have provoked considerable comment at the time. However, traces of Jesus' marital status and clues to the identity of his wife can be found in the Gospels.

One English scholar, A. N. Wilson, suggests that, "The story of the wedding feast at Cana contains a hazy memory of Jesus' own wedding,"[7] and the Muslim scholar Professor Fida Hassnain says of it:

> The question arises who is the guest and who is the bride? I would suggest Mary is the host for she orders the procuring of the wine or the guests, which Jesus deals with. One wonders whether it is *his* own marriage with Mary Magdalene, and whether the whole episode has been kept under camouflage . . . I believe that Mary Magdalene behaved as the chief consort of Jesus, and he also took her as his spouse.[8]

The story of the wedding is found in the Gospel of John:

> And the third day there was a marriage in Cana of Galilee; and the mother of Jesus was there:
> And both Jesus was called, and his disciples, to the marriage.
> And when they wanted wine, the mother of Jesus sayeth

unto him, they have no wine, Jesus sayeth unto her, Woman, what have I to do with thee? Mine hour is not yet come.

His mother sayeth unto the servants, whatsoever he sayeth unto you, do it (John 2:1–5).

The story continues with changing the water into wine and Jesus ordering the servants to distribute it. A study of Jewish custom of the time reveals that only the bridegroom or the groom's mother would have the necessary authority to give orders to the servants at a wedding feast,[9]—which indicates that this was indeed Jesus' own wedding being described.

Later in the same Gospel, we read of circumstances that, again interpreted in the light of the strict legalistic customs of the time, reveal the true nature of the relationship between Jesus the Nazorean and Mary Magdalene.

Then Martha, as soon as she heard that Jesus was coming, went and met him: but Mary sat still in the house . . .

And when she had so said, she went her way, and called her sister secretly, saying, the Master is come and calleth for thee. As soon as she heard that, she arose quickly, and came unto him. (John 11:20, 28–29)

The Mary in question is Mary of Bethany, better known as Mary Magdalene, who is clearly playing the role of dutiful wife, the only woman permitted to sit at a man's feet. In the Gospel of Luke, we find the following: "And she had a sister called Mary, which also sat at Jesus' feet and heard his word" (Luke 10:39), indicating, according to Jewish custom, that Jesus and Mary Magdalene were husband and wife.

The Catholic theologian Margaret Starbird was so incensed at the apparent heresy of Jesus' marriage as described in *Holy Blood, Holy Grail*, that she set out to refute it. It is a credit to her spiritual and intellectual integrity that the book she published after several years of detailed research, *The Woman with the Alabaster Jar*,[10] is a superbly argued and detailed exposition of the conclusive evidence proving the marriage of Jesus to Mary Magdalene and their founding of a dynasty. The alabaster jar in question contained expensive perfume that Mary poured on Jesus' head:

While Jesus was in Bethany in the home of a man known as Simon the Leper, a woman came to him with an alabaster jar of very expensive perfume, which she poured on his head as he was reclining at table.[11]

According to Jewish custom, and to other Near Eastern traditions from Sumer, Babylon, and Canaan, the king's head was ritually anointed with oil, usually by the royal priestess or royal bride in her ancient role of goddess. The Greeks called this ritual *hieros gamos*, or the sacred marriage. This ritual union with the priestess was crucial if the king were to be recognized in his divinely blessed and royal status, as the true "anointed one," or the messiah.[12] As a result, Western art and Church iconography nearly always portray Mary Magdalene as the lady with the alabaster jar.

THE FIRST CHURCH IN JERUSALEM

The large corpus of material describing the beliefs of James the Just and the Essenes helps us clarify the basis for the true teachings of Jesus. It is also a vital aid in stripping away the veneer of theological obfuscation that resulted from the mythologizing of this gifted spiritual teacher. Despite its later marked divergence from the initiatory teachings of Jesus, the social structure of the early Christian Church was largely shaped by Essene teaching, tradition, and practice.[13]

The early Church is known to have used a handbook known as the *Didache*, or "the teaching of the Lord." Regulations drawn from this were often quoted in letters to new Christian communities. The similarities between the *Didache* and the *Community Rule* found among the Dead Sea Scrolls is quite startling—particularly in view of the Church's determined attempt to date the latter to an earlier era. Both begin with information describing "the two ways"—the way of light and the way of darkness—and proceed in a manner that leaves no doubt as to which is the parent document.

The first "Christian Church" in Jerusalem was led by a triumvirate of elders, based clearly on the model of the Essene community. The three leaders of the followers of Jesus were known as "the Pillars," and they are listed in the New Testament as James, the brother of Jesus and the so-called "first bishop of Jerusalem," Simon-

Peter, and John (Galatians 2:9). This demonstrates that the well-established use of pillar symbolism had evolved even further from its original Egyptian use as a sign of divinely inspired wisdom or gnosis, through its signification of the divine presence during the forty years in the wilderness, to a symbolic representation of an individual who has attained enlightenment or righteousness. The Dead Sea Scrolls scholar Robert Eisenman equates James the Just with the Teacher of Righteousness of the Essenes.[14]

JAMES THE JUST

As a hereditary member of the ma'madot, Epiphanius described James' function as high priest in the following terms:

> I find that he also exercised the Priesthood according to the Ancient Priesthood, [the Rechabite or Nazorite one—possibly even the one Hebrews are calling the "Priesthood after the Order of Melchizedek"]. For this reason he was permitted to enter the Holy of Holies once a year, as the Bible lays down in the Law commanding the High Priests. He was also allowed to wear the High Priestly diadem on his head as the aforementioned trustworthy men—Eusabius, Clement and others have related—in their accounts.[15]

Another early Church father, Hegesippus, describes James being brought to the temple by the Scribes and Pharisees to quiet the Passover crowd hungering after the messiah. These establishment figures were, of course, intent on pacifying the crowd in order to coexist peacefully with the Roman occupiers.

James was of a different persuasion, however, for he was at the center of agitation at the temple in the years leading up to the war against Rome.[16] Far from quieting the crowd, he did the reverse and fanned the flames of revolt.[17] In *The Antiquities of the Jews* cited above, Josephus describes the beliefs and activities of the "fourth philosophy," those zealous for freedom and liberty, merging part of his earlier descriptions of the Essenes in *War of the Jews* with that of this nationalistic group. He confirms, thereby, that the Essenes and the Zealots were either following the same religious and political direction or, more probably, had become almost indistinguishable from one another. It is also indicative of this trend that Josephus only uses the term *Zealots* when referring to the people opposed to the high-priest Ananus, who eventually murdered James.

James, the leader of a group of strict, deeply religious, national-istic Jews, was the man to whom Jesus entrusted the leadership of his own disciples. So could there have been any major difference between the true teachings of Jesus and those of James? No! Major or sig-nificant deviations are inconceivable. This poses a question, how-ever: How and why is the version of Jesus' teaching reported in the canonical Gospels so different from the sectarian, Torah-based, ultra-orthodox practices revered by James the Righteous and the Essenes? To understand that, we must look at the character of a man whose changes of direction were baffling in their complexity—one who started by persecuting the followers of Jesus, was "miraculously con-verted," joined James and the others, and later, betrayed them.

SAUL OF TARSUS

The man who, in later centuries, became known as the Father of Christianity was the strange and complex Saulus, or Saul, of Tarsus, better known as St. Paul. Paul's own writings confirm that he was both a Roman citizen and a Pharisee who spent some time perse-cuting the followers of Jesus after the crucifixion (Acts 7:59). After his miraculous conversion on the road to Damascus, did a religious volte-face and changed, not only his religion, but also his name. After a mys-terious three years spent in Arabia (Galatians 1:17), he joined James in Jerusalem, learning the "true Way" as taught by Jesus (Acts 24:14), before setting out on a series of prolonged evangelical journeys.

Paul's missionary travels took him to many of the important cities of the eastern Mediterranean, so neither his persistence nor his energy can be faulted. However, within a remarkably short time, he was subject to scathing criticism by James and the original dis-ciples in Jerusalem. It is clear, both from the New Testament accounts and from other sources, that there was a major and fundamental dif-ference between the Way as interpreted by James and his Essene companions and the version preached by Paul. Conflict was inevitable and is mentioned, although in a glossed-over manner, in the account of the Council of Jerusalem in the Acts of the Apostles. This rather diplomatic version of events implies that, after some discussion, Paul's version of the message was deemed acceptable and valid (Acts 11). However, knowing that James the Just and the disciples who walked with Jesus had a righteous and absolute dedication to the Torah, the strict prohibition against mixing with Gentiles, keeping strictly to the dietary laws of Judaism, and trying to create a purified "elite within the elite of Israel" in preparation for the eventual victory of the power of light over the powers of darkness in the Last Days, we must see this as an incredible scenario—particularly when we read Paul's personal beliefs, which are expressed so clearly in his epistles.

Paul mixed with Gentiles. According to him, the covenant and its laws no longer applied, circumcision was not necessary for converts, and faith alone was all that was needed for salvation in the run up to the Parousia, or End of Times, when Jesus would come again. In his study of the Dead Sea Scrolls and related documents, Robert Eisenman has found records of this dispute that have enabled him to reconstruct a more accurate version of these events. In this, it becomes obvious that the dispute hinges on Paul's preaching to the Gentiles and his denial of the validity of the Torah. This led to a dramatic confrontation between a man called the Liar and those of his persuasion on one side, and the Righteous Teacher and the disciples on the other.

The importance of this bitter dispute is stressed by the reference to treachery in the underlying text, which refers to factional strife within the community.[18] The insistence of the Essenes on ritual purity, doing Torah, refusing to eat food sacrificed to idols, and forbidding social contact with Gentiles was rigidly enforced within the group. In the Qumran Community Rule it is stated that:

> Any man who enters the Council of Holiness walking in the
> Way of Perfection as commanded by God and, whether overtly
> or covertly, transgresses one word of the *Torah* of Moses on any
> point whatsoever . . . shall be expelled from the Council of the
> Community and return no more. No Man of Holiness shall
> associate with him in monetary matters or in approach *on any
> matter whatsoever.*[19]

This is exactly what happened to Paul and, after his expulsion, even his closest associate, Barnabas, deserted him, as he recounts in the Epistle to the Galatians (2:11–13). His total repudiation of the Law and his insistence that salvation is by faith alone and not by doing Torah, which he holds as worthless, is made explicit later in the same letter (2:15–16). The Catholic historian Paul Johnson states that, from the time of this dispute, the evangelical mission of St. Paul steadily lost ground to that of the evangelists duly accredited by James the Just in Jerusalem.

Paul makes dismissive mention of this practice of accreditation when he writes: "Or do we need, like some people, letters of recommendation to you . . ." (II Corinthians 3:1). Johnson is quite clear that, if it had not been not for the destruction of Jerusalem by the Romans a few years later, Paul's monumental effort would have been consigned to a minor footnote of history or, more likely, forgotten altogether.[20] From this point onward, few, if any, Jewish disciples have anything more to do with Paul. His traveling companions and collaborators after his expulsion are Judeo-Greeks such as Timothy, "whose mother was a believing Jewess" (Acts 16:1), a remarkably similar description to the one he applies to another of his companions and converts, the Herodian Princess Drusilla (Acts 24:24). Drusilla, like Paul, was a Roman citizen. Nearly all of Paul's own letters written after this event express resentment and bitterness about his treatment and express his pain at the charge that he is a liar and not a true apostle. For example:

> Am I not free? Am I not an apostle? Have I not seen Jesus our Lord? . . . Even though I may not be an apostle to others, surely I am to you! (I Corinthians 9:1–2)

In a later letter, he writes:

> . . . and for this purpose I was appointed a herald and an apostle—I am telling the truth I am not lying . . .(I Timothy 2:7)

If one reads all of Paul's epistles one after another, it is impossible to miss the constant self-pitying tone and the sense of resentful defensiveness that emerges. Read them all in sequence and you may well begin to perceive Paul in a very different light.[21]

In the light of his anti-Torah teaching, for James and his followers in Jerusalem, Paul was a false prophet. One early Church father, Iraneus, Bishop of Lyon, quotes an Ebionite document that describes Paul as "an apostate of the Law."[22] The Ebionites, or "the Poor" were the names by which Jesus' followers became known during and after James' ministry. Another Ebionite document dated to the early years of the 2nd century C.E., the *Kerygmata Petrou*, describes Paul as "an apostate of the Law" a "Spouter of wickedness and lies," and "the distorter of the true teachings of Jesus." The same document gives short shrift to Paul's description of the visions leading to his miraculous conversion on the road to Damascus, classifying them as "dreams and illusions inspired by devils."

All in all, it seems reasonable to suggest that the family and disciples of Jesus viewed Paul with considerable contempt. From Paul's letters, we can sense that this distrust and dislike were mutual. He describes his own position vis-à-vis the community in Jerusalem in these terms:

> Therefore stand fast in the freedom with which Christ has
> made us free and do not [submit] again to the yoke of slavery . . .
> Everyone who accepts circumcision is obliged to do the whole
> Law. Whosoever is justified by the Law are set aside from
> Christ. (Galatians 5:1–4)

Paul's epistles were viewed by James and his brethren as full of blasphemous ideas and peppered with gratuitous insults denigrating circumcision, circumcisers, and the Torah generally. They accused him of adopting the two-faced approach, to use Paul's own words, of being simultaneously a "Law-Keeper to those who keep the Law" and a "Law breaker to those" who do not (I Corinthians 9:24–26). So it is not surprising that the quarrel between Paul and James did not end with Paul's expulsion from the true disciples in Jerusalem. It turned from verbal antagonism to murderous violence.

THE ARREST OF PAUL

Paul physically assaulted James and tried to murder him. James was thrown headlong down the steps of the temple and broke his legs. This attempted murder is recorded in the *Pseudo-Clementine Recognitions* and is also part of the subject matter of a lost work about James from which Epiphanius quotes several passages, the *Anabathmoi Jacobou*, or *The Ascent of Jacob*. The most scholarly and conclusive study of these events can be found in Robert Eisenman's master-work, *James the Brother of Jesus*.[23]

After the assault, Paul was arrested,[24] supposedly because he had incensed the mob at the temple by his blasphemy in preaching the Gospel. It appears that the real reason for this arrest was protective, since the mob wished to kill him in revenge for his attempt on James's life. While in custody, he was warned of another plot to kill him, so he then warned the Roman arresting officer (Acts 23:20–21), who took him to Caesarea under a large military escort of two hundred soldiers, seventy cavalrymen, and two hundred spearmen (Acts 23:23–24)—a suspiciously large escort for a simple blasphemer whom the Romans would normally have left to the none-too-tender mercies of the Sanhedrin, who would have sentenced him to death by stoning. Yet no one in the Christian world seems to question why so much importance is attached to Paul or why such an expenditure of military resources is committed to his removal at a time of potential rebellion. Yet a clue exists in the New Testament: Paul is not just a Roman citizen. He is a Herodian, a member of the ruling family and a long-term friend of Rome.

The first mention we have of this pivotal relationship with the Herodians occurs in one of Paul's own letters. In a reference whose importance has signally failed to register on modern Christians of any denomination, Paul writes:

> Greet those who belong to the household of Aristobulus.
> Greet Herodian my relative. (Romans 16:10–11)

The Aristobulus he mentions was the son of Agrippa I's brother, Herod of Chalcis, who had a son called Herod, known as Herodian, or the Littlest Herod. These family and political links explain how, as a comparatively young man, Paul wielded power in Jerusalem as a member of the temple guard authorized by the high priest to persecute the followers of Jesus. As a group of nationalistic, zealous Jews, the Jesus group would have been a prime target for temple authorities bent on suppressing rebellion against their Roman masters. The English author A. N. Wilson suggests: "It does not seem unreasonable to suppose that he was in the same position in the temple guard when Jesus was arrested."[25]

The important political clout that goes with royal connections may explain Paul's comfortable status during his two year imprisonment at Caesarea at the behest of the Roman governor, Felix (Acts 24:1–27). Within the same account, we learn that Felix was married to a lady called Drusilla, who was a Jewess, the third daughter of Agrippa I, and the sister of Agrippa II. She had divorced her first husband to marry Felix (Acts 8:9ff.), who was also well connected, being the brother of Nero's favorite freedman, Pallas. This is the same Drusilla mentioned earlier who was among those who loyally followed Paul after his expulsion by James. Josephus records that the original Antipater, the father of Herod the Great, was awarded hereditary Roman citizenship for services to Caesar,[26] so Paul and Drusilla, as Herodians, both relatives of King Agrippa II,[27] were born into a highly privileged position that they exploited to the full.

In his epistle to the Philippians, Paul mentions one of his important converts, Epaphroditus, who was a senior advisor to the Roman Emperor Nero (Philippians 4:18)—an important connection he stresses later in the same letter with, "Greetings, especially those in Caesar's household" (Philippians 4:21). Paul, or Saul, as the Romans and Herodians knew him, had contacts in very high places. These important relationships tell us how Paul, a supposedly simple tentmaker, traveled the world with ease, had so many miraculous escapes from prison, and was treated as the welcome guest of people of considerable power and political influence. It is no accident, therefore, that the community at Antioch, who were the first believers to be called Christians, mainly consisted of other Herodians; Paul was getting considerable support from his family.

These strong Herodian and Roman pro-establishment links explain the neutering of Jesus' message that occurred when Paul stripped it of all nationalistic fervor and substituted so many calls to obey lawful authorities. Paul, like his ancestor Herod the Great, wore his Judaism very lightly, otherwise it would be impossible to conceive how any Jew of his supposedly Pharisaic background could have indulged in the kind of anti-Semitic and anti-Torah teaching he promoted.

The contrast between Paul's message of subservience to lawful, i.e. Roman, authority and his preaching of a New Covenant that denied most of the strictures of the Torah was the complete negation of the teaching of James and the original disciples of Jesus in

Jerusalem. James' zealous and intrinsically Jewish stance had a very political dimension. He was at the center of agitation at the temple, actively promoting a pro-Torah, distinctly nationalistic, anti-Herodian, and anti-Roman policy that led to a head-on collision with the authorities in Jerusalem, namely the Saducee high priests and their principal ally, Paul's close relative, King Agrippa II.

The Murder of James the Just

The confrontation came to crisis point after King Agrippa appointed a new Saducee high priest, Ananus. Acting on his orders, the Sanhedrin was convened to try James for blasphemy. Procedures existed for the execution of men deemed popular with the people. These are listed in the *Mishna Sanhedrin*, which recommends that the priests gather around the condemned, jostle him, and cause him to fall from the temple wall. Then they stone him and beat out his brains with clubs.[28] This is precisely what happened to James the Just. He was cast down from the temple wall, stoned, and then given the coup de grace with a fuller's club.

James' murder occurred despite his popularity and the fact that eighty Pharisees petitioned Rome on his behalf and volunteered to die with him.[29] Jerome, the early Church father who translated the Bible into Latin, records that, "James was of such great Holiness and enjoyed so great a reputation among the people that the downfall of Jerusalem was believed to be on account of his death."[30] The 3rd-century Christian theologian Origen, and Eusebius, bishop of Caesarea, both claim to have seen a copy of Josephus different from the one we presently possess, probably the Slavonic version, which stated that the fall of Jerusalem was a consequence of the death of James, not the death of Jesus—a significant admission for two of the most respected early fathers of the Church.[31]

It was after this traumatic event that the Ebionites and the other members of the ma'madot, now under the leadership of James' "cousin," Simeon, decided to leave Jerusalem and cross the Jordan into Pella.[32] Leadership of this group remained among the descendants of the family of Jesus known as the *Desposyni* for over 150 years after their flight to Pella.[33]

In Jerusalem and Judea, opinion among the other Jews was sharply divided. Those of the Zealot faction actively fomented immediate rebellion against Rome, the Sadducees, "Hellenizers," and Herodians. Others wanted to maintain the status quo and keep the peace. By 66 C.E., the die was cast and the move to war came into the open.

At this point, Saul, the kinsman of Agrippa, comes back into the picture. Josephus notes that, when the war broke out in 66 C.E. and the Jewish Zealot forces occupied Jerusalem:

> The men of power [the Sadducees], perceiving that the sedition was too hard for them to subdue ... endeavoured to save themselves, and sent ambassadors, some to Florus [the Roman Procurator] ... and others to Agrippa, among whom the most eminent was Saul, and Antipas, and Costobarus, who were of the king's kindred.[34]

The object of sending messengers to Florus and Agrippa was to ensure prompt military action by the Romans in order to subdue the rebellion before it got out of hand—a motivation totally consistent with the general thrust of Paul's "obey lawful authorities" philosophy expressed so clearly in his writings. When this ploy failed, the insurrection became unstoppable and, when the Jews repeatedly defeated the Romans, a deputation was sent to the Emperor Nero at Corinth—then called Achia. Again Josephus provides the details:

> Cestius sent Saul and his friends, at their own desire, to Achia, to Nero, to inform him of the great distress they were in ...[35]

After this meeting, Nero appointed Vespasian as general in command of the legions in Palestine, thereby sealing the fate of Jerusalem. Eventually, after four years of prolonged and bitter fighting, Jerusalem was besieged and fell to the Romans amid scenes of unprecedented carnage and brutality. Its surviving inhabitants were put to the sword, crucified, or sold into slavery, and the city itself and the temple were razed to the ground. In this brutal manner, the Jews were finally deprived of their cultic center, the home of the Lord God of Israel, and the heart was brutally ripped out of their culture and traditions. Despite the prophecies and the righteous behavior of the Essenes and the bravery of the Zealots, the forces of darkness had triumphed over the sons of light. Now everything had changed, not only for the Jews, but for the entire world.

CHAPTER 7

THE FOUNDING OF CHRISTIANITY, RABBINICAL JUDAISM, AND REX DEUS

With the fall of Jerusalem, followed by the self-immolation of the defenders of Masada, Rome's reconquest of its rebellious subjects was complete. The holy city was a smoking charnel house, the temple destroyed, the streets, alleyways, and underground passages choked with putrefying corpses, and the city limits marked by a ring of unfortunates crucified after their failed attempts to escape. Thousands of survivors were paraded in chains through the streets of Rome behind the triumphal procession of their conquerors bearing the treasures of the temple, commemorating the triumph of Rome and the humiliation of the Jews. The parade finished with the ritual execution of the leaders. Then the mass of captives was dispatched to the slave markets, the arena, or to end their days in the galleys and mines of the empire.

The failure of the Jewish revolt, for which the people of Israel paid such a horrendous price, changed international history. The full impact of the failed revolution of 66–73 C.E. is impossible to assess, for, with the passage of time, its far-reaching results have shaped the history of Europe, the people of the Middle East, and, ultimately, the Americas. The historian Neil Faulkner describes one such immediate outcome:

> The defeat of apocalyptic hope and the physical destruction of the Judaeo-Christian sect cleared the way for Pauline Christians

to de-nationalise Jesus, cauterise his revolutionary message and repackage him as a "saviour-god" dispensing opiate for the masses.[1]

It was not only the followers of Paul's distorted message who had to conform to the changed political situation. In order to survive, any Jewish religious or cultural activity had to be completely recast in complete subservience to the ever-present realities of Roman power.[2] The temple, the main place acceptable to the Jewish people for sacrifice, was destroyed. As a result, mainstream Judaism itself had to be substantially changed to avoid being absorbed by the ravening maw of Roman power.

The Pharisees had always preached accommodation with the Romans and, like many of his fellow Pharisees, Rabbi Yohanen ben Zakkai had been totally opposed to the revolution and the extremes of the Zealots. During the early stages of the siege of Jerusalem, he was smuggled out of the city in a coffin. As a result of his moderation, after the fall of city, he and his companions were the only Jewish leaders to retain credibility. Rabbi Yohanen approached Emperor Vespasian and asked permission to found a school at Jamnia where Jews could study, pray, and begin the task of restructuring their religion. The school, he insisted, would be a spiritual center and not a hotbed of revolutionary fervor.

Judaism was to be stripped of its messianic and intensely nationalistic zeal.[3] Now that the temple was gone, the rabbis taught their fellow Jews to experience God in their neighbors. Some taught that the *mitzvah*, ("Thou shalt love thy neighbor as thyself,") was the greatest principle of the Torah.[4] The founding rabbis of this new form of Judaism altered the emphasis, but not the substance, of their religion to create a new style of worship and ritual acceptable to the Romans. They drew heavily on established tenets of belief and the vast store of Scriptures and exegesis their predecessors had accumulated, and continued to speak of Jerusalem in the present tense, even though the temple building no longer existed. The reality the temple had symbolized, that of God's mystical presence on Earth, was an eternal truth that became the heart of Judaism from that day onward.[5]

THE DISPERSAL OF THE REX DEUS FAMILIES

The Ebionites and surviving members of the ma'madot returned from Pella under the leadership of Simeon, the cousin of Jesus, and took up residence near Mount Sion in the ruined city of Jerusalem.[6] However, this was not to be a permanent move. Several successive Roman emperors, including Vespasian, Titus, Domitian, and Trajan, repeatedly ordered the tenth legion, the main occupying force, to hunt down and execute any Jew who claimed to be a descendant of King David.[7]

This persecution was simply an extension of a far older threat. The Rex Deus sagas recount that, years earlier, the children of Jesus were parted and sent to separate places of safety in order to ensure their survival.[8] Jesus' two-and-a-half-year-old son, James, was entrusted to the care of Judas Thomas Didymus, Jesus' twin brother, and sent for safekeeping to King Abgar of Edessa.[9] Mary Magdalene, the pregnant wife of the messiah, fled to Egypt, where she gave birth to a daughter called Sarah before seeking refuge in southern France.[10]

Now it was time for the descendants of the Davidic line to disperse to avoid persecution and death. They scattered to France, England, Spain, Italy, Eastern Europe, and throughout the Middle East. Before doing so, however, they used their time in the ruins of Jerusalem to reinforce their Cohenite marital practices in order to preserve their sacred bloodlines and began to transform their beliefs and practices to ensure their survival. They had long since rejected formal worship at the Jerusalem Temple as, in their eyes, it was polluted. Now all they had to do was to discard their fervent nationalism and anti-Roman stance, laying even greater emphasis on behavior and—creating an elite within the elite dedicated to the principles of sacred brotherhood founded firmly on the gnostic principles of justice and truth. In this way, they hoped to preserve the spiritual core of their initiatory message and its insistence on "doing Torah" without fear of persecution by the Romans.

Thanks to the works of an early father of the Church, Epiphanius, we have a clear idea of their outward beliefs about Jesus. Epiphanius wrote of them:

> Beside a daily ritual bath, they have a baptism of initiation and each year they celebrate certain mysteries . . . In these mysteries

they use unleavened bread and, for the other part, pure water . . .
They say that Jesus was begotten of human seed . . . that he was
not begotten by god the Father, but that he was created . . . and
they too receive the Gospel of Matthew and this they use . . . to
the exclusion of all others. But they call it the Gospel according
to the Hebrews.[11]

One modern historian, Karen Armstrong, confirmed that they
knew Jesus had been human and not divine when she wrote, "After
all, some of them had known him since he was a child and could
not see him as a god."[12]

The followers of St. Paul had no trouble bringing their beliefs in
line with the reality of Roman power. Paul, in his capacity as a
Roman citizen, friend of Caesar, and kinsman of Herod, had already
transformed the Way into a subservient form of worship that encouraged its followers to obey lawful authorities and "render unto Caesar
what is Caesar's." In Pauline Christianity, the Law of Moses was
superseded by faith, the nationalistic and apocalyptic vision of the
original disciples was ignored, and the esoteric pathway to the god
of the Jews, who had been looking after the people of Israel since the
time of Abraham, was hijacked and perverted.[13]

THE FIRST CHRISTIANS

In the aftermath of the failed Jewish revolt, the followers of Jesus
fell into two main groups: the original apostles, known as the
Nazoreans or Ebionites, led first by James and then by Simeon, and
their theological opponents, the Christians, who followed the teaching of Paul. The Ebionites were scattered or in the process of rapid
dispersal to escape the unwelcome attention of the Roman authorities. The Pauline Christians were relatively settled and the battle for
supremacy among them was eventually won by those centered in
Rome. The thinking and beliefs of this group of Roman Christians
began to dominate and ultimately shaped the belief structure and
the future of this "new" religion.

The Ebionites were totally dependant upon the oral transmission
of the teachings of Jesus that they had received directly from the
original apostles or from the brothers of Jesus—direct instruction

Tomb of Mary Magdalene, St. Maximin la Baume, Provence.

Ceiling painting of Mary Magdalene with a child
in her arms, Sacre Monte near Varese, northern Italy.

from the very people who had walked and talked with Jesus when he was alive. The Pauline Christians, on the other hand, had received instruction directly or indirectly from Paul who, on his own admission, had never met the living Jesus. Paul's disputed claim to apostleship was based on his visionary instruction that he claimed was directly from "the risen Lord."

It is widely recognized that Paul's prolific letter-writing provides the earliest documentation of this period and that his letters began to circulate among the communities he served from about 47 C.E., more than thirty years before the first of the canonical Gospels appeared.[14] Prior to the writing of the Gospels, these were the only documents circulating among Paul's converts. There were others, now vanished or suppressed, known in scholarly circles as the Q documents, that gave written expression to the recorded teachings of Jesus and possibly to descriptions of aspects of his ministry. The biblical scholar Robert Eisenman writes:

> In using the letters of Paul as our primary source material, we are on the firmest ground conceivable, for these are indisputably the earliest reliable documents of Christianity and can be dated with a high degree of certainty. They are patently earlier than the Gospels or the Book of Acts, which precede them in the present arrangement of the New Testament and which are themselves in large part doctrinally dependant upon Paul. Acts to some extent is dependant on Paul's letters for historical information as well.[15]

This almost total doctrinal dependence of Acts and the Gospels upon the work of Paul has been the cause of considerable confusion to the vast majority of believers simply because, in the New Testament, the Gospels come first, followed by Acts and then by the Epistles. This ordering, which is the result of decisions made centuries later, is taken to reflect the chronological order of composition, a mistake that distorts any real appreciation of the relative theological importance of the Scriptures concerned.

It is difficult to penetrate and expose the original ingredients of Christian belief, because the activities and teaching of Paul predominate excessively in the New Testament accounts of Christian beginnings. Indeed, they completely overshadow and virtually exclude the contribution of the real apostles and their view of the true doctrine of Jesus. In the New Testament, dominated as it is by Pauline material, we are only shown brief, inadequate, and misleading glimpses of the very substantial Nazorean movement to which the true apostles belonged.[16]

THE WRITING OF THE GOSPELS

There is now a scholarly consensus regarding the probable dating of the composition of the four canonical Gospels. Mark is agreed to have been the first to appear and was written between 70 and 80 C.E. Matthew is generally believed to have made its appearance about ten years later with the Gospel of Luke and the Acts of the Apostles in the first decade of the 2nd century. The first written version of the Gospel of John is variously dated from 100 to 120 C.E.[17]

The Synoptic Gospels of Matthew, Mark, and Luke are, according to the modern scholarly view, founded, to a considerable extent, on an earlier lost common source that is known as Q. There is a startling consensus among scholars regarding Q's content and style that has resulted in the virtual re-creation of the document. Burton L. Mack, Professor of New Testament Studies at the Claremont School of Theology in California, writes:

> The remarkable thing is that the authors of Q did not think
> about Jesus as the Messiah or the Christ, nor did they understand
> his teachings to be an indictment of Judaism. They certainly did
> not regard his crucifixion as a divinely inspired, or saving event.
> Nor did they believe that he had been raised from the dead to
> rule over the world. They thought of him as a Jewish prophet
> whose teaching made it possible to live an attainable and right-
> eous life in very troubled times. As a result they neither gathered
> to worship in his name, honoured him as a god—which to them,
> as devout Jews would have been the ultimate blasphemy—nor
> celebrate his memory through hymns, prayers or rituals.[18]

Yet the Gospels, largely based on information from the Q document, speak of Jesus as a divine figure. Close and unbiased examination of this concept, however, soon displays the a priori improbability of the doctrine of the deity of Jesus.

Jesus was born, raised, and taught as a Jew; his followers regarded themselves as a Jewish movement. The doctrine of a divine human being is diametrically opposed to the Jewish concept of God at the time of Jesus. No Jew subscribing to the Hebrew Scriptures and seeking acceptance by other Jews could present himself in such a manner without being stoned to death for blasphemy. However, the deification of humans was agreeable to current heathen notions, as the history of the Roman Empire confirms. Therefore, the obvious inference is that the deification of Jesus was an intrusion from Gentile or heretical sources and not fundamental to the integrity of Jesus' message. Proof of this is found in the fact that Jesus' deification was staunchly resisted by the original apostles and those Jews who believed that he was the Messiah. This fact confirms that it was alien in origin and that Jesus himself could not have entertained it.[19]

CHAPTER 8

THE DARK AGES AND THE REPRESSIVE CHURCH

The marriage of secular and political power that resulted from the Edict of Milan and the Council of Nicea spawned a repressive church/state alliance that was described in somewhat pungent terms by a modern Catholic theologian as "an abortion in the womb of the Church."

> The mother church of Western Christianity inherited the Roman Empire with the Edict of Milan in 312. In that century the patriarchal and dualistic theologian Augustine of Hippo put forward a theology that legitimized the . . . conscription of Christians into the military, "just wars" in the name of Christ, coercion of minority groups such as Donatists, and rendering women into shadows and scapegoats. "Man but not woman is made in the image and likeness of God"[1] Only today are we beginning to free ourselves from this abortion of the maternal in the womb of the church begun sixteen centuries ago.[2]

Soon after the Council of Nicea, Constantine made it clear that the benefits he had granted to the Christian Church "must benefit only adherents of the Catholic Faith,"[3] which he defined as those who accepted without reservation the doctrine enunciated in the new creed and the supreme ecclesiastical authority of the bishop of Rome. He stated: "Heretics and schismatics shall not only be alien from these privileges but shall be bound and subjected to various public services." The emperors who followed continued the same policy, and membership in a heretical sect incurred a degree of infamy and a loss of civil rights. The first specific laws against heresy were promulgated in the 380s[4] and, by the time of Emperor Theodosius in the 5th century, had multiplied until there were over 100 statutes aimed at heretics.

HERESY

Theodosius I barred all heretics from public office and conducted purges against them.[5] He was responsible for the exile and expulsion of Nestorius, the Patriarch of Constantinople, who made the assertion that to argue about whether Jesus was God or the Son of God was irrelevant, as everyone knew that he had been born to a human father and mother like anyone else. Exiled with Nestorius was a large group of Greek classical scholars; in this manner, all the benefits of centuries of Greek intellectual speculation and learning, philosophy, mathematics, and science were wiped from the memory of European man as if they had never existed.[6] Thus the Church, which claimed to be based upon the redemptive sacrifice of the risen Christ, was unmerciful to those who disagreed with it on matters of faith.

The Church historian David Christie-Murray defines heresy as "an opinion held by a minority of men which the majority declares unacceptable and is powerful enough to punish."[7] The necessity for punishment, however, created the need for a far tighter and more precise definition, which was provided by St. Augustine (354–430), the Christian theologian who became Bishop of Hippo in 396 C.E. He described all women as "vessels of excrement," and failed to clarify whether or not he included Mary the Mother of God in that category. His other doctrines of "the just war" and "compel them to come in" became the foundation for a repressive and persecuting society that, under the direction of the popes, grew rapidly.[8]

Augustine redefined heresy as "the distortion of a revealed truth by a believer or an unbeliever." The ambiguous term "revealed truth" was simply defined, by the Church of course, as what the Church itself had declared to be revealed truth. The hierarchy used this circular argument, along with St. Augustine's other pronouncements on heresy, to establish a total monopoly on all access to the sacred.[9] The Church has always seemed to believe that heresy exists wherever and whenever any man exercises his God-given gift of free will in matters of faith. Even in 1990, Cardinal Ratzinger, who is in charge of the Congregation of the Doctrine of the Faith, the modern equivalent of the Inquisition, claimed: "The freedom of the act of faith cannot justify the right to dissent."[10] To show how little has changed over two millennia, the New Catholic Catechism, published in 1990, states, "The task of giving an authentic interpretation of the Word of God ... has been entrusted to the living teaching office of the Church alone."

After their rebuke from Pope Sylvester, the Desposyni and other members of the Ebionites went underground to ensure their survival.[11] Scattered throughout Europe, Arabia, Egypt, and the Near East, these descendants of the ma'madot, the twenty-four high-priestly families of biblical Judaism, learned to dissemble in order to survive. Outwardly, they followed the prevailing religion of their place and time; in secret they preserved the true initiatory teachings of Jesus and spread the fruits of their gnostic insight to benefit the communities within which they moved. Like all the high-priestly families before them, they kept strictly to the marriage laws that bound the Cohen clan. Levites, the hereditary holders of minor priestly duties at the temple, were allowed to marry outside their clan: the Cohens, as hereditary high priests, could only marry other Cohens. As heirs to a hereditary office that traced its origins back to the first dynasties of Egypt, this restriction was sacrosanct and inviolable. Henceforth, they called themselves Rex Deus or, more simply, "the Families."

THE CHURCH TIGHTENS ITS GRIP

The Rex Deus families, the last truly authoritative group that could give lie to the Church's dogmatic and blasphemous assertion that Jesus was God, were now scattered and silent—a silence necessary for survival, for the Church could brook no rivals and swept away all other sources of knowledge of the spiritual world. It campaigned vigorously throughout the empire for the destruction or closure of all the temples and centers of worship of rival faiths, wherever possible hijacking these sacred sites for its own use. The Greek mystery temples were rendered defunct and the oracles silenced for all time.[12]

The Church slammed the doors that gave access to the spiritual and cultural heritage of the people firmly shut. Moreover, in its deliberate march toward absolute power and authority, it feared any access to the realms of either sacred or secular knowledge that it did not control.[13] Who knows what might happen if people were encouraged into education, intellectual adventure, and inquiry? Education was therefore restricted to the clergy and holy orders became the essential prerequisite for basic literacy.

By restricting access to books, education, understanding, and the world of the spirit, the Church revealed its real aims and objectives—total power and control over kings, emperors, and princes; over territories, peoples, and individuals; over this life and entrance to the next. With the Church's stranglehold on all forms of education, intellectual adventure was stifled and the superstitious populace remained quiescent in a state of ignorance and fear. Thus, with the effective end of the Arian faith in the 5th century, a period of calm and unity of religious belief appeared to pervade the intellectual and spiritual desert that was Europe in the Dark Ages.

With the collapse of the Roman Empire, the Church was the only surviving institution with any determined sense of purpose allied to the organizational skills necessary for survival. As it extended its influence over the barbarian tribes, it also became the major lawmaker in the declining empire. The clergy, who were not only the scribes but also the final arbiters against whose decisions there was no appeal, codified the traditional laws of the tribes of Europe. The Church clergy wrote down the oral legends, myths, and stories of the various tribal groups, adding their own dogmatic gloss, omitting all that was offensive to accepted doctrine, retaining this, adding that, subtly changing the histories and forming the mold for a new, essentially Christian, culture. Tribal myths and legends were reduced to stories—mere fiction stripped of all power and validity.

Thus the Church was able to distort the histories of entire cultures, increasing its grip not only on the current reality of the tribes, but also on their past and their ancient cultural heritage.[14] This process was reinforced by the wholesale incorporation of pagan festivals into the new Christian calendar. The festival of Astarte, the Phoenician goddess of love and fertility, became Easter; the Summer Solstice became the feast of St. John the Baptist; the pagan feast of the Winter

Solstice, amalgamated with the birthday of Mithras, the Persian god of light on 25 December, came to be celebrated as the birthday of Christ, or Christmas.

The fathers of the expanding Church believed they could legislate away all knowledge of the spiritual world, and that they alone could control all access to spiritual powers. This delusion continued to influence the thinking of Church leaders and popes for many centuries to come. The only evidence that has come down to us is found in the truly horrendous stories of the persistent and vicious persecutions that were the inevitable result of such an illusion.[15] However, even in the well-named Dark Ages, there were glimmers of hope—little points of light battling against the seemingly all-pervading darkness imposed by the Church's monopoly on education and salvation. This hope sprang from the Ebionite/Rex Deus tradition that preserved the true teachings of Jesus.

CELTIC CHRISTIANITY

The first of these portents of truth was found on an island in the far west of Europe—in Ireland, the seat of the Celtic Church. The first evangelization of the British Isles took place only four years after the crucifixion, long before the first Christian heretic, St. Paul, confected the blasphemous dogma of the deification of Jesus. Evangelists accredited by James the Just, who promulgated the true teachings of Jesus, founded the Church in Britain.

According to two authorities recognized by the Roman Church—St. Gildas, writing in 542 C.E.,[16] and the early Christian historian Freculpus[17]—this evangelical effort spawned a distinctive religion known as Celtic Christianity. In the tolerant atmosphere created by this new religion, the older Celtic religion of Druidism lasted for several centuries in Britain after the advent of the new faith. Most Druids had no difficulty with this form of initiatory Christianity, and even became priests of the new religion while continuing in their privileged position as members of an intellectual class created by their ancestors 1,000 years before. Columba, the great Celtic saint, is on record as preaching that "Jesus is my Druid,"[18] perhaps the most accurate delineation of the initiatory form of Jesus' teaching made in the West.

The Celtic Church developed a form of monasticism characterized by spiritual purity and simplicity. Priests were encouraged to marry and the priesthood was, like that in the early Jerusalem Church, a hereditary office.[19] Like all true initiates of this tradition, they used their spiritual insight for the benefit of the community they served, and not for the benefit of their own person or position. No images of the crucifixion were used in their churches and infant baptism was forbidden.[20] The Celtic Church rejected all the trappings and benefits of temporal power, unlike its power-hungry rivals in Rome, and the simplicity and humility of the Celtic monks stood in stark contrast to the pomp and circumstance of the priesthood in the rest of Europe.

This situation was given force and point by the vibrant cultural dynamism of these long-haired Celtic mystics and monks, whose artwork, scholarship, and scriptural learning were exemplary. Education was treasured and the monasteries accumulated large and well-used libraries. Nomadic by nature, the Celts evangelized much of Western Europe,[21] crossing from Scandinavia in the north to Switzerland in the east. The 17th-century historian Thomas Fuller described these peripatetic missionaries as the "wandering scholars." They were as learned in the classics as they were in Holy Writ, another point that distinguished them from their Roman Catholic counterparts. Such was the quality and range of their classical learning that Professor H. Zimmer claims: "It is almost a truism to state that whoever knew Greek on the continent of Europe in the days of Charles the Bald was an Irishman or had been taught by an Irishman."[22] In fact, they were known as the "snail men," who left a silver trail of knowledge behind them wherever they went.

Their efforts were soon swamped by the pervasive and repressive attitudes of the corrupt Church in Rome, but all was not yet lost in Dark Age Europe. Beyond the reach of Rome, there was a country whose prosperity, respect for learning, and religious tolerance shone as a bright beacon in the intellectual and spiritual darkness that had fallen over the rest of Europe.

MOORISH SPAIN

In stark contrast to the Christian Church's intense distrust of education, in Moorish Spain between 755 and 1492, learning was prized and respected. Art and architecture flourished, as did centers of education, both secular and religious. The religious tolerance of the Islamic invaders allowed Christian, Muslim, and Jew to live together in peace and harmony. The Sufi mystery schools in Spain were one of the principal open and accessible sources of mystical teaching in an otherwise barren continent.[23] Volumes of study devoted to the ancient and revered initiatory wisdom of the Kabbala were produced by the Jewish rabbinical schools and later made their way slowly into Christian Europe. The classical learning of Greek civilization slowly seeped back into Christian consciousness from Muslim Spain, a movement that gathered speed with the Scholastic revival in Paris in the 13th century.[24]

Moors from North Africa invaded the crumbling Visigothic Empire in Spain in 711 C.E.[25] Under the rule of, first, the Umayyad dynasty and, later, the Abassids,[26] most of Spain came under the rule of Islam and developed its own distinctive, tolerant, and highly sophisticated culture. Both Christians and Jews were respected by the Muslims as "people of the Book," for these faiths had given prophets such as Abraham and Jesus to early Islam.[27] They were treated with a degree of tolerance and understanding that was completely alien to Christian culture in the rest of Europe.

For the next 750 years, members of all three great monotheistic religions of the world lived together in relative peace and harmony. The Jews, who were being hounded to death or treated as second-class citizens in the rest of Europe, enjoyed a rich cultural renaissance of their own[28] and, like the Jews, Christians were allowed full religious liberty, not merely in Spain, but also throughout the Islamic Empire. Most Spanish Christians were extremely proud to belong to a highly advanced and sophisticated culture that was light-years ahead of the rest of Europe.[29]

The legacy of Moorish Spain to the medieval West is considerable. The Christians evolved a Mozarabic culture and Spanish scholars and texts later supplied much of the raw material for the adolescent culture of the West.[30] By the 10th century, Cordova was one of the most sophisticated cities in Europe and was held to rival Constantinople in the richness of its culture. It may possibly have even exceeded that city as a center of scholarship and learning,[31] for, under the rule of the Umayyads, Islamic Spain achieved considerable international renown for the poetry, literature, and learning of both Cordova and Granada. The well-attended and richly endowed colleges in Andalusia later provided a model for those of Oxford and Cambridge in England.[32] At a time when most European nobles, kings, and emperors were barely literate, the Umayyad court was the most splendid in Europe and provided a haven for philosophers, poets, artists, mathematicians, and astronomers.[33] This tradition continued and, later, at the height of Abassid power, Spain enjoyed a period of unexampled, independent prosperity.[34]

Under its Islamic rulers, Spain knew growing prosperity. The Moors had brought knowledge of efficient irrigation systems that transformed large swathes of barren land into highly productive farmland. Sugar cane, cotton, rice, and several varieties of fruit such as figs, olives, and oranges were planted along with new vegetables and spices. Mulberry trees were imported and a thriving silk industry was soon established. Granaries were established, stocked, and maintained to alleviate times of shortage.[35] The arts flourished along with agriculture, and Muslim sophistication paved the way for the new rulers to found trade guilds, for skilled craftsmen were prized and well rewarded.[36]

By the early 10th century, the previously unified Islamic empire was fragmenting into smaller states, mostly highly sophisticated centers of wealth and learning that continued to provide a fertile environment for economic and cultural life.[37] As a result of their integration into the Islamic free-trade zone, both Spain and North Africa developed lucrative trade deals with the Levant.[38] This sustained prosperity lasted for nearly seven centuries and left an architectural and artistic heritage that is still a source of wonder to the modern world. Yet this magnificent flowering of art and architecture, important though it is, pales to insignificance when compared to the cultural achievements in literature, poetry, medicine, mathematics, and philosophy that accompanied it.

Emirs owned great libraries and attracted poets, philosophers, and mathematicians to their courts.[39] Cordova became home to one of the greatest libraries in Europe, second only to the greatest in the world, which was located at the heart of the Muslim empire in Baghdad. The almost insatiable passion for learning in Muslim Spain stimulated the production of between 70,000 and 80,000 bound volumes each year. This not only reflected local demand, but also demonstrated the capacity for high-quality production. One Caliph alone built up a collection of over 400,000 volumes.[40] With the expulsion of the persecuted Nestorian scholars from Europe as a result of religious intolerance, the Arabic world became home to the vast collection of Greek learning in mathematics, philosophy, and science they had accumulated. This now flourished in Spain, along with knowledge of classical medicine.[41] Thus it was in translation from Arabic, not the original Greek, that knowledge of the Greek philosophers crept cautiously back into the mainstream of Christian thought via schools in Spain.

It was not just the fruits of Greek civilization that came by this circuitous route into Europe. Along with philosophy, mathematics, and science came more recent advances in medicine, art, and architecture. Many of the branches of knowledge we now treasure and take for granted would have withered away had they not been preserved and enhanced by our Arab brethren.[42] Jewish scholars made a major contribution to this translation from Arabic to European languages, for they could move with ease between Latin, Hebrew, and Arabic, and provided a vital link in the international dissemination of knowledge.[43] Under the leadership of Gerard of Cremona (1114–1187), an influential school of translation that attracted scholars from all over Europe developed in Toledo. Its main area of interest was scientific and mathematical works, which included the work of the Muslim Averröes of Cordova (1126–1198). It was from this school that the distinguished Abbot of Cluny, Peter the Venerable, commissioned a translation of the Holy Qur'an into Latin in 1141. His motive was to create a scholarly basis for the refutation of Islam.[44]

The contrast in attitudes to learning and religious toleration between Christian and Islamic cultures was made brutally obvious at the time of the Crusades. While Christian knights were butchering "infidels" after the capture of Jerusalem, other, more enlightened, members of the same religion were sitting at the feet of Muslim scholars in Spain so that they might bring the learning of the Islamic world to the West and return to Europe the classical and ancient wisdom that had been suppressed in the Dark Ages.[45]

THE PROPHET MUHAMMED AND ISLAM

The religion that founded and sustained this impressive degree of tolerance, and the flourishing intellectual and artistic milieu in which it flowered, maintained similar regimes throughout its empire. Islam is founded on the series of revelations granted to the great Prophet Muhammad in Arabia in the early years of the 7th century. The Prophet dictated these visions to scribes who recorded them as the Qur'an.

Muhammad grew up in an area that was heavily influenced by a considerable Jewish population, descendants of those who had fled there after the fall of Jerusalem in 70 C.E. They had kept strictly to their Judaic faith and had prospered. By the time of Muhammed's birth, almost half the population of Yathrib, now Medina, was Jewish. Impressive though the Jewish influence was in that area, the influence of Christianity was even stronger—not Christianity of the Pauline variety, however, but of the Monophysite heresey, a doctrine held by Coptic or Syrian Christians who believed that, in the person of Jesus, there was only a single nature.[46] A variety of apocryphal writings were also circulating in Arabia, most probably those associated with James and the Ebionim.

It is known that the Prophet, who underwent a period of self-doubt after his initial visionary experiences, soon became absolutely convinced of the innate truth of his revelations and that he was indeed a "messenger of God" in the prophetic tradition of Abraham, Moses, Elijah, John the Baptist, and Jesus.[47] Furthermore, Muhammad no more perceived himself as founding a new religion than had Jesus before him. Muhammad was convinced that he was simply restoring the true and age-old monotheism that had existed since ancient times, that he was simply the last in a long line of divine messengers or prophets who testified to the same religion of the one true God. According to the Prophet, the One Truth had been revealed to both Jews and Christians, but they had either distorted the message or ignored it.[48]

The great Prophet Muhammad, who preached simple monotheism, beautiful yet simple instructions to "do Torah" in the *suras* of the Qur'an, was a direct descendant of Simon, one of the younger brothers of Jesus. The implications are obvious and, as we shall see later, indicate very strongly that he was of the Rex Deus line and tradition. Knowing the religious influences that touched him in his early youth, and bearing in mind his descent from the family of Jesus, it is not surprising that the Qur'an reads like an Arabicized, highly poetic, and detailed version of the teaching of the Ebionim. In addition, the most influential mystical streams within Islam, the various Sufi orders, were all founded by men of inspired spiritual vision who, in their turn, were descended from Muhammad and, therefore, from the family of Jesus. The fact that the Sufis had prolonged contact with the biblical people of Israel is given substance by a remark made by the grandson of Judaism's greatest philospher, Moses Maimonides, who wrote: "The greatest gift given by the People of Israel to the world is Sufism."

CHAPTER 9

THE RISE OF REX DEUS
ARISTOCRACY IN EUROPE

Throughout the early years of the Dark Ages, the scattered members of the Rex Deus families kept their heads down. The families, who were descended from the ma'madot, including the Desposyni—the direct descendants of Jesus—spread throughout Europe, Asia Minor, and the East, and used their natural talents, literacy, and Jewish contacts to gain and consolidate positions of power among the emerging trading and landowning classes. By keeping their own beliefs secret and outwardly conforming to the religious and social practices of their district and time, the Rex Deus members in Christian Europe succeeded in escaping the unwelcome attention of the increasingly powerful Catholic Church. Several of the Rex Deus families gained positions of power close to minor and sometimes major kings, power they exploited to ensure that other members of the family group were, in turn, appointed to positions of influence and aristocratic privilege.[1]

While great stress is placed on the French Merovingian connections to the Rex Deus families, in those families' own traditions this apparent liaison does not assume the overwhelming importance placed upon it by the authors of *The Holy Blood and the Holy Grail*.[2] Baigent, Leigh, and Lincoln signally ignore the family that truly wielded all power in the rule of the later Rex Deus generations of that era. This family, identified over fifty years ago by Dr. Walter Johannes Stein as a true "family of the Grail,"[3] and stewards of the palace who eventually usurped the crown, were—the Carolingians.

The Carolingians were all illustrious and experienced individuals in their own right, both as statesmen and generals. When Charles Martel, Charles the Hammer, led the Franks to victory over Abd-el-Rhaman at Poitiers in 732 C.E. and halted the Islamic expansion into France and the whole of Europe, he was nominally only the Mayor of the Palace. Pepin the Short, who finally deposed the Merovingian dynasty and won papal recognition for the Carolingian house, went on to conquer Aquitaine, limit Lombard power in northern Italy, and finally drive the Moors from Languedoc.[4] On his death in 768, the kingdom was divided between his son Charles, later known as "the Great," or Charlemagne, and his younger son, Carloman. However, when Carloman died in December 771, Charlemagne reunited the kingdom and began a series of wars to expand it. Eventually he ruled over a territory that reached from the Danube to the Mediterranean. He made forays into Moorish Spain—unsuccessful in the north, but capturing the important areas known as the Spanish Marches in the south—and he consolidated the hold on Septimania, now Languedoc/Rousillion, which was first established by his father.

JEWISH SEPTIMANIA

Not long before the Moorish invasion, Jews fleeing from persecution in Visigothic Spain settled Septimania. This influential Jewish community lived under the guidance of their own *nasi*, or prince, whose appointment was authorized by Pepin after the capture of Narbonne in 759.[5] One Latin romance supported by several Hebrew and papal documents claims that the Jews of Narbonne delivered the city to the Franks in return for a promise of self-government under their own king.[6]

What is beyond dispute is that, after the capture of Narbonne, the Jews of Septimania emerged from the shadows into the limelight and were clearly seen as a highly privileged group, richly endowed with freehold estates granted to them by the Carolingian kings.[7] Their protection was certainly assured under the reign of Charlemagne, for he was an astute ruler who could see where the commercial interests of his empire lay. He knew that the Jews were the keys to success in international trade, so he and his nobles encouraged their immigration into the empire as a matter of consistent policy. Many charters testifying to the granting of protection and privileges to Jewish merchants are still extant.[8] Furthermore, it was under the rule of the Carolingians that the office of *magister Judaeorum* was instituted. This was an imperial officer appointed to regulate all matters within the empire regarding the Jewish community.[9]

It is also a matter of record that the emperor used a Jew, Isaac by name, as an interpreter for the ambassador he sent to Haroun-al-Rashid, Caliph of Baghdad, in 797. As a result of this ambassadorial visit, the first *nasi*, or Jewish prince of Narbonne, Rabbi Makhi, was sent from Baghdad to Septimania, where Charlemagne endowed him with great possessions.[10] There is a long-standing tradition among European Jews that Charlemagne also encouraged the transfer of the main center of Torah studies from Baghdad to Narbonne.[11]

There may well have been another, more important, reason for his determined protection of the Jews, however. One historian of the Carolingian era, P. Munz, writing long before any disclosure of the Rex Deus traditions, asserted that Charlemagne claimed succession from the biblical kings of Israel. Furthermore, Munz concludes that Charlemagne deliberately engineered the situation in Septimania in order to arrange intermarriage between his family and that of the nasi, who also descended from the Davidic line. This alliance, he hoped, would demonstrate that the Carolingian dynasty had divine sanction as rulers.[12]

The major responsibility of the new Nasi Makhir was to lead the Jews of Septimania and the Toulousians in the defense of the Spanish frontier and the Mediterranean coast against raids by the Umayyad Moors of Spain and North Africa.[13] Thus Charlemagne's motivation was many-faceted. It was commercial and directed toward trade; it encouraged Jewish scholarship as well as commerce; it had a strong defensive element; and it provided an opportunity for the reunion in marriage of two royal houses, both claiming descent from the House of David. This complex range of aims and objectives succeeded beyond all expectations.

The descendants of the nasi were, with one exception, loyal and brave supporters of the Carolingian dynasty throughout their long reign, a loyalty that was maintained for generations, sometimes against all odds. The Jewish community in Narbonne prospered and grew steadily, and lasted until the expulsion of the Jews from France under

King Philippe le Bel in 1306. The records disclose that the Jews continued to maintain considerable estates in the Narbonnais from the time of Pepin the Short until at least the middle of the 11th century. They owned a substantial portion of the city of Narbonne—villages, vineyards, saltworks, mills, fishponds, and public ovens.[14] One Christian commentator, Peter the Venerable, wrote in 1143 denigrating the "Jewish king" of Narbonne and claiming that he could not accept any king of the Jews unless he reigned in the Holy Land.[15] The noted Jewish traveler and chronicler, Benjamin of Tudela, also writing in the 12th century, stated:

> Narbonne is an ancient city of the Torah. From it the Torah
> goes out to all lands. Therein there are sages, magnates and
> princes (nas'im) at the head of whom is R. Kalonymo . . . a
> descendant of the House of David as stated in his family tree.
> He holds hereditaments and [other] landed properties from the
> rulers of the country and no one may dispossess him by force.[16]

The extensive properties held by the Jews and their nasi at the time of their expulsion indicates that they occupied a sizeable portion of the countryside and city until the early years of the 14th century.[17]

Charlemagne's protection of the Jews, along with his statesmanship, military prowess, and commercial acumen, led to a growing reputation and an ever-expanding kingdom. He became the perfect ally for any ruler under pressure. On his election as pope, Leo III, who was under threat from the Lombards to the north of Rome, wrote to Charlemagne in strange terms, assuring the king of the Franks of his humble obedience and promising fidelity to his person.[18] After a series of successful forays into the Lombard kingdoms of northern Italy, which relieved the pressure on Rome, Charlemagne was crowned and anointed as the new Holy Roman Emperor by pope Leo III in 800. The great historian Edward Gibbon recounts that:

> . . . at his Imperial Coronation, Rome, which had been deliv-
> ered by the sword, was subject, as his own, to the sceptre of
> Charlemagne. The people swore allegiance to his person and
> family: in his name money was coined and justice was adminis-
> tered; and the election of Popes was examined and confirmed
> by his authority.[19]

Charlemagne continued to expand his empire by a series of campaigns against the Saxons and a variety of internal wars suppressing rebellion within its boundaries.

Like all absolute monarchs, he practiced the royal prerogative of *bannum*, the right to punish those who rebelled against him, albeit in a remarkably merciful manner by the standards of the time, and that of *gratia*, the donation of lavish gifts to loyal friends.[20] To keep order within his sprawling dominions, he used the royal prerogative of gratia in a manner common in Europe since the early 7th century by creating a warrior aristocracy,[21] rewarding his supporters and loyal aids by the granting of rank and lands. Throughout the empire, Charlemagne created over 600 counties[22] that enabled his orders to be implemented with considerable efficiency by his newly created and loyal counts. Who were the most trustworthy people he could appoint to these positions of power? Other members of the Rex Deus family group were the obvious choice, especially in the regions of greatest potential danger, the Marches or borderlands, which were ruled by a marquess and, under him, a number of counts.

The onerous duties of a count, particularly in Gaul, were such that they often had to be assisted by viscounts who acted as deputies if the count were called away on official duties or had to go to war beside the emperor. Charlemagne and his successor, Louis the Pious, allowed smaller kingdoms to continue in a subordinate manner within the empire, most notably those of Aquitaine, Italy, and Bavaria. Each had its own central administration and royal court, and was allowed to follow its own policies, unless the emperor decreed otherwise.[23] Thus, by the time of Charlemagne's death in 814, much of Europe—particularly France, Septimania, Provence, northern Italy, and Saxony—were administered by nobility of the Rex Deus line.

REX DEUS IN EUROPE

Several branches of the Rex Deus families had sought refuge in parts of Europe that lay far beyond even the boundaries of Charlemagne's expanded empire and thus were well out of reach of the evergrowing tentacles of Holy Mother the Church. We can identify some of these by their later marriage into known Rex Deus families within Christian Europe, for the Cohenite marriage habits provide reliable evidence of their membership in this secretive group of hereditary high priests. Another indication of their origins lies in records that disclose that identifiable members of the Rex Deus group awarded them positions of trust.

Our first Rex Deus informant, Michael, told us that one important branch of the families could be identified as the Saxon royal house of England in the 11th century.[24] In light of the influence of Charlemagne in Saxony, this is highly credible. Following the Norman conquest of England in 1066, Princess Margaret, the daughter of the deposed Saxon heir to the throne, fled for safety to Hungary. This Saxon descendant of both the Hasmonean and Davidic lines of Israel then became engaged to marry King Malcolm Canmore of Scotland. During her long and dangerous journey from Hungary to Scotland, she was placed under the protection of two trusted knights, one from Normandy, the other from Hungary. It is most unlikely that this important princess would have been entrusted to the care of anyone outside the Rex Deus families who, for both dynastic and spiritual reasons, would have protected her with their lives. On the successful completion of their escort duties, the two noblemen were rewarded by King Malcolm with grants of estates in Scotland, where they both founded dynasties that later played a major role in Scottish history. The first of these Rex Deus knights was the Hungarian Sir Bartholomew Ladislaus Leslyn, the founder of the Leslie Clan.[25] The other, a Norman knight, was Sir William "the Seemly" St. Clair, who originated from the St. Clair estates near St. Lo in Normandy.[26]

THE LORDLY LINE OF THE ST. CLAIRS

William the Seemly St. Clair was a descendant of Røgnvald the Mighty, Earl of Möre, an area of Norway on the northwest coast near the present city of Trondheim.[27] Røgnvald's second son, Rollo, invaded the northwestern area of present-day France, the lands surrounding the river Seine, and conquered Normandy. His possession of this land was legalized by a treaty with King Charles the Simple of France, made at the castle of St. Clair-sur-Epte in 912. Charles, like all the Carolingian kings of France, was a member of one of the leading Rex Deus families.

Statue of the headless St. Clair over the
altar at the Church of St. Clair-sur-Epte.

Tim Wallace-Murphy

Statue of Rollo, first Duke of Normandy, Raven, France.

Part of the treaty shows that the king gave his daughter, Gisele, as wife to Rollo, the first duke of Normandy.[28] This is a strong indication that Rollo was indeed a member of the Rex Deus group.

Despite a long-held belief among the St. Clair family, St. Clair-sur-Epte, as important as it was to Norman history, never actually belonged to Rollo or any of his successors. The Chaumont family owned the castle and land for several centuries and the lands themselves were part of the Isle de France under the rule of the king and not part of the Duchy of Normandy.[29] According to the geneologist L-A de St. Clair, writing in 1905:

> It is therefore highly unlikely the any family used the name of St. Clare-sur-Epte as its family name. It is the town of St. Clair near Saint-Lo, near the western limit of the Bessin, that is the true origin of the name of the noble house of St. Clair. [30]

The use of the family name of St. Clair can be traced to the reign of the fourth duke of Normandy, Richard II, when the names of the territory they occupied began to be applied to the individuals who ruled them.[31]

Rollo resided in the town of Caen and the lands near the seat of government were given to his relatives and trusted companions-in-arms. As Rollo and Gisele had no children, he later married Popee, the daughter of the count of Bayeaux, who bore him a son, known as William Long-Sword. William was succeeded by Richard I, whose daughter, Emma, married King Ethelred the Unready of England, providing yet another example of intermarriage between Rex Deus families. More were to follow, for another of his daughters married the Count of Brittany, while a third, Mathild, became the wife of Eudes, Count of Chartres.[32]

Not content with joining with the royal house of Saxon England and the family of the count of Brittany, they also married into the aristocratic families of Chaumont, Gisors, d'Evereaux, and Blois, the family of the Counts of Champagne. They were linked to the ducal House of Burgundy and to the Royal House of France, the Capetians, who claim descent from Mary Magdalene. Later marriages linked the dukes of Normandy to the House of Flanders and, as a result, to Godfroi de Bouillon, the first Christian ruler of the kingdom of Jerusalem and an ancestor of the Habsburgs.[33]

When one considers the reputation of the Vikings as fearsome raiders and uncouth barbarians, the unseemly haste of the leading aristocratic families of France to marry into this bunch of piratical warriors would be, under normal circumstances, difficult to understand. The lands of Normandy, important though they may have been, do not of themselves explain this headlong charge into matrimonial alliance by some of the oldest families in Europe. When we study the genealogies of these families, we find that they made repeated dynastic alliances with each other and that the same patterns of alliance occur time and again. All of their marriages are conducted from within a select group, and the same family names repeatedly appear in the genealogies of all of them every third or fourth generation. One explanation for these almost incestuous matrimonial arrangements is that they were all known members of the Rex Deus group who, like the Cohens before them, could take their marriage partners only from among their own small, select group. The persistent interbreeding of these families is more like the creation of bloodstock in the farming world than normal human behavior

Thus William the Seemly St. Clair was clearly a member of the Rex Deus families. On his arrival in Scotland, he was granted lands at Roslin and also became the queen's cupbearer. The first St. Clair to be born in Scotland, Henri de St. Clair, William's son, accompanied Godfroi de Bouillon to the Holy Land in 1096 and was present at the fall of Jerusalem.[34] Knights from eleven other leading Scottish aristocratic families accompanied him. Representatives of all twelve families met regularly at Roslin prior to that crusade and for many centuries afterward. The group included ancestors of the Stuarts (with whom the St. Clairs intermarried), Montgomerys, Setons, Douglases, Dalhousies, Ramseys, Leslies, and Lindsays—all families linked by marriage, shared loyalties and beliefs, and a common ancestry that reached back in time through biblical Israel to ancient Egypt.

The Rex Deus families extended their influence throughout the ranks of European nobility and, by acts of protection to various churches and cathedrals, began tentatively to spread their tentacles into the very organization that stood as its main opponent, namely the Church. After an unsuccessful siege of Chartres in 911, Rollo, the first Duke of Normandy, swore that the cathedral and city of Chartres would remain under his protection. He attested to the following declaration:

> I, Rollon, Duke of Normandy, give to the brotherhood of the church of Notre Dame de Chartres my castle at Malmaison, which I too with my sword, and with my sword I shall be their guarantor.[35]

THE CHARTRES MASTERS

In 1007, the great Bishop Fulbertus was installed as Bishop of Chartres and, under the protection of the Rex Deus nobility of the area, made the cathedral city an important center of learning as well as a focus of pilgrimage.[36] The school soon attained international renown and, during the 200 years of its major influence, attracted pupils from all over Europe, including Bernardus, Thierry of Chartres, William of Conches, and John of Salisbury.[37] Fulbertus' pupils were probably the first in Christian Western Europe to read the works of Plato, Aristotle, Pythagoras, and Cicero, as well as being familiar with mathematics, science, and recent Arabic inventions such as the astrolabe.[38]

The knowledge of the Greek Classics, mathematics, science, and invention taught at Chartres came from that beacon of light in the Dark Ages, Moorish Spain. The Classics were translated, not from Greek, but from Arabic, and the translations were made by Jewish scholars working in Yeshiva under the protection of the tolerant rule of Islam. How did this knowledge get from Spain to Chartres? The answer lies in the Rex Deus connection. We find a strong indication of this when we learn that, under the outward guise of teaching the seven liberal arts of *grammatica, dialectica, logica, musica, mathematica, geometrica*, and *astronomia*, Fulbertus taught the seven steps of initiation based on the ancient Egyptian model, the same tried and tested initiatory pathway preserved by the twenty-four families of the ma'madot throughout the history of ancient Israel and preserved by the Rex Deus families of Europe.[39] Thus the mystery school at Chartres was able to practice an initiatory pathway right under the noses of the repressive Church authorities.

The Rebuilding of Chartres Cathedral

When fire destroyed the cathedral in 1020, Fulbertus set about a rebuilding program with the financial aid of the kings and nobles who had acted as patrons to his academy. The list of these financial backers begins with King Robert, the Capetian king of France, and included most of the Rex Deus nobility of northern France, as well as William, Duke of Aquitaine.[40] Fulbertus' new Romanesque cathedral was dedicated by his successor, Thierry of Chartres, in 1037, eight years after the founder's death.

The central personality in the initiation school at Chartres after Thierry's death was one of his pupils and another member of the families, Bernardus.[41] He continued the initiatory teaching and based it on the work of one of Jesus' leading disciples, St. John the Divine. Thus we can see how Rex Deus teaching and tradition began its first slow and careful infiltration of European society in a manner that exerted far more real influence than the families' numbers might suggest, for, from Chartres, sprang the scholastic movement that eventually led to the foundation of a university in Paris.

St. Bernard of Clairvaux

Protection and patronage of churches and cathedrals was not the only path to influence within the Church used by the Rex Deus families. Some of them joined the Church itself and took holy orders in an attempt to influence their corrupt enemy from within. The bizarre antics of one family in the county of Champagne provide a fascinating illustration of some of the tensions that this strategy provoked.

Bernard de Fontaine, later canonized as St. Bernard of Clairvaux, expressed a wish to join the struggling Cistercian order, which was relatively new and in imminent danger of collapse. His family was horrified when he first announced his intention, but their attitude was abruptly and completely transformed for reasons that are now a matter of pure speculation. Family opposition to his plans evaporated at the speed of light and, stranger still, a large number of his male relatives and friends chose to follow him into the order. No less than thirty-two of them became novices with Bernard when he joined in 1112.[42]

Bernard rose within the Church with incredible speed and, although he never led the Cistercian order, he, nonetheless, attained an almost unbelievable position of influence throughout the religious world, becoming the principal personal adviser to the pope. He exerted almost equal power over temporal affairs, advising kings, emperors, and the nobility. His membership in the Rex Deus network of families was an obvious asset in attaining this power and influence.

Bernard's deep commitment to initiatory teaching is openly expressed in the 120 sermons he preached based on the *Song of Songs* by King Solomon.[43] He extended this teaching by enhancing the spiritual tradition of the branch of the Compagnonnage, the craft-masons known as the Children of Solomon. No documentary evidence exists that can adequately explain the bizarre burst of collective enthusiasm leading so many of his family and friends to join the Cistercians, but later events do provide certain clues. As we shall see, it appears that Bernard conspired with other members of the Rex Deus group to achieve a common aim that left an indelible mark on the course of European history. This conspiracy was wide-ranging and encompassed the actions of a variety of people, including his cousin (who later became patriarch of Jerusalem), his uncle André de Montbard, Hughes de Payen, the St. Clairs, the Setons, the Royal House of Flanders, and one of the most important noblemen in Europe at that time, Count Hughes of Champagne.

HUGHES OF CHAMPAGNE

Hughes I of Champagne ruled over an area somewhat larger than Wales that lay to the east of Paris. He was the godson of King Philippe I of France, who was nominally his sovereign. He also owed allegiance to the Holy Roman Emperor and the Duke of Burgundy. The Counts of Champagne were linked both by blood and marriage to the St. Clairs,[44] the Capetian kings of France, the Duke of Burgundy, the Duke of Normandy, and the Norman and Plantagenet kings of England. Hughes' main seat of power, Troyes, in the county of Champagne, became a renowned center of learning and culture attracting scholars, knights, and intellectuals of considerable stature. At this time, large Jewish families, often led by rabbinical scholars, began to migrate from southern Europe and settle in the Paris basin, the lands of Champagne, and on the banks of the River Rhine.[45] One family among these settled in Troyes and produced a son who was destined to become one of the greatest Jewish biblical scholars of all time—Rabbi Solomon ben Isaac, known as Rachi.

Born in Troyes, Rachi studied at *yeshivot* in both Worms and Mainz before returning to Champagne to establish his own *yeshiva* in the city of his birth.[46] Rachi was a frequent and welcome guest at the court of Hughes de Champagne and attained such intellectual repute that, as a biblical scholar, he is still unequalled, and, as a philosopher, he is considered second only to the incomparable Maimonides. The tolerance of Hughes de Champagne was such that Rachi was able to maintain a Kabbalistic school of considerable stature in the city.[47] The Kabbala was the principal spiritual pathway encompassing the traditional Hebraic/Egyptian pathway of initiation. Hughes de Champagne and his descendants gave shelter and protection to the Jews, as did most Rex Deus nobles, and when, in the later part of the 12th century, the Jews were expelled from the Isle de France, they retained their security and residence in Champagne.

In 1104, Hughes I de Champagne met in a secret conclave with the leading noble members of the families of Brienne, De Joinville, Chaumont, and Anjou, all members of the Rex Deus dynasties.[48] Shortly afterward, he left for the Holy Land and did not return to Champagne until 1108. In 1114, he made another brief and mysterious visit to Jerusalem and, on this return, made a donation of land to the Cistercian order, land upon which the monks built a new monastery, the Abbey of Clairvaux. Bernard de Fontaine was immediately appointed as its first abbot.

Hughes de Champagne's mysterious visits to the Holy Land and his donation of land to the Cistercians were merely the prologue to concerted action by the families, which were about to go public for the first time. The resurrection of Rex Deus was to take place, not in the county of Champagne or even in Europe, but in the holy city of Jerusalem with the foundation of an order of warrior monks whose name was to resound through the annals of European history down to the present day—*The Poor Knights of Christ and the Temple of Solomon*, otherwise known as the Knights Templar.

CHAPTER 10

†HE KႶİGH†S †EMPLAR

Bernard of Clairvaux rose to a position of great power and influence both in the medieval church and in the world of temporal politics, not only because of his useful family connections, but also as a result of his immense energy. Despite suffering from ill health throughout his life, he instigated the foundation of at least sixty-eight Cistercian houses from his base at Clairvaux. His personal example and deep spirituality had such profound influence on the Cistercian order that he is sometimes called its second founder. His reach into other branches of the initiatory tradition was wide-ranging, for Bernardus of Chartres and later leaders of the mystery school there like John of Salisbury and Alanus ab Insulis were Cistercians, as were many of the other Chartres masters.[1]

One of the many Cistercian houses founded by Bernard stands in the principality of Seborga in northern Italy. According to local tradition, it was established in 1113 to protect "a great secret."[2] Under the direction of its abbot, Edouard, were two men, Gondemar and Rossal, who had been knights before they became monks. In company with Edouard, they had joined the order at the same time as Bernard. A document in the archives at Seborga claims that, in February 1117, Bernard came to the abbey with seven companions, released Gondemar and Rossal from their vows, and gave a solemn blessing to the whole group, which departed for Jerusalem in 1118. The document records that, prior to their departure, Bernard nominated Hughes de Payen as the Grand Master of "the Poor Militia of Christ," and that he was consecrated in that rank by Abbot Edouard.[3]

THE FOUNDATION OF THE ORDER

An account by Guillaume de Tyre, written over seventy years after the events it describes, places the foundation of the order that came to be known as the Knights Templar in Jerusalem in 1118.[4] Granted quarters on the Temple Mount by King Baldwin II within a few weeks of the new king's accession to the throne,[5] they took the name of the "Poor Fellow-Soldiers of Jesus Christ" and were recognized as "the Knighthood of the Temple of Solomon."[6] The founding members of the order were its first Grand Master, Hughes de Payen, André de Montbard, Geoffroi de St. Omer, Payen de Montdidier, Achambaud de St.-Amand, Geoffroi Bisol, Godfroi, Gondemar, and Rossal.[7]

This supposedly randomly assembled group of knights, apparently united only by their common religious purpose was, in fact, a tightly knit group of relatives who all belonged to Rex Deus and were closely associated with Count Hughes I of Champagne. Hughes, as we have already mentioned, made several visits to the Holy Land prior to the foundation of the Templars. Indeed, when he returned to the East in 1114, Ivo, Bishop of Chartres, wrote to him rebuking him for abandoning his wife and vowing himself to the "knight-hood of Christ" in order to take up "that gospel knighthood by which two thousand may fight securely against him who rushes to attack us with two hundred thousand."[8] This is not the only puzzling mention of the order prior to the generally accepted date of its foundation. All that may reasonably be inferred from this confusion, however, is the long-standing nature of the conspiracy and planning that underpinned the creation of the Knights Templar.

There is one further anomaly regarding Hughes de Champagne. It is a matter of record that, in 1125, he returned to the Holy Land and joined the Order of the Knights Templar, thereby swearing unquestioning obedience to its first Grand Master, his own vassal, Hughes de Payen.

THE FOUNDING MEMBERS

Hughes de Payen was born in 1070 at the De Payen chateau on the banks of the Seine, one of the principal castles defending Champagne.[9] Sometime between 1085 and 1090, he received the fiefdom of Montigny near Lagesse in the county of Champagne.[10]

Hughes was the cousin of two of Europe's most powerful men, Bernard of Clairvaux[11] and the Count of Champagne, who was also his overlord.[12] He was known as Hughes the Moor because of his lineal descent from the Prophet Muhammad, which, of course, indicates that he was not merely Rex Deus, but one of the Desposyni, a descendant of one of the brothers of Jesus.

It has often been asserted that Hughes de Payen was married to a certain Catherine de St. Clair, a marriage to which we have given some credence in previous works. However, having searched through countless archives, we have to admit that we have not found any valid document confirming or even inferring any matrimonial alliance between Hughes and the wider St. Clair family. The French author Thierry Leroy has found documents confirming that Hughes de Payen was indeed married, but to a lady called Elisabeth, and that the marriage took place sometime between 1108 and 1114. Unfortunately, there is no absolute indication of her maiden name.[13] Despite assertions that Hughes died childless, he did, in fact, father at least one son, Thibaud de Payen, who was eventually elected abbot of the monastery of Sainte-Colombe in 1139. In the one of the contemporary chronicles, the following words are used to describe the new abbot: "Theo Aldus de Pahens, filius Hugonis primi magistri templi Jerosolymitani," which translates as "Thibaud de Payen, son of Hughes, first master of the Temple in Jerusalem." André de Montbard, one of Hughes' closest associates in the new knightly enterprise, was the uncle of Bernard of Clairvaux,[14] a kinsman of the Duke of Burgundy, and yet another vassal of the house of Champagne. Geoffroi de St. Omer was the son of a leading Flemish nobleman, Hughes de St. Omer.[15] Payen de Montdidier and Achambaud de St.-Amand were both closely related to the Royal House of Flanders, whose sons, Godfroi de Boullion and his younger brother Baudouin of Brittany, were rulers of the kingdom of Jerusalem—Godfroi as protector of the Holy Sepulchre and, after his death, Baudouin as King Baldwin I.

RECOGNITION OF THE ORDER

The Knights Templar received recognition from the patriarch of Jerusalem at the Council of Nablus in 1120.[16] The patriarch, yet another distant cousin of Bernard of Clairvaux, gave the order its first insignia—a red two-barred cross that later developed into the Cross of Lorraine. The insignia was later used to good effect by General de Gaulle as a symbol of Free France during the Second World War. Orderic Vitalis (1075–c. 1141), writing in the Norman monastery of St. Évroul, recorded that, in the 1120s, Count Fulk V of Anjou joined the "knights of the Temple" for a period of time during his pilgrimage to Jerusalem. On his return to Europe, he continued to pay them thirty pounds of Anjou for their support. Orderic described the Templars as *venerandi mitlites*, knights who should be held in great respect or admiration, and wrote that they devoted their lives to the physical and spiritual service of God, despised all worldly things, and faced martyrdom daily.[17]

The stated, primary purpose of the new order of warrior monks was the protection of pilgrims en route from the Mediterranean coastal port of Jaffa to Jerusalem. When we consider that Hughes de Payen was at least forty-eight years old at the time of the order's foundation and that most of his companions were of similar age, it is difficult to envisage quite how nine knights, none of whom could be described as being in the first bloom of youth, were going to accomplish this mammoth task—a problem that is rendered particularly intractable when one studies their main course of action during the first nine years of the order's existence. Far from patrolling the bandit-infested roads between the coast and Jerusalem, they spent their time excavating beneath the Temple Mount, directly under their headquarters.[18]

Lieutenant Warren of the Royal Engineers excavated the eighty-foot vertical shaft that they dug and the system of radiating tunnels to which it led during the later years of the 19th and the early years of the 20th centuries. Warren discovered a variety of Templar artefacts in the tunnels he explored, including a spur, the remains of a lance, a small Templar cross, and the major part of a Templar sword. These fascinating relics now rest in Edinburgh with the Templar archivist, Robert Brydon, along with a letter from Captain Parker who accompanied Warren on his explorations. Parker wrote to Brydon's grandfather in 1912 and gave the finds to him for safekeeping.

Several questions arise from the discovery of these tunnels: Were these excavations the primary purpose that lay behind the founding of the Order? What exactly were they seeking? Did they find it? How did they know precisely where to excavate? How did they obtain quarters immediately above their chosen site of excavation? Most of these questions are impossible to answer with any precision, but it is possible to speculate on the probable answers to some of them based upon a foundation of fact.

One clue appears carved on a pillar in the north porch of Chartres Cathedral, the porch known as the Portal of the Initiates. The carving depicts the Ark of the Covenant being transported upon a wheeled cart.[19] Legend from biblical times recounts that the Ark of the Covenant was buried deep beneath the temple in Jerusalem long before the Babylonian invasion. A long-standing esoteric legend within Europe claims that Hughes de Payen was chosen to retrieve it and bring it back to Europe.[20] The same legend goes on to tell us that, on its arrival in Europe, it was at first hidden beneath the crypt of Chartres Cathedral, which was, at that time, under the control of the Chartres masters.

Along with the Ark, it was further claimed, a vast quantity of ancient documents was uncovered. Over the years, there has been considerable speculation as to the nature of these documents and a reasonable consensus has emerged that they probably contained, among other things, copies of the Dead Sea Scrolls material found at Qumran, and treatises on sacred geometry, ancient science, and other aspects of the Hebraic/Egyptian gnostic tradition. The translation of the Copper Scroll found at Qumran tends to confirm this, as it lists a variety of sites where temple treasure and items of sacred import were hidden immediately prior to the destruction of the temple in 70 C.E. Furthermore, many of the other sites listed in the Copper Scroll were excavated by John Allegro, the Dead Sea Scrolls scholar. In several of these, he found many artefacts relating to the 12th-century Knights Templar, but nothing whatsoever from the era of the destruction by the Romans.

The only rational scenario to explain these circumstances is that the knowledge of these secret hiding places was passed down through the generations for over 1,000 years via the oral traditions of the Rex Deus families. In the matter of the careful positioning of their quarters immediately above the treasure they sought, King Baldwin was obviously part of the conspiracy, and it is indicative of this that the order first "went public" within a few weeks of his accession. Yet, despite several visits to the Holy Land by both Hughes de Champagne and Hughes de Payen during the reigns of Godfroi de Boullion and his brother Baldwin I, no attempt whatsoever had been made to found the order.

THE RETURN TO EUROPE

At the new Grand Master's request, King Baldwin II wrote to Bernard of Clairvaux asking him to intercede with the pope for formal papal recognition of the order, for Bernard was, at that time, not only advisor to Pope Honorius II, but his former teacher.[21] Hughes de Payen and his fellow cofounders set sail for Provence, then Normandy, where he met the English King Stephen, who gave him permission to travel through England and on to Scotland, where he stayed with the St. Clairs of Roslin.

King David of Scotland gave a donation of land at Ballantrodoch that became the headquarters of the order in Scotland and has since been renamed Temple. This land bordered on the St. Clair estates so that communication between the ancient family of the St. Clairs and the new Knights Templar could be easily maintained. As an immediate result of these travels, the order was granted estates not only in Scotland, but also in England, Champagne, and Provence. To this day, there is still considerable dispute as to which of these was the first to be given. The most likely estimate is that the lands around Les Arcs-sur-Argens in Provence were first, Temple Cressing in England shortly after, Ballantrodoch third, and Troyes fourth. The matter is complicated, as the gifts were first communicated orally and often only confirmed in writing long after the knights had actually taken possession of their new properties. The fact is that these first donations of land had been long planned and were soon followed by a veritable cascade of gifts of estates, castles, towns, farms, and villages throughout Christian Europe. These other gifts of property and money followed the pope's official recognition of the order and the award of its first "rule."

THE RULE OF THE TEMPLARS

In response to King Baldwin's letter, Bernard of Clairvaux did bring the order to the attention of the pope, who willingly gave his blessing to the warrior monks and commanded his papal legate in France, Cardinal Matthew d'Albano, to call a council of Church and temporal dignitaries to legalize the new order and give the knights their first religious rule. The council opened at Troyes on 14 January 1128 under the direction and presidency of Cardinal d'Albano. It was attended by the archbishops of Rheims and Sens, and the bishops

Roslin Castle, the ancestral home of the St. Clairs of Roslin.

Templar castle, Grimaud Ville, Var, Provence.

The Templar village of Les Arcs-sur-Argens, Provence.

of Orleans, Paris, Soissons, Auxerre, Meaux, Chalons, Laon, and Samur. Also present were the abbots of Vezelay, Citeaux, Pontigny, Trois-Fontaines, Saint-Remy de Rheims, Dijon, Molesmes, and, according to some accounts, the abbot of Clairvaux.[22] There is some dispute in the records as to whether Bernard actually attended in person for all or even part of the council in view of his bad health. However, the entire event was certainly dominated by his thinking. Temporal power was also well represented by the new Count of Champagne, Thibaud IV, William II, the Count of Nevers, and another nobleman, André de Baudemant.

On 31 January 1128, the Grand Master, Hughes de Payen, and his fellow knights were called to appear before the council to receive the new rule that had been written by Bernard of Clairvaux.[23] Ten years after the Council of Troyes, Pope Innocent II issued the papal bull *Omne datum optimum*, which made the Templars responsible, through their Grand Master, to the pope and the pope alone, thus freeing them from the authority of bishops, archbishops, kings, and emperors. This papal action, less than twenty years after the Templars' foundation, made it wholly independent of all prelates and princes, and thereby the most independent religious order in the Christian world. It was soon to become the most powerful, both in wealth and military might.

GROWTH OF THE ORDER

Within two years of the Council of Troyes, the Knights Templar had acquired land in Portugal and established close relations with the rulers of that country. Donations on the eastern side of Spain came more slowly, but followed a similar pattern. The Templars owned property in Aragon soon after 1130. As a result, by the early 1140s, they had acquired enough land and had recruited sufficient members to sustain simultaneous military operations on two fronts—in the Holy Land and the Iberian Peninsula. They fought in most of the King of Aragon's campaigns against the Moors and acted in an advisory capacity to him. Their numbers in these campaigns were never great, but they could mobilize quickly and remained in the field as long as required.[24] In fact, both in Europe and the Holy Land, they were the first full-time, professional, standing army since the fall of the Roman Empire.

The grants of land, castles, and other property came in so fast in the early years after the Council of Troyes that, in some cases, the order had to defer garrisoning their new lands for several years due to a shortage of manpower. Their main focus was, however, the protection of the kingdom of Jerusalem. All the early recruits, both knights and others who were capable of military service, were sent to the East as soon as possible. They were following their Grand Master's example, for Hughes himself, accompanied by 300 knights drawn from the noblest families in Europe who had rushed to become members of the order, returned to the Holy Land in 1129.[25] Bearing in mind the difficulties in communication that existed in Europe in the early years of the 12th century, to say nothing of the time it took to arm and equip these men, much less transport them to a rendezvous point within Europe, this massive influx of recruits and their rapid transportation to the Holy Land is yet another clear example of prolonged and efficient planning on a very large scale.

The influx of recruits and the ever-growing list of donations of land and property did not all originate directly from the families of Rex Deus. Bernard of Clairvaux was, in modern parlance, a master of the art of public relations and publicity. He wrote a tract, *In Praise of the New Knighthood*, that extolled the virtues of the Knights Templar and delineated the immense spiritual benefits that would accrue to those who supported its aims with acts of personal service, donations of land, or good old-fashioned money. One enigmatic paragraph toward the end of this document almost gives the game away, as to the true purpose of this knightly order whose sworn objective was to protect, not only the pilgrims to the Holy Land, but the Holy Land itself. Bernard wrote:

> Hail, land of promise, which, formerly flowing only with milk and honey for thy possessors, now stretchest forth the food of life and the means of salvation for the entire world.[26]

The central tenet of Church dogma was the belief that, more than 1100 years before, Jesus had died on the cross at Golgotha in the supreme sacrificial act of salvation. By his death, he had already redeemed mankind and saved us all from sin. Bernard, Abbot of Clairvaux, was a senior member of the Church, the advisor to a series of popes, at least two of whom had been his pupils, and had supposedly dedicated his life to furthering mankind's understanding of this dogma, which the Church regards as a fact. So what did he mean when he wrote:"Now stretchest forth the food of life and the means of salvation for the entire world"? Or, as rendered in alternative translations:"from which will come salvation for the entire world"? Was Bernard referring obliquely to the documents found under the Temple Mount and their translation? Or was he referring to the reappearance of the original teachings of Jesus that he hoped for in this era of Rex Deus resurgence?

We shall probably never know, unless further documentary evidence comes to light. What is certain is that, following the circulation of his tract, *In Praise of the New Knighthood*, recruits, gifts of land, and money flowed into the arms of the Knights Templar. Nor were they the only beneficiaries; the previously struggling Cistercian order, which had revived appreciably after Bernard and his companions joined its ranks, also underwent an extraordinary period of expansion. In Bernard's lifetime, they established over 300 new abbeys, the most rapid expansion on record of any monastic order before or since. Furthermore, during his lifetime at least, the Cistercians and the Knights Templar were widely regarded as two arms of the same body—one a contemplative monastic arm, the other the strong, swift, military arm.

France, Provence, Champagne, Bar, England, Tuscany, and the present area known as Languedoc/Roussillon became the major centers of Templar power and influence within Europe, closely followed by Aragon, Gallicia, Portugal, Scotland, Normandy, and the Holy Roman Empire. Eventually, their estates, castles, and churches stretched from the Baltic to the Mediterranean, and from the Atlantic coastline to the Holy Land. All the profits and income from these vast holdings were devoted to one aim: maintaining the standing army and fortifications in the Holy Land. Every means possible was devoted to this one end, and, in fulfilling this aim, the order left no stone unturned in its endeavor to maximize its profits and increase its efficiency and power.

TEMPLAR ESTATES

The vast majority of Templar properties in Europe were not great castles, with the exception of Spain and Portugal, where these were a necessity in their battles against the Moors. The Templars instead held farmhouses, mills, barns, small apsidal chapels, and commanderies—administrative centers usually combined with agricultural buildings. In the main cities, strongholds were erected to act as secure places for treasure in transit or to hold troops en route to the Holy Land. The knights were warriors who needed servants, farriers for their horses, and armorers; the farms needed general laborers, blacksmiths, carpenters, and herdsmen; their ships needed crews, carpenters, sailmakers, oarsmen, and senior officers and navigators; their churches had their own chaplains and, as we shall see later, they needed masons and craftsmen in stone. The so-called warrior monks owned land in every climatic zone in Europe; they owned farms, vineyards, pasturage for sheep and cattle, quarries, mines, mills, smithies, and stud farms. They became, in effect, the first multinational conglomerate in history.

One modern consultant in business management, the American S. T. Bruno, described them in the following terms:

> The fact of the matter is that the Templars ran a "world wide" system of farms, shipping concerns and financial services. They pressed olives in the Jordan Valley, made wine in France and traded wool in Ireland. Agriculture was, of course, only one activity. They also shipped lumber from Edessa, and carried pilgrims across the Mediterranean from Lombardy to Acre. They even provided a medieval form of "travellers cheque" to pilgrims and loaned money to kings. Although one might envisage their primary military "product" as singularly focused on the conquest of the Holy Land, the resource branch of the order operated in a number of different markets.[27]

The organizational skill required to manage this vast, international, multifaceted enterprise and keep a standing army in the field at the same time was staggering. Yet they did it—and still some of their clerical critics within the modern Church call them "illiterates"! Bruno claims that, for almost 180 years, the Templars managed their organization in a manner consistent with some of the most sophisticated and best management practices understood today in the 21st century.[28]

LONG-DISTANCE TRADE

At the time of the Templars' foundation, long-distance trade, mainly conducted by sea, centered on the northern Italian cities of Venice, Genoa, and Pisa. These cities exploited their geographical position and prospered greatly from trade with both the Byzantine and Islamic empires to the east. Northern Europe, in its turn, slowly but steadily improved in wealth and offered timber and woollen cloth in exchange for the spices and silks of the East.

At first, long-distance overland trade was fraught with difficulty, as local barons imposed heavy tolls on goods passing through their lands and all goods and money in transit were prey to bandits who infested the countryside. The coming of the Templars changed all that. Their estates, scattered throughout Europe as they were, gave them ideal bases from which to fulfil their primary function of protecting the pilgrimage routes. As a result, long-distance travel and trade became safer and far more feasible. Large regional markets began to appear. This, in turn, further stimulated mercantile activity. The Counts of Champagne were sufficiently independent of their nominal overlords, the Kings of France and the Dukes of Burgundy, to ignore any royal restrictions on trade and they began to encourage merchants to bring their business to the market at Troyes. They created a climate of stability, security, and freedom that facilitated the growth of this international market situated near the midpoint between the emerging trading centers of the Low Countries in the northwest and the prosperous trading cities of Venice, Genoa, and Pisa in northern Italy. Other powerful nobles soon followed this example, and trade was further facilitated by Templar action.

TEMPLAR BANKING

Trade of this nature cannot flourish unless the financial infrastructure to sustain it is present,[29] and the warrior monks added another string to their bow. The Templars, who were used to working in many currencies and organizing the safe transport of gold and money across Europe to finance their military activities in the Holy Land, now began to offer financial services to the emerging trading classes. They set themselves up as bankers, using a device they had learned from the Sufis of Islam—namely the "note of hand"—to arrange financial transfers from one part of Europe to another. This gave further impetus to trade and led to more profitable business for them. They lent money to merchants, the nobility, princes, and prelates, and all their financial dealings were backed by their reputation for probity, accuracy, and safety. They soon rose to be the wealthiest financial institution in the Christian world.

Travel and the transport of goods could not take place in safety if the roads and trade routes were not effectively protected. The Order of the Knights Templar fulfilled both functions and, as a result, played a significant part in creating the fundamental necessary conditions for the accumulation of capital. These conditions already applied in the great trading centers of northern Italy and, thanks to the services and security provided by the Knights Templar, they spread rapidly throughout the main centers of population in Europe.

The political results that flowed from the commercial success of the trading cities of northern Europe—namely an increasing independence and autonomy from their nominal rulers in the Papal States or the Holy Roman Empire—were soon reflected in a sustained and cumulative shift in the balance of power in the rest of Europe. Power began to move from the feudal barons of old to the emerging mercantile class in the towns and cities. In some areas under the rule of Rex Deus nobility, this developed into an embryonic form of democracy, as city councils in one form or another began to flex their muscles and, at first, complement and, later, rival the power of their nominal overlords.

This novel mixture of fearsome reputation as fighting men and renown as defenders of Christianity, along with their ownership of large estates in every corner of Europe and their financial acumen and reliability, led to Templars being appointed as ambassadors, advisors to kings, popes, and emperors, and positions of responsibility in nearly every kingdom in which they operated. All in all, the Templars rose to positions of almost incalculable power and influence throughout the European continent. They wielded power and influence in military matters, in diplomacy, in international politics, and, above all, in financial matters. What made them so different from other religious orders of great reputation, many of which were of far greater antiquity? To begin to understand the possible answers to this question, we must examine their belief system.

CHAPTER 11

THE BELIEFS OF THE
KNIGHTS TEMPLAR

The comparison between the impressive achievements of the Templars in their brief 180-year history and those of other orders that were established long before them and who outlasted them by many centuries, is startling. Yet the obvious lines of inquiry that could explain these differences are usually ignored or brushed under the academic carpet as irrelevant. The Knights Templar were suppressed, ignominiously, at the beginning of the 14th century after a controversial trial for heresy conducted by the French Inquisition at the behest of King Philippe le Bel of France. Their internal records were either stolen by the Inquisitors, hidden by the knights themselves, or destroyed. The resultant information vacuum has had two detrimental effects: to give free reign to speculation, and to provide academic historians with an excuse for ignoring the real cause of the Templars' prodigious growth.

The apparent information vacuum is not quite as complete as it may seem, however. The Templars have, in fact, left us a considerable legacy that can be used as a guide to their true beliefs. It exists in their involvement with a form of veneration that is almost invariably associated with Templar activity—namely the cult of the Black Madonna. Additional clues to their beliefs can be found hidden, albeit in allegorical form, within another example of Rex Deus activity that originated in the city of Troyes—a literary work that still fascinates millions of people today, *The Search for the Holy Grail*. The warrior-monks also left us an indelible guide to their main principles of belief, carved as three-dimensional teaching boards in the great Gothic cathedrals they built or financed during the explosion of creativity that one perceptive British author, William Anderson, called *The Rise of the Gothic*.

THE CULT OF THE BLACK MADONNA

The cult of Mariolatry received its main impetus from Chartres, though its true origins are rooted in the pagan worship of a variety of mother goddesses. For example, Notre Dame Sous-Terre at Chartres Cathedral is a Christianized variation on the ancient Druidic practice of worshipping the fire-blackened figure of a virgin about to give birth, *Virginibus pariturae*, described by Julius Caesar in the *de Bello Gallico*, book 4. Throughout Europe, many such assimilations occurred that retained older, pagan forms of worship and incorporated them into Catholic practice.

Veneration of the Black Madonna started in a similar manner. The sites of several important Black Madonnas either predate the foundation of the Templar order or are situated geographically far beyond their reach. However, the peak years of the development of this strange cult coincide with the time of the order's power, and the majority of the effigies are located in areas of Templar influence. Furthermore, the cult is intimately entwined with veneration of Mary Magdalene.

The Catholic Church, while it has always been happy to rake in the financial benefits of pilgrimage to these sites, has consistently felt uncomfortable with the cult of the Black Madonna. Since Mariolatry plays such an important role in the Catholic faith, this obvious discomfort with the intense local, national, and sometimes international, veneration of Black Madonnas seems difficult to understand. What on earth can this effigy represent that causes the hierarchy so much embarrassment?

One clue to the acute discomfort felt by the Church in this matter is found in the words of Bernard of Clairvaux. At the time of the Council of Troyes, Bernard laid down a specific requirement for all the members of the new knighthood to make "obedience to Bethany and the House of Mary and Martha"—in other words, obedience and loyalty to the dynasty founded by Mary Magdalene and Jesus. Many scholars of the esoteric have come to the conclusion that the great Notre Dame cathedrals built or financed by the Templars were dedicated, not to Mary the mother of Jesus, but to Mary Magdalene and the son of Jesus—an idea that, when viewed from the Church's perspective, is plainly heretical.

The Templar veneration of the Magdalene in the guise of the Black Madonna was widespread throughout the lands they controlled. The perceptive Scottish researcher and author Ean Begg lists over fifty centers of veneration found in churches dedicated to Mary Magdalene.[1] In the European esoteric tradition, the Magdalene is described as "the symbol of divine wisdom" and, according to the Nazorean tradition, she was depicted garbed in black like the priestess Isis, surmounted by Sophia's crown of stars. Her infant wore the golden crown of royalty.[2]

According to the 20th-century initiate, Rudolf Steiner, symbolism can be interpreted at up to at least nine different levels, depending on the perception and initiatory status of the viewer. The Black Madonna is no exception to this. At the first exoteric level, she is simply the mother of Jesus with her only child; at the second, she is Mary, the seat of wisdom. At the esoteric level, the same symbolism can be held to represent the Magdalene and the child of Jesus. At a deeper level, as in ancient Egyptian symbolism, the color black indicates wisdom, so the Templars were venerating the goddess of wisdom, Sophia, embodied in the form of the goddess Isis and the Horus child, which is then camouflaged as the Christian holy mother and the infant Jesus.[3] At yet another level of understanding, Isis was venerated as "the Initiate of Light,"[4] or enlightenment.

Harking back to the Christianization of pagan deities, the Black Virgin can also be held to represent the Earth Mother, the Egyptian goddess Anna, who was always represented in Egyptian tradition as black.[5] Ean Begg, who has dedicated several years to the study of the Black Madonna and the hidden streams of spirituality within Christian Europe, claims that the study of the history and legends of the Black Virgin may reveal a heretical sect with the power to shock and astonish even current post-Christian attitudes, and a secret involving political forces still influential in modern Europe.[6] His comment, when judged in the light of the Rex Deus tradition, is right on the mark!

THE HOLY GRAIL

Despite the existence of the Rex Deus families being held as a closely guarded secret not revealed until the later decades of the 20th century, Rex Deus beliefs, legends, and stories had been widely known for more than nine centuries without anyone recognizing their true origins. The creation and dissemination of the stories of the search for the Holy Grail was the masterstroke that immortalized the Rex Deus tradition. This literary genre was deliberately and successfully created to serve the purposes of the descendants of Jesus. The grail sagas of the 12th and 13th centuries are a clever amalgam of pre-Christian traditions with a Christian gloss, and containing a coded guide to the true teachings of Jesus.

Variously described as a chalice, a cup, a stone that fell from heaven, a stone within a cup, or a magical bowl,[7] the Grail is believed to be capable of restoring life to the dead, or good health to the wounded or infirm. Pre-Christian and Celtic legends describe the Grail as a cauldron with similar magical qualities.[8] The Grail is carved as the "stone within the cup" carried by Melchizedek in the carving of this priest-king of Jerusalem that has place of honor by the north door of Chartres Cathedral, in the porch known as the Portal of the Initiates.[9]

The Grail sagas acquired their Christian gloss through the inspired genius of two remarkable men—Wolfram von Essenbach,[10] who spent some years in the Holy Land and is believed by some scholars to have been a Templar knight, and Chrétien de Troyes. Their stories were a clever mixture of pagan legend, Celtic folklore, Jewish mystical symbolism, Rex Deus tradition, and alchemical and Kabbalistic nuance, masked by a thin veneer of mainstream Christian veneration for the holiest relic in the Christian tradition—the cup used at the Last Supper and supposedly used by Joseph of Arimathea to catch the blood of Jesus after the crucifixion.

The first Grail romance appeared on the European literary, religious, and chivalric scene around 1190 in the form of an unfinished epic, *Perceval*, or *Le Conte del Graal*, written by Chrétien de Troyes.[11] Chrétien, who was a relative of Hughes de Payen,[12] trained for the priesthood and became a noted translator and a writer of considerable repute. He dedicated three of his early works to Marie, Countess of Champagne, the daughter of King Louis VII of France and Eleanor of Aquitaine.[13] Some claim that he originally intended to dedicate *Le Conte del Graal* to Marie. However, when Marie's husband, Count Henry of Champagne, died shortly after returning from the Holy Land, she retired from public life. Chrétien immediately sought a new patron from the ranks of Rex Deus, Phillipe d'Alsace, the Count of Flanders and a close relative of the early Christian kings of Jerusalem,[14] who was also the son of a cofounder of the Knights Templar, Payen de Montdidier.

The collection of legends that Geoffrey of Monmouth wrote concerning King Arthur, which came to public notice in 1136, eighteen years after the foundation of the Knights Templar, and those of the Holy Grail, while separate and distinct to begin with, soon became inextricably mixed. Both genres share similar ideals of chivalry and speak movingly of a spiritual search for perfection played out against a backdrop of brutal reality that was all too tangible and familiar to the enthralled listeners and readers.

It is ironic that, in the opinion of many scholars, both the Arthurian and Grail traditions seem to share a common source that has long since been lost. Comparisons have been made between this alleged "common source" and its relationship to the resulting sagas, and the similar relationship between the Q document and the Synoptic Gospels. We are not in a position to dispute the theory that there may have been some common written source linking these two chivalric legends—one that was perhaps known to both Chrétien and Wolfram. We do know, however, that both authors' works were indeed linked by another, far more important and lasting, common source—the teachings and traditions of Rex Deus. One Grail scholar, Malcolm Godwin, came remarkably close to identifying this linkage when he wrote:

> The Legend of the Grail, more than any other western myth,
> has retained the vital magic that marks it as a living legend
> capable of touching both imagination and the spirit. No other
> myth is so rich in symbolism, so diverse and often contradictory
> in meaning. And at its core there exists a secret which has sus-
> tained the mystical appeal of the Grail for the last nine hundred
> years, while other myths and legends have slipped into oblivion
> and been forgotten.[15]

The most widespread description of the Holy Grail depicts it as a relic, a cup used by Joseph of Arimathea to collect the blood of Jesus after the crucifixion. This is obviously a story concocted by someone with no knowledge whatsoever of Jewish burial practice at the time, for, apart from anything else, any men who handled a corpse would be obliged to undergo a prolonged period of purification, which is hardly likely on the eve of Passover. The Jewish aversion to men handling corpses, much less blood, in biblical times renders this story absolutely incredible. Furthermore, orthodox Jewish burial traditions of that era demand that the corpse be interred with the entire body and blood together in order to guarantee life in the hereafter. This practice continues among the Hassidim to this day and would absolutely bar against the taking of blood from any corpse.

THE GRAIL QUEST

When the first Grail romance was written, Europe was, in many respects, a police state; anyone perceived as spiritually or religiously different was liable to be burned at the stake. The Rex Deus families, in order to survive, had learned the art of dissembling and perfected it to a high degree. Therefore, while the Grail sagas purport to describe a long and dangerous quest for that most holy of all relics—the cup of Jesus—encoded within it is another, very different, message.

The Grail romances describe a long, arduous search by a knight subjected to many temptations and physical dangers—a somewhat romanticized story based on the well-known perils of prolonged pilgrimage. Set, as it is, during the supreme age of the veneration of holy relics, what is so different about the story of the quest for the Holy Grail? Behind the standard description of the quest, one that was perfectly acceptable to the hierarchy of the time, lies another story. The Grail saga is an allegory for an alchemical quest,[16] a heretical guide to a spiritual pathway to enlightenment.

In the 12th century, any knight seeking salvation merely had to volunteer for duty in the Holy Land. The indulgence promised for this exercise in Christian virtue granted absolution for all sins, both those already committed and any that might be committed in the future. Service in the Knights Templar ensured that, if killed in battle, the knight would go immediately to heaven, bypassing purgatory. So why seek the Grail? Another reason to question the basic overt message of the Grail sagas is that, by going to any church or cathedral, anyone could, by the miracle of transubstantiation, get direct access to the actual body and blood of Jesus through the simple act of communion—without great trial or danger, merely the mild embarrassment of making an act of confession.

The original Grail romances carry coded clues to a heretical belief system that contradicted the monolithic power of the oppressive Church of that time. The king of the Grail castle, the Fisher King, is wounded. He imperfectly serves his impoverished realm, just as the usurpers of the true teachings of Jesus, those who lead the Christian Church, despoil the spiritual lives of those they claim to serve. When someone pure enough to see the Grail restores the Fisher King to full health, his wasted kingdom will be restored. When the true teachings of Jesus triumph over greed, lies, hypocrisy, and distortion, the realization of heaven on Earth will be made manifest.

As to the initiatory qualities hidden within the romances, Tim's first literary collaborator, the late Trevor Ravenscroft, composed his masterwork, *The Cup of Destiny*,[17] around just these themes. His motivation was to reveal to the younger generation that, within their drama and symbolism, these sagas veil signposts to a unique path of intitiation into the deepest mysteries of the true message of Jesus. He was not alone in this conclusion, for one of the world's leading mythologists, the late Professor Joseph Campbell, writing of the importance of the Grail, cites a passage from the *Gospel of Thomas*: "He who drinks from my mouth will become as I am, and I shall be he."[18] Campbell came to the conclusion that this represented the ultimate form of enlightenment that can arise from a successful Grail quest.[19]

The actual words, "Holy Grail," are said to be a corruption of the term "Holy Gradual"—gradual in the sense of a gradual spiritual ascent or ascending initiatory way leading to eventual enlightenment. In the last two decades, another meaning has been ascribed to the term. *Sangraal*, as it is written in French, is claimed to be a disguised version of *Sang Real*, or Holy Blood.[20] This was first brought to the notice of the English-speaking world in 1981 with the publication of *Holy Blood, Holy Grail*, which claimed that Jesus, suppos-

edly the celibate Son of God, was, in fact, as mortal as we and that
he married and founded a dynasty.

MYTH AND ALLEGORY

The use of myth and legend to carry spiritual allegories and uncomfortable truths into the public consciousness in an acceptable manner
is as old as speech and memory. Those who dismiss these cultural
vehicles as some form of inspired fiction suitable only for children
or the credulous ignore the fact that every meaningful part of life—
heroic deeds, family and national traditions, and all religions, including Christianity—have always generated a colorful mythology of
their own. Thanks to the great work of Joseph Campbell and others,
the value that is attached to mythology has undergone significant
change.[21]

Myths, like symbolism, can be understood at a variety of levels
and, if viewed with discernment, can be signposts to hidden truths.
Campbell himself claimed: "Mythology is the penultimate truth,
because the ultimate cannot be put into words."[22] The Indian scholar
Ananda Coomeraswamy wrote: "Myth embodies the nearest approach
to absolute truth that can be stated in words."[23] The poet Kathleen
Raine put a similar point far more succinctly when she said: "Fact
is not the truth of myth; myth is the truth of fact."[24] However, to
reach a viable understanding of Templar beliefs, we need not rely
solely on cultic practices that have outlasted them, or on allegorical
literature, or even on myth and legend, for we have a far more tangible and visible source of reference—the architectural heritage that
they created.

The mysterious and sudden outburst of cathedral building in
the 12th century in Christian Europe gave us those majestic and
powerful "prayers in stone" that still adorn the European landscape.
The questions that arise in the mind of any tourist or pilgrim who
sees them today are: What provoked this enormous expenditure of
resources at this particular time? And where did the new architectural skills that spawned the rise of the Gothic come from? To answer
these questions, we turn to one of the Church's traditional enemies,
the Rex Deus families and their offspring and associates, the Knights
Templar and the craftmasons.

The Medieval Craftmasons

Initiatory orders had, apparently, always existed among the crafts-men who built the churches, cathedrals, and castles of Europe. Known in England simply as the craftmasons, in France, they went by a variety of names: The Children of Father Soubise, the Children of Master Jacques, and the Children of Solomon, whose heirs are known today as Les Compagnons des Devoirs du Tour de France, or the Compagnonnage. All three brotherhoods held certain beliefs in common: they observed a moral tradition of chivalry within their craft, they had a humility toward the work that must be done, and they were men who knew how to use a pair of compasses.[25]

Moreover, according to Raoul Vergez, a companion-carpenter of the Duties who rebuilt most of the church spires in Brittany and Normandy after the Second World War,[26] they all shared the same bread. Sharing the same bread is one of the hallmarks of a community or fraternity, and those who know how to use a pair of compasses are men who have been initiated into the secret knowledge of sacred geometry. These were the qualifications that admitted them to the status of mason. The divine origin of their skills was described by the English author Ian Dunlop, when he wrote: "It is not uncommon in medieval illumination to find God the Father represented as the 'elegans architectus' holding a large pair of compasses."[27]

The initiated masons gained qualification into a hierarchy of three ascending degrees: apprentice, companion, and master mason. Apprentices learned their trade in a peripatetic manner, moving from yard to yard throughout the country in what was described as a *Tour de France*, receiving instruction from skilled and initiated men known as companions. When they attained the required degree of skill, they were initiated by their masters in secret conclaves known as *cayennes*. The three fraternities that, centuries later, merged into one, had different duties, skills, and traditions. The Children of Father Soubise, who mainly built in the Romanesque style, were found at the very heart of the Benedictine monastic system. Their masons' marks, or "signatures," differ greatly from those of their brethren who built in the Gothic style, even when their work is contemporary. Master Jacques, the son of Jacquin who, according to tradition, was made a master craftmason after an apprenticeship served in Greece, Egypt, and Jerusalem, supposedly founded the *Compagnons*

Passants du Devoir, or the Children of Master Jacques. The same tradition states that he made the two pillars of the temple of Solomon—Boaz and the one that is actually called Jacquin.

THE CHILDREN OF SOLOMON

The third fraternity, the Children of Solomon, are the most important in our investigations into the great Gothic cathedrals. They built Chartres Cathedral and most of the other Gothic Notre Dames, such as those at Rheims and Amiens. These glorious buildings are all marked with their signature, the *chrisme à l'epée*—a Celtic cross enclosed in a circle. Cistercian monks taught the principles of sacred geometry to the Children of Solomon, who were named after King Solomon, the prime mover behind the construction of the first temple in Jerusalem. Another branch of the Compagnonnage built many of the Templar churches in the south of France, in both Languedoc and Provence. They were known as the *Compagnonnage Tuscana*, whose traditions and rituals traced their mysteries back to Egypt and biblical Israel via their Roman and Greek roots. According to their secret traditions, they were part of a *collegia* of constructors known as *Les Tignarii*, reputedly founded by the Roman initiate Numa Pompilius.[28]

The precise nature of the relationship between the Children of Solomon and the Order of the Templars is far from clear. No one can discern whether the craftsmen were an integral part of the knightly order, affiliated with it in some unspecified way, or just associated with it by usage. With the encouragement of Bernard of Clairvaux, the Templars gave a rule to this fraternity in March 1145 that was prefaced by the words:

> We the Knights of Christ and of the Temple follow the destiny
> that prepares us to die for Christ. We have the wish to give this
> rule of living, of work and of honour to the constructors of
> churches so that Christianity can spread throughout the earth
> not so that our name should be remembered, Oh Lord, but that
> Your Name should live.[29]

It is highly probable that this fraternity of skilled masons working in the new Gothic style were indeed affiliated in some way with the Order of the Templars. They were granted great privileges by the establishment of that time, including freedom from all taxes and protection against any form of prosecution by the constructors of other buildings. It is also instructive to note that, at the time of the suppression of the Templars, the Children of Solomon lost all the privileges and immunities granted to them.

Both the Knights Templar and the Children of Solomon were intimately involved in that fantastic and productive era of cathedral construction known as the Rise of the Gothic. Fred Gettings, the English architectural historian, makes this point abundantly clear:

> The Knights Templar who were founded ostensibly to protect
> the pilgrimage routes to the Holy Land, were almost openly
> involved in financing and lending moral support to the building
> of Cathedrals throughout Europe.[30]

Both the early 20th-century initiate Fulcanelli and his biographer, Kenneth Rayner Johnson, claim that Gothic architecture, which was the fruit of the Templar's knowledge of sacred geometry, was not merely an example of architectural beauty, but also a three-dimensional code that passed a hidden message in architectural form of *la langue verte*—the green language, or the language of initiation. They were not alone in this belief, for earlier, toward the end of the 19th century, J. F. Colfs wrote: "The language of stones spoken by this new art, [Gothic architecture] is at the same time clear and sublime, speaking alike to the humblest and to the most cultured heart."[31]

La langue verte arose from an understandable desire of initiates to mask the details of their conversations from casual eavesdroppers such as the Church hierarchy. Thus heretics could communicate using a verbal code, without putting either their lives or their freedom in jeopardy. This useful defense against persecution became the language, not only of the initiates, but also of all the poor and oppressed. It was the direct medieval ancestor of cockney rhyming slang and the "hip-talk" or "rap" of the American inner-city ghettos.[32]

SACRED GEOMETRY

Sacred geometry is a divinely inspired art form that involves the skills of engineering, building, and design. Its practitioners claim it was handed down from master to novice in an unbroken chain from the earliest times until the fall of Jerusalem in 70 C.E. This chain of communication preserved, enhanced, and transmitted the secret knowledge used by the ancient Egyptians and biblical Israelites to construct their sacred buildings. After the fall of Jerusalem, the knowledge of sacred geometry was apparently lost, until the Knights Templar returned to Europe from Jerusalem in 1128 after completing their excavations under the Temple Mount. Intriguing questions arise from the strange juxtaposition of the Templars' return from Jerusalem and the sudden explosion of building in the Gothic style that followed. Did the Templars find the keys to this new form of building under the Temple Mount? Were other influences at play in Jerusalem that can explain this new form of architecture? There is no discernable transition period in Europe between the prevailing form of Romanesque architecture and the new, tall, graceful form of the Gothic cathedrals. The Gothic style was a startlingly new development, but what were its true origins?

THE RISE OF THE GOTHIC

In earlier works, we have suggested one possible source for Gothic architecture—namely documentation discovered under the Temple Mount. Since we have proposed this idea in the absence of evidence of any viable alternative, however, we have always had some reservations about it. These originate from the fact that architectural development at the time any such documents might have been buried would not have included arches of any kind. Egyptian and Hebraic architecture were both based on transverse lintels, not arches. In fact, the only influence that might have stimulated the creation of an arch at that time was Roman.

A colleague, Gordon Strachan, has now proposed a far more credible theory. Gordon is a long-time associate of Keith Critchlow, who has devoted most of his life to an in-depth study of sacred architecture. His research knows no boundaries of faith, culture, or time. Strachan's conclusion has the merit of simplicity and credibility. Moreover, it is totally consistent with what we know of the cultural interchange occurring at the time of the First Crusade and thereafter.

He firmly believes that the pointed arch that is the foundation of the Gothic style came from outside Europe. Furthermore, he agrees that the country from which it came was the Holy Land. He claims that it resulted from "a unique blending of indigenous building skills with the architectural genius of Islam."[33] The Templars, during their initial nine-year residence in Jerusalem, met many Sufis. Sufism itself was experiencing a revival at that time.[34] As mentioned earlier, the Sufis were devout believers in a form of interfaith pluralism and, like their Rex Deus counterparts in Europe, followed an initiatory spiritual pathway. It was from contact with the Sufis, Strachan claims, that the Templars first became aware of the manner of designing the Islamic *mukhammas* pointed arch. Indeed, before bringing this knowledge back to Europe, they used it in the Holy Land to build a three-bayed doorway with pointed arches on the Temple Mount, arches that can still be seen today.[35] Thus knowledge of sacred geometry gained an immense boost from contact between the initiatory orders of both faiths—the Templars and the Sufis. If Strachan is correct, this interfaith architectural legacy bequeathed to us by the Templars can still be seen and appreciated in the flowering of artistic and religious expression of the medieval Gothic cathedrals.

Two mystical writers also noted the importance of Templar influence on these buildings in the last century:

> The building of cathedrals was part of a colossal and cleverly devised plan which permitted the existence of entirely free philosophical and psychological schools in the rude, absurd, cruel, superstitious, bigoted and scholastic Middle Ages. These schools have left us an immense heritage, almost all of which we have already wasted without understanding its meaning and value.[36]

In his work *Le Mystère des Cathédrales*, Fulcanelli wrote that a church or cathedral was not merely a place of worship or a sanctuary for the sick and deprived, but also a place of commercial activity, public theatre, and secular beliefs.

> The gothic cathedral, that sanctuary of the Tradition, Science and Art, should not be regarded as a work dedicated solely to the glory of Christianity, but rather as a vast concretion of ideas, of tendencies, of popular beliefs; a perfect whole to which we can refer without fear, whenever we would penetrate the religious, secular, philosophic or social thoughts of our ancestors.[37]

He described these Gothic cathedrals as a form of philosophical "stock exchange," where lingering pockets of arcana and heresy were flouted under the noses of an unsuspecting clergy.[38]

CHARTRES CATHEDRAL

One example of this can be found at Chartres, where the cathedral is a superb statement of the truths that lead man closer to God. The structure stands as a hymn to gnostic initiatory spirituality—a melodic symphony in stone that is a visible celebration of divine harmony. Each pilgrim or tourist, regardless of his or her faith or lack of it, leaves the building spiritually uplifted, inspired, and transformed. This is the true measure of the enduring magic of the cathedral, which is known as the Golden Book, for inspired sages have inscribed their wisdom therein as a lasting legacy to all who seek spiritual truth.[39]

The west front of Chartres cathedral, built as an addition to Fulbertus' 11th-century structure, houses the three main doors. In a small, narrow frieze that runs just above the lintels of all three doors, thirty-eight scenes from the life of Jesus are carved in detail. Significantly, however, these depictions do not include the crucifixion. Indeed, there is not one single carving of the crucifixion that dates from the 12th century in the entire cathedral.[40] This startling omission of any commemoration of the central tenet of Christian dogma is quite deliberate: it is a reflection of the Templar belief that Jesus came to reveal and not to redeem.

The magnificent stained-glass windows transform the natural daylight into a shimmering haze of subtle color that pervade the interior. The stained glass of Chartres does not react like ordinary glass. It was made using scientific knowledge—true gnosis—brought back by the Templars from their excavations in Jerusalem.[41] Scholars of the esoteric claim that this form of glass was deliberately created so that it would filter out light rays or luminous particles that were deemed harmful to humankind's innate capacity for spiritual activity. This selective filtering of cosmic rays, they claim, creates a wavelength of light that can harmonize with the natural vibrations of human cellular tissue and maximize the effect of initiatory energy.[42]

Jesus enthroned in glory showing Templar cross in
his halo, the main portal, west front of Chartres Cathedral.

In the central lancet, immediately below the huge rose window in the north transept, Saint Anne, the mother of the Virgin, is depicted wearing a halo that is usually associated with the Magdalene. The lancets flanking it are all initiates: Melchizedek, the King of Righteousness, whose teaching inspired the Kibeiri and their spiritual heirs, the Druids and the Essenes; Aaron, the brother of Moses and a priest of the Egyptian temple mysteries; King David and lastly, King Solomon, who was "wiser than Moses and full of the wisdom of Egypt."

There are three Black Madonnas in Chartres. A modern replica of the medieval copy based upon the Druidic figure Virginibus Pariturae is in the crypt, which the official guide states was used as an initiation chamber. There is another in the main cathedral—the Virgin of the Pillar, clothed according to tradition in heavy, ornate robes formally shaped in a triangle.[43] Immediately in front of the statue is a tangible level of energy, a place of God-given power where the vibration is especially low and induces a fainting feeling indicating that this is a point of spiritual transformation.

The third initiatory Black Madonna is depicted in stained glass. Notre Dame de la Belle Verrière miraculously survived not only the fire that destroyed Fulbertus' Romanesque cathedral, but centuries of strife, the French Revolution, and two World Wars. Within the cathedral are many other points of telluric power that have the capacity to raise one to a point of etheric enhancement, to a true "state of grace"—a quality that was recognized, used, and enhanced by the craftsmen who created this magnificent building. Initiation is further commemorated by figures flanking the entrance to the north door in the Portal of the Initiates. On the left is a carving of Melchizedek holding a chalice—the Grail from which the stone protrudes. He is handing the cup to Abraham. Next comes Moses, who received the two tablets of the Law that some claim are represented by the pillars of the temple of Solomon, Jacquin and Boaz.

One of the most intriguing symbols in Chartres is the labyrinth—a circular design made of black-and-white flagstones occupying over one-third of the floor of the nave. This is not just a Christian symbol, as several Neolithic labyrinths of identical pattern have been found. One day after visiting Chartres, Tim visited a folk festival in Brittany and watched a dance that gave a clear indication of the initiatory nature of the labyrinth. The music was pure North African Arab

Notre Dame du Pilar, Chartres Cathedral.

Statues of Melchizedek, Abraham, and
Moses, Portal of the Initiates, Chartres Cathedral.

music—slow, reedy, rhythmic, and entrancing. The entire village, led by the mayor and his wife, danced with their arms linked so closely that their sides seemed to touch, shuffling sideways in a curving formal design that replicated the exact pattern of the labyrinth. Tim recognized in their movements a variation of a Sufi dance designed to bring about a shift in consciousness. Thus, Chartres Cathedral is a hymn to the hidden streams of spirituality—an instruction book of initiation carved in stone and masked by an outward display of Christian worship.

AMIENS CATHEDRAL

At Amiens, the largest cathedral in France, there is a vault that soars 140 feet heavenward. The west front is dominated by a statue of Jesus known as the Beau Dieu of Amiens. Here, Jesus is depicted with his feet resting on a lion and a dragon. So here, in pride of place, is a representation of Jesus and the *Wouivre*, the initiatory telluric energy of the Druids.

Immediately below this is a statue of that supreme adept of the Old Testament, King Solomon. The walls leading into all three doors are, like those at Notre Dame de Paris, decorated with quatrefoils depicting alchemical symbolism representing, not the transmutation of base metals into gold, but the spiritual transformation of base humanity into the gold of spiritual enlightenment.[44]

According to the French mystical writer François Cali, in traveling from Chartres to Amiens one makes an almost imperceptible transition—"from the love of God to the love of Wisdom—which is in order, number and harmony—which can be equated with God, but which need not be."[45] Order, number, and harmony are all attributes of the divine gnosis so treasured by the Templar knights. This cathedral, a wondrous, symphonic blend of space, stone, and light, was designed and constructed to celebrate the gnostic principle of Sophia, or sacred wisdom, and to house the Knights Templar's most precious relic—the reliquary containing the severed head of John the Baptist. According to our friend and colleague, Guy Jourdan, the noted Provençal scholar of Templarism, this object of veneration is nothing less than *la vrai tête Baphometique Templier*—the true Baphometic head of the Templars.

In the transept, there is a series of carved panels depicting the biblical story of John the Baptist, all colored in the medieval fashion. To reinforce the point, the outer wall of the choir is decorated with superbly sculpted bas-reliefs that depict his life and death, including one where the top of his severed head is being pierced by a knife. The significance of this piercing is not known, but its importance to the Templars can be seen in their burial practices. One Templar church in Bargemon, Provence, has had part of its floor replaced with a transparent Perspex sheet, allowing a clear view of the human remains in the crypt beneath. A row of skulls and long bones can be seen and each skull is pierced in the manner depicted at Amiens.

The importance of John the Baptist to the Templars can be discerned in this passage from the Gospel of Thomas, where Jesus is quoted as saying:

> Among those born of women, from Adam until John the
> Baptist, there is no one so superior to John the Baptist that his
> eyes should not be lowered (before him).

Throughout Languedoc and Provence, in the lands once subject to Templar rule, churches dedicated to St. John the Baptist abound. In one, at Trigance, Provence, an ingenious arrangement allows a beam of light to illuminate the altar with a golden glow at dawn on the Baptist's feast day. In most of these churches and chapels, carvings of John the Baptist take precedence, yet contemporary carvings of the crucifixion are notable by their absence. In many cases, these buildings are noted, not only for their alchemical symbolism, but also as homes to the Black Madonna.

THE INITIATED LEADERS

Like the Rex Deus families from which they sprang, the Knights Templar were, from the very first, masters of dissembling. From their inception, as we have seen, they purported to be a devout and militant Christian order founded to protect pilgrims and the Holy Land. They claimed to be responsible, through their Grand Master, to the pope alone. The vast majority of the knights and all the sergeants, craftsmen, and auxiliary members were undoubtedly staunch followers of the Catholic faith. The founders and the real leaders thereafter were

Carving of Jesus being baptized
by John the Baptist, Amiens Cathedral.

Carving of John the Baptist preaching, Amiens Cathedral.

the "heretics" and Gnostics. This was a matter of supreme secrecy, however. According to French scholars Georges Caggar and Jean Robin:

> The Order of the Temple was indeed constituted of seven "exterior" circles dedicated to the minor mysteries, and of three "interior" circles corresponding to the initiation into the great mysteries. The nucleus was composed of seventy Templars . . .[46]

It is reasonable to conclude from this that the devout Christian members of the order belonged to the exterior circles of insight and would rarely be allowed to rise to a status that entitled them to join

En mïlon fu faïnct Jhan decapïte ·
Pour auoïr dïct et prefche verïte ·

The Beheading of John the Baptist, Amiens Cathedral.

the inner ruling circles. Membership of the secretive ruling clique was restricted to known members of Rex Deus who had proved their worth, or who came from an impeccable background. Exceptions might possibly have been made for the admission of outsiders who had earned the trust and respect of their leaders. The nucleus, however, would have been solely recruited from Rex Deus. These leaders of the Templar order were dedicated to the quest for gnostic enlightenment, whose fruits they used to improve the quality of the lives of all who lived in their territories.

Salome piercing the temple of John the Baptist,
Amiens Cathedral.

CHAPTER 12

GENOCIDE AND REPRESSION

The land of Septimania, ruled by nobles drawn from the Rex Deus families, stood as a bulwark against Moorish invasion for centuries after the Carolingian era. The large and prosperous Jewish population under the rule of their semi-autonomous nasi, or prince, lived in harmony with their Christian neighbors, despite the choleric fulminations of a succession of popes and archbishops. Only nine years after the fall of Narbonne to Pepin the Short, Pope Stephen III bitterly condemned royal concessions of property to the Jews of Septimania. In a letter addressed to Archbishop Aribert of Narbonne, he expressed extreme displeasure at these gifts and stated that he was distressed by them to "the point of death."[1]

Stephen was not alone. Later, Pope Gregory the Great protested against the Jewish ownership of Christian slaves. Acts of various Church councils in the 6th and 7th centuries show continuing unease at the Jewish ownership of properties in and around Narbonne.[2] In the 11th century, acts of the second and third Councils of Gerona, held in 1068 and 1078, claim that the Jews of Septimania were in possession of lands that had, at one time, been subject to the tithes of the Church.[3] The noted world traveler and Jewish chronicler Benjamin of Tudela reported that the nasi still had significant land holdings as late as the middle of the 12th century,[4] but that, shortly after that, they surrendered most of the political power they had possessed during the Carolingian era.[5]

Regular contact between Septimania and the Moslem world was established by the activities of Arab merchants and doctors, who reached the province from the East or from across the Pyrenees. Jewish doctors and scholars were held in high regard. In Narbonne and Montpellier,[6] they had their own *yeshiva*, or religious schools, that helped create the first written versions of the Kabbala. The influence of Jewish and Moslem apocryphal writings was widespread among the Catholic clergy, and sometimes even reached the common people. In some towns, Jews were appointed to the office of consul or magistrate,[7] for here they were not barred from public life as they generally were elsewhere.

The tolerance and acceptance of the Jewish communities in Septimania, however, stood in stark contrast to their treatment in most parts of Christian Europe where, by the late 12th century, the Jews were regarded as an alien minority, tolerated only when under the protection of the lord of the town. They were feared because of their prominence as moneylenders or because they often acted as government officials.[8] In most of Europe, the Jews were ritually, publicly humiliated and, intermittently, viciously persecuted in the same way as heretical groups.

The almost innate attitude of toleration that prevailed in old Septimania, now Languedoc, had a pronounced and discernible effect on both education and trade. By the middle of the 12th century, Montpellier had developed a reputation as a center of medical learning because of the Jewish community's reputation for producing skilled doctors steeped in the medical traditions of Islam.[9] By the end of that century, long before the foundation of the university, there were students of art and law studying in the town.

The climate of religious tolerance in Languedoc had its origins in the actions of that farsighted statesman, Charlemagne, and was maintained by the Rex Deus nobility he installed throughout the region. By the end of the 10th century, Languedoc was under the rule of a number of great families descended from these nobles. Under them, a tightly knit group of Pyrenean lords, although not nobles of the highest rank, were able to maintain a large degree of independence. They were all closely linked by marriage in the manner we have come to recognize as the Rex Deus tradition.[10]

Normally, the nobility throughout Christendom was bound by

responsibilities of vassalage, kinship, or both.[11] Trapped within this complex web of obligations, they were subservient to Holy Mother the Church, especially in the prosecution of heretics. Circumstances in Languedoc conspired to dilute the effectiveness of these feudal and religious burdens. The area was remote and ruled by nobles of considerable power who were intimately connected by marriage to the local lords who served under them. Moreover, and perhaps most important, the Church itself was in a state of almost terminal decline at this time.

THE DECLINE OF THE CHURCH

At this time in Languedoc, many churches were empty and unused, as there were not enough priests to service them. Some ecclesiastical buildings were used simply to hold dances or local revels. Clerical corruption and lassitude had brought about a state of religious indifference in most people. Acts of Church councils held at that time ordered abbots and bishops to wear the tonsure and habit of their order and forbade them to wear furs, play at games of chance, swear, have actors or musicians as guests, hear matins in bed, indulge in frivolous gossip during divine office, or use excommunication to gain personal advantage.

The Councils charged the clergy with laxity in convoking synods, taking fees for conferring holy orders, celebrating illegal marriages, and quashing legitimate wills. Corruption and negligence reached such a pitch that no respectable citizen would dream of having their son trained for the priesthood. The lower clergy that did exist were poorly chosen, largely ignored by their bishops, and held in contempt by the people at large. They lived such a miserable life that, according to Pope Innocent III, they deserted their calling en masse for richer and potentially more profitable occupations.[12]

The Church hierarchy largely ignored their parish priests; they were blatantly indifferent to papal authority, making them extremely unpopular in their own dioceses. The people refused to back them against the barons, and reviled them for their lack of concern for the poor. The abbots, in their richly endowed monasteries, were equally unpopular with the peasantry and townspeople. According to the testimony of contemporary Catholic writers, the Church in

Languedoc at that time completely lacked authority and prestige, and was, as a result, spiritually dead. The area was ripe for change, and that change proved religious in nature. Languedoc, although Catholic in both theory and fact, had, by a wholly natural process, quietly and without any overt rebellion, become the perfect breeding ground for heresy—a heresy that claimed to follow the true teachings of Jesus, an initiatory religion preached by priests who clearly followed the apostolic path of simplicity and service.

THE RISE OF CATHARISM

Where did this new religion originate? In assessing this, we must proceed with a degree of caution, as much of our information comes from a very suspect source indeed—namely the Church. According to Malcolm Barber, Professor of Medieval History at the University of Reading:

> It is notoriously difficult to trace the path of ideas over centuries, especially when those ideas run counter to prevailing orthodoxy and are therefore subject to vilification, distortion, and suppression. Some historians . . . have been prepared to accept the essential continuity of dualism, tracing it from Gnosticism and Manichaeism to the Paulicians and thence to the Bogomils and Cathars.[13]

This viewpoint appears to be confirmed by William of Tudela, who asserts that heresy was rife all the way from Béziers to Bordeaux—a heresy that came to be known as Catharism.

The Cathars were not dissident Catholics. They drew their strength from a faith far more ancient and authentic than that of the Church.[14] This made them increasingly dangerous to Rome, because the nobles of Languedoc were not merely tolerant of the new religion; they became its most steadfast and notable supporters. William of Tudela's only hint about the origin of Catharism occurs when he refers to a meeting in Carcassonne between the bishop of Osma and those he calls Bulgars. There is a degree of consensus that Catharism may have originated in Bulgaria and traveled along routes created by the Crusaders. The Cathar faith took firm root in northern Italy and Languedoc and began to spread through parts of France.

In Catharism, the pope was confronted with a rival religion in the very heart of Europe—one that was gaining ground fast and presenting itself as the custodian of the true teachings of Jesus. Catharism had won over the one class of the population that, under normal circumstances, would have been obliged to defend the Church's cause by force of arms.[15] Support for Cathar beliefs was not restricted to the nobility, however, for many members of the bourgeoisie in the towns had joined the new religion, and they controlled town governments almost everywhere.

Catholic merchants and traders of the 12th century faced acute theological problems posed by their business dealings. The Church fulminated against usury, yet credit was necessary to facilitate trade. Thus pressure from the Church competed with the profit motive. Some, such as Fulk of Marseilles, solved this problem by abandoning his trade and joining the Cistercians, along with his wife and son. A more attractive alternative was to become a Cathar believer since, unlike the papacy, Catharism did not preach against usury.[16]

CATHAR BELIEFS

The Cathar religion expounded a dualist, gnostic, and initiatory form of Christianity. It preached a gospel—the Gospel of Love—that was allegedly the secret Gospel of St. John the Divine. Though strongly colored by a rich vein of dualism, this teaching would, nonetheless, have been readily recognized by Jesus and James the Just.

The Cathars preached that the Earth and all that was in it, including our bodies, was the creation of an evil god, the *demi-urge*, who existed in opposition to a good god that was pure spirit. They believed that, if they followed the true teachings of Jesus and lived a life of simplicity, their souls, as spiritually perfected believers, would unite with this good god after death. Sinners, on the other hand, would reincarnate into this evil world.[17] Thus Cathars denied the existence of hell, and thereby removed the principal source of fear—that of hellfire and damnation—from ordinary people.

In the Cathar faith, Jesus was not described as a redeemer, but as a revealer of divine truth—the first person to perform the baptism by the Holy Spirit that had been proclaimed by John the Baptist.[18]

Cathars believed that John the Baptist taught Jesus, who, in his turn, taught John the Divine, who wrote the only scripture in which they put any credence—the Gospel of Love. They taught that Jesus brought salvation through his teaching, not by his sacrificial death.[19] In the light of Rex Deus beliefs and what we know of the true teaching of Jesus, it is hardly surprising that the Rex Deus nobility of Languedoc not only protected the Cathars but, in many cases, also joined them.

The Cathars "knew" that the god of the Old Testament could not have been a righteous god, since he had drowned so many people in the Flood, annihilated pharaoh and his army, destroyed the inhabitants of Sodom, and actually approved of murder by ordering the Israelites to massacre the people of Canaan.[20] They were thus seditious in the eyes of the Church hierarchy. What the Catholics found intolerable was the outright denial of the One True Church, for, if Cathar teaching were true, the sacraments of the Church were null and void and the Church itself founded on deception and lies. Why, then, should anyone pay any attention to it? Or pay taxes and tithes? The Church's trappings of wealth and worldly power simply demonstrated that it belonged to the evil world of matter and that the pope was an active agent of satanic powers.[21]

The Cathars, on the other hand, could offer their flock the true teachings of Jesus and the Gospel of Love, read and taught in a language ordinary people could understand. Their teachings stripped away the accretions of dogma, tradition, and superstition that had, over the centuries, obscured the simple words and actions of Jesus and the apostles. Furthermore, the Church had staunchly resisted any attempt to translate the Scriptures or its liturgy into the local languages of Christian Europe. Any Catholic who displayed the desire to read the Gospels in his own tongue inevitably risked an accusation of heresy.[22]

THE PERFECTI

Within the Cathar faith, the laity were known simply as *credentes*, or believers, the priests as *les bonhommes*,[23] or good men. Their critics, on the other hand, called them *perfecti*—a corruption of the Latin term *hereticus perfectus*, also known as the *Cathari*, or the pure ones.[24] The *perfecti* were, in every sense, "good men" who caught people's imagination through their sheer goodness. They were drawn from both sexes and went forth to visit country cottage, village, chateau, or city street, where they were received with universal veneration and respect.[25] As ministers to the Cathar community, the perfecti stood closer to their flocks than any Catholic priest had ever done. They were poor; they mixed with people in their daily lives and shared their labors at the loom or in the fields. They embodied an authority that needed neither pomp nor ceremony to impose its will. They proclaimed the Church of Love, lived their beliefs, and did violence to no man. As a result, the Cathar Church flourished and grew prosperous, and those who were converted to it felt that they were part of a community that offered a richer spiritual life and far more earthly fraternity than the corrupt and indifferent Catholic Church.[26]

Professor Barber identifies another factor that contributed to the appeal of the new church—its lack of doctrinal dogmatism, which stood in startling contrast to the bitter theological quarrels of the Catholic clergy.[27] One example of this lack of doctrinal rigidity is found in the one ritual obligation that was laid upon the credentes—to perform *melioramentum*, or *melhorer*, an act of respect and veneration to any perfectus they might meet. This consisted of bowing three times to the perfectus and saying: "Pray to God to make a good Christian of me, and bring me to a good end." The perfectus would give a blessing and say: "May God make a good Christian of you, and bring you to a good end." Other than this simple act, the believers had no other religious obligations, and could even continue to attend Mass in Catholic churches if they wished.[28]

Perfecti lived in working communities regardless of their previous social status, traveling in pairs to tend to the pastoral needs of the credentes, preaching and healing as they went. Their healing skills, like those of their Essene predecessors, were based on spiritual insight moderated by their skill as herbalists.[29] As initiates, they knew that Jesus had promised his disciples they would all become capable of everything he did.[30] The perfecti knew this to be true, for they knew that sacred knowledge came directly from the good god and that, as a result of following the teaching of Jesus, spiritual union with God would result from their divine gift of gnosis.

THE CONSOLAMENTUM

The one sacrament within Cathar practice was that of the *consola-mentum*—a ritual laying on of hands invoking baptism by the Holy Spirit that was granted to those credentes who had served a three-year novitiate proving their humility and dedication. This was merely the beginning of the formal initiatory process that continued for a lifetime as the perfecti ascended through the degrees of enlighten-ment, receiving increasing levels of spiritual knowledge as they pro-gressed.[31] The imparting of the consolamentum took place in a private house with other perfecti as witnesses. The officiating per-fectus ritually washed his or her hands before either touching the Gospel or laying hands on the candidate—again consciously reflect-ing the emphasis on ritual purity of their Essene precursors.

The life of a perfectus demanded total abstention from all sexual activity. They refrained from eating meat or any by-product of repro-duction such as eggs, cheese, milk, or butter. This practice stemmed from their belief in the transmigration of human souls into animals; an animal might contain an imperfect human soul awaiting revela-tion. They could drink wine and eat fish, which were believed to be the result of spontaneous generation in water. Credentes, on the other hand, were faced with no such dietary or sexual restrictions. Their role was to prepare themselves to receive the consolamentum on their deathbed.

THE STRUCTURE OF THE CATHAR CHURCH

Despite these severe limitations on the lives of the perfecti, there was no shortage of candidates. Indeed, the Cathar Church flour-ished to such an extent that it required a formalized set of dioceses with properly recognized boundaries. This not only indicates the massive growth of the Cathar faith, but also their intention to estab-lish a structured church on this Earth, whatever their views about the corruption and excesses of the Catholic clergy.[32]

There were four Cathar dioceses established in Languedoc by 1167: Albi, Agen, Carcassonne, and Toulouse.[33] Later, another was founded at Razès.[34] In view of our earlier descriptions of the ances-try of the nobility of Languedoc, it will come as little surprise that

Cathar castle of Queribus, Languedoc.

Cathar castle of Puilaurens, Languedoc.

a further diocese was established in the County of Champagne, one that soon received a companion, the diocese of France. Lombardy and Tuscany contained six more Cathar episcopal sees, with a further six in the Balkans. Each was led by a bishop served by two assistants—a "major" and a "minor" son, both elected from the deaconate of perfecti. When a bishop died, the major son became bishop, whereupon the minor son was promoted and another elected.[35] This sophisticated structure would not have been necessary, nor would it have been created, except for the widespread support from both the populace and the local counts.

REX DEUS AND THE CATHARS

The literate and sophisticated Rex Deus nobility of Languedoc had become overtly anticlerical by the mid 12th century. They did not merely tolerate the Cathar Church; they supported and encouraged it from the first. Count Raymond IV of Toulouse, who died in 1222, was particularly well-disposed toward the new religion and took a perfectus with him wherever he traveled. The Count of Foix and his family were renowned for their support of the Cathars. The count's wife, after raising her family, became a member of the perfecti.[36] Roger Trençavel, Viscount of Carcassonne and Béziers, was tutored by perfecti and became a staunch defender of the Cathars throughout his lands—a crime in the eyes of the Catholic Church for which he eventually paid with his life. Giraud, the Catholic historian, claims that all the minor nobility of the Lauragais, the prosperous and populous district between Carcassonne and Toulouse, were Cathars, as were their subjects.[37] A contemporary historian of the Albigensian Crusade and a staunch supporter of the Roman Church, Pierre des Vaux-de-Chernay, wrote: "The Lords of Languedoc almost all protected and harboured heretics ... defending them against God and the Church."[38]

PROSPERITY IN LANGUEDOC

By the close of the 12th century, the Cathar community was not only numerous, but extremely prosperous. The perfecti, nearly all drawn from the richer echelons of society, donated all their property

Rex Deus symbolism on a plaque at Béziers Cathedral.

to their church, while credentes, many of whom were members of mercantile families, sometimes bequeathed their entire fortunes to the new faith. Other rich and influential credentes made donations of money and property within their lifetime.

Despite the vow of absolute poverty they took and never broke, perfecti accepted these gifts and disposed of them according to the best interests of the local population. The communities of perfecti provided emergency relief for the poor and needy, and maintained communal houses that fulfilled the roles of schools, monasteries, and hospitals. They founded working craft guilds, large weaving establishments, leather works, and paper mills.[39] These establishments served as educational centers for the young and training establishments for the novitiate. A number of noble ladies surrendered their homes and wealth to the community for use as Cathar convents that were used to give aid to the daughters of the poorer credentes. They also provided refuge and spiritual guidance to children of the nobility who chose to spend their lives in God's service.[40]

The result of this infusion of tolerance and spirituality was the reinvigoration of religious and creative life throughout Languedoc. It spawned a truly dazzling civilization founded upon spiritual principles that encouraged commerce, the beginnings of democracy in the cities, economic stability, creative freedom, love, and religious toleration.[41] If it had not been for the prolonged and genocidal response of the Church to this new faith, it has been seriously suggested that the Renaissance might well have happened two centuries before it did, in Languedoc and not in Italy.

THE RESPONSE OF THE PAPACY

The reaction of the Church of Rome to the Cathar religion was prolonged and, at first, apparently reasonable. In 1145, Bernard of Clairvaux was sent to Toulouse in response to an appeal from Prior Eberwin of Steinfield to investigate the activities of a group known as the "Cologne heretics," who were led by an apostate monk called Henry. Bernard wrote to the Count of Toulouse and commented about the state of the Church in the region and the activities of Henry:

> The Churches are without congregations, congregations are
> without priests, priests are without proper reverence, and,
> finally, Christians are without Christ . . . Henry revels in all his
> fury among the flock of Christ.[42]

Despite encountering a discernible degree of heretical and anticlerical attitudes both in Toulouse and among the nobility of
Languedoc, Bernard described the Cathars as a people of simple and
devout spirituality led by a gifted priesthood. He said of the perfecti: "No one's sermons are more spiritual."[43] At about this time,
the pope was informed by clergy in Liège that a new heresy had
manifested itself that seemed "to have overflowed various regions
of France. One so varied and so manifold that it seems impossible to
characterise it under a single name."[44] It is plain that the descriptions of this multifaceted heresy referred to the Cathar faith.

The Cathar religion continued to grow and began to displace the
Catholic faith, a situation that was completely intolerable to the
Church hierarchy and the pope in Rome. The Church tried persuasion first, and despatched a preaching mission to Languedoc led
by a fanatical Spanish priest, Dominic Guzman.[45] The Spaniard's pastoral activities were spectacularly unsuccessful, for a house he founded
for repentant Cathar women in Prouille in 1206 was hardly used.[46]
Guzman's prolonged preaching and proselytizing must also have
fallen on deaf ears, for the terrifying finale to his verbal crusade was
a brutal warning couched in clear and unambiguous terms:

> For years I have brought you words of peace, I have preached, I
> have implored, I have wept. But, now as the common people
> say in Spain, if a blessing will not work, then it must be the
> stick. Now we shall stir up princes and bishops against you and
> they, alas, will call together nations and peoples and many will
> perish by the sword. Towers will be destroyed, walls overturned
> and you will be reduced to slavery. Thus force will prevail
> where gentleness has failed.[47]

This prophetic statement had, at the very least, the merit of honesty—although, when judged in the light of subsequent events, it
could be described as the understatement of the century. Despite
the fact that the Council of Narbonne had ruled in 1054 that "No

Christian should kill another Christian, for whoever kills a Christian undoubtedly sheds the blood of Christ,"[48] this was deemed inapplicable to the Cathars, as they were not Christians in the eyes of the Roman clergy. They were merely heretics and could be killed or brutalized at will.

THE ALBIGENSIAN CRUSADE

The murder of the papal legate, Peter de Castlenau, on 14 January 1208 triggered the campaign against the Cathar communities. A vassal of Count Raymond IV, Toulouse allegedly killed Peter. The pope responded two months later with the following call to arms:

> Attack the followers of heresy more fearlessly than the Saracens—since they are more evil—with a strong hand and a stretched out arm . . . avenge this righteous blood . . . Forward then soldiers of Christ! Forward brave recruits to the Christian army! Let the universal cry of grief of the Holy Church arouse you, let pious zeal inspire you to avenge this monstrous crime against your God![49]

Thus came the call for a crusade against the Cathars, who were judged to be a far greater danger to Christianity than all the armies of Islam. The pronouncements made it clear that every recruit for this holy war would be granted absolution for all their sins—past, present, and future—in return for a mere forty days service in the crusade.[50] Those who went to war in the name of the "Prince of Peace" were also given license to seize the property of any heretic, noble or peasant, and implied permission to steal, murder, rape, plunder, and pillage in the name of God. The crusading army was accompanied by a variety of clergy and papal representatives to ensure that all suspected heretics were dealt with appropriately and tortured before being dispatched to the warm embrace of the stake. Yet, despite the fact that this was an official crusade started at the behest of the pope, neither the Knights Templar nor the Knights Hospitaller played a significant part in it.[51] We have no records that indicate how the pope reacted to this abstention by the main body of warrior-monks, but we do have some insight into the arguments the orders deployed to justify their strange decision.

Languedoc was home to nearly 30 percent of the Templars' European holdings, and also contained a large number of establishments owned by the Knights Hospitaller. Despite the overt rivalry that inevitably colored the relationship between these two orders, there was a surprising, and perhaps suspicious, degree of unanimity in their response to the call for a crusade against the Cathars. Both claimed that their holdings in the province were purely commercial and agricultural, understaffed, unfortified, and not garrisoned in a military manner. They would, therefore, be unsuitable as bases or defensive strongholds in time of war. Furthermore, the deeds of donation granting them these estates specifically forbade their use for any warlike activity.[52] The Rex Deus foundation of the Templars, the fact that nobles from the same groups of families in Languedoc had donated the lands in question, and that these same nobles supported the Cathars, all help to explain the strange reluctance of the warrior orders to join in the war.

THE KNIGHTS TEMPLAR AND THE CATHARS

The records disclose that there were clear links between the Knights Templar and the Cathars that extended well beyond mere family loyalty. As the crusade reached its height, Templars gave assistance to knights who actively defended the Cathars against the crusading armies.[53] There is also a remarkable degree of correspondence between the names of leading Cathar families in the records of the Inquisition and those of leading Templars from that area.[54] Cathars fleeing from the crusaders were sometimes given shelter by the Templars, who, in direct contravention of papal instructions, allowed them to be buried on consecrated ground. This led to the obscene practice of disinterment, followed by trials on charges of heresy of rotting corpses carried out at the behest of the Inquisition. When convicted, the heretical cadavers were ritually burned at the stake. The political leader who apparently had most to gain by the crusade, the king of France, took no part in the campaign itself until very late in the day—until 1229, in fact, as he was busily occupied in preparing for war against the English. The French king only participated at that point because, by then, he realized that the outcome was inevitable and he saw an opportunity to annex Languedoc.[55]

THE MASSACRE AT BÉZIERS

The crusading army marched down the Rhone Valley and arrived outside the walled city of Béziers in July 1209. The lord of Béziers and Carcassonne, Viscount Raimond-Roger Trençavel, was convinced that Béziers was indefensible and left to supervise the defenses of Carcassonne. The Jews of the city, knowing only too well how their coreligionists were treated in the north of France, joined him in flight. The bishop appealed to the citizens to surrender to the forces of the papacy, but the enraged people chose to ignore him and prepared to defend their homes.[56]

The siege was short. On the eve of battle, the leaders of the crusading army, aware that the majority of the citizens of Béziers were Catholics, sought advice from the papal legate, the Cistercian Arnauld Aimery, as to how they should behave if the city fell. They received instructions that clearly displayed the teachings of a church founded on principles voiced by Jesus—teachings like: Love thy neighbor as thyself, or Love thine enemies. The papal legate's instructions were simple: "Show mercy neither to order, nor to age, nor to sex . . . Cathar or Catholic—kill them all . . . God will know his own when they get to him!"[57] The crusaders, all staunch and obedient Catholics, followed the legate's advice to the letter. The city fell the morning after these instructions were given, and over 20,000 people were slaughtered without mercy, including more than 7,000 men, women, children, and priests who had taken sanctuary in the sacred and normally inviolable precincts of the cathedral. Pierre des Vaux-de-Chernay wrote that the massacre was a punishment for the sins of the heretics:

> Béziers was taken on St. Mary Magdalene's day. Oh, supreme justice of providence! . . . the heretics claim that St. Mary Magdalene was the concubine of Jesus Christ . . . it was therefore with just cause that these disgusting dogs were taken and massacred during the feast of the one that they had insulted . . .[58]

This harsh attitude set the scene for all that was to follow for the next thirty years. Béziers acted as a vivid example of what would befall those who resisted the pope's army. Narbonne surrendered without demur, and the viscount and the bishop offered material support to the crusaders and volunteered to surrender any perfecti within the city, as well as any property belonging to the Jews of Béziers.

THE FALL OF CARCASSONNE

Carcassonne was next to be besieged. After a two-week investment, the water supply ran dangerously low and Viscount Trençavel was offered safe-conduct to discuss surrender terms. Despite the safe-conduct, he was imprisoned[59] and his son's inheritance rights set aside. He died in prison in November 1209. In the estimation of the majority of historians, his death was the result of foul play. At the surrender of the city, the inhabitants were spared without exception and with no signs of religious discrimination, but they were forced to vacate the city in their underwear and leave their homes and possessions for the profit of the invading army.[60] With the fall of Carcassonne, the newly appointed leader of the crusading army, Simon de Montfort, was awarded all the feudal rights, titles, and lands of the Trençavel family.

THE BRUTALITY CONTINUES

The sieges of Béziers and Carcassonne were simply the opening acts of the long-drawn-out agony hidden behind the innocuous title of the Albigensian Crusade. The war continued for nearly thirty years, with the ebb and flow of its bloody tide punctuated by acts of gross brutality, individual and collective bravery, and mass burnings of perfecti of both sexes. This all played out against the backdrop of a deliberate scorched-earth policy that brought starvation and financial ruin in its train.

The first public burning of perfecti took place at Castres. After the fall of Minerve, 140 perfecti of both sexes were consigned to the flames. To the great delight of the crusaders, 400 more were burned after the fall of Lavaur, sixty were incinerated at Les Casses, and 5,000 men, women, and children were hacked to death after the fall of Marmande. Simon de Montfort distinguished himself by his cruelty and, in 1210, after capturing the fortress of Bram, he sen-

Ramparts at Carcassonne.

Main gateway to the city of Carcassonne.

tenced 100 of its defenders to have their noses, lips, and ears sliced off. He then ordered ninety-nine of them to have both eyes gouged out; the last was left with one eye so that he could lead his maimed and bleeding companions to the nearby Cathar stronghold of Cabaret to encourage its defenders to surrender.

Cabaret did not fall.[61] The unsuccessful defenders of Lavaur were treated with the usual Christian chivalry. The eighty knights who had fought so valiantly were sentenced to be hanged, but the gallows collapsed, so their sentences were commuted to having their throats cut. The chatelaine, Lady Guiraude, was given to the conquering soldiers for their sexual pleasure, and, in conformity with biblical tradition, cast down a well and stoned to death for adultery.[62] The crusaders justified these acts of obscene barbarity by claiming they were defending the true religion against heresy. This was reason enough to justify a brutal campaign of expropriation conducted with the express approval of several popes and the active encouragement of the local hierarchy, who benefited enormously from the requisition of property belonging to the heretics they hated so much.

THE FALL OF MONTSÉGUR

This thirty-year war officially ended with the fall of the last Cathar stronghold of Montségur in 1244. The siege had lasted nearly a year and, for once, the crusaders acted with some semblance of chivalry. The surrender terms permitted a two-week truce before the victors entered the castle.[63] The fighting men of the garrison were spared, but not, of course, the perfecti. It has been alleged that, during the truce, several perfecti made their escape from the castle, supposedly carrying the Cathar treasure,[64] the true nature of which is a matter of pure speculation. As the defenders marched down the mountainside to freedom, their path was illuminated by a huge conflagration as 225 perfecti, men and women, were consigned to the flames.

The long-drawn-out agony of the crusade against the Cathars was ended. Catharism, however, still survived. It had not been extirpated by the brutality of the Albigensian Crusade; it flourished in secret in many parts of Languedoc. The nobility of the area who had survived largely became *faudits*, or little more than bandits. The suffering of the people was not yet over, however, for the Church had another plan for the heretical populace of Languedoc—one that would finally put an end to the Cathar heresy, and the name of which would live in infamy for centuries to come—the Holy Inquisition.

CHAPTER 13

†HE HOLY ÎNQUISITION

Pope Gregory IX was well-satisfied with the results of the Albigensian Crusade. In a letter to his bishops in the south of France, he announced his intention of using the teaching friars to discover and repress heresy. In July 1233, he appointed two Dominican friars as full-time Inquisitors. Thus, the Inquisition began. These two Inquisitors were later described by Peter de Rosa, a historian of the papacy, as the first of "a long line of serene untroubled persecutors of the human race."[1]

The Holy Office of the Inquisition was led and largely staffed by members of the Dominican order founded by Dominic Guzman. Its intent was to create a perpetual climate of fear in which heresy would not dare to rear its head. Inquisitors now had legal authority to convict suspected heretics without any possibility of appeal and, in effect, to pronounce summary death sentences.[2] Their primary target was the Cathars.[3]

The activities of the Inquisition ensured that, in Languedoc and throughout Europe, the pope's gift of peace was far more terrifying than the horrors of the recent war. He lost no time in extending the reach of the new organization. In the same year the office was created, he appointed Peter of Verona as Inquisitor in Lombardy.[4] In 1246, Pope Innocent IV instructed the Franciscans to join the Dominicans in the work of the Inquisition and divided Italy into two inquisitorial provinces.[5] In the bull *Super Extirpatione*, the Franciscans were given responsibility in Tuscany, Umbria, and the

Veneto, while the Dominicans were charged with the remainder of the country. Inquisitorial duties in the rest of Christendom were apportioned as follows: the Franciscans were given responsibility for eastern France south of the Loire, Poland, Dalmatia, Bohemia, Croatia, Serbia, Hungary, Jerusalem, and the Holy Land; the Dominicans operated in northern France, western France south of the Loire, Germany, and Austria; the two orders would work together in Aragon, Navarre, Burgundy, and Italy. Thus the Inquisition was set in motion throughout much of Christendom from the midpoint of the 13th century onward.[6]

Using procedures banned in other courts, the Inquisition rode roughshod over the established canons of justice and ignored all written, state, and customary laws that granted some semblance of protection to the accused. Thus it developed a system of jurisprudence that, in time, infected, not only ecclesiastical practice and canon law, but also the criminal law of the lands subjected to its malign influence. It made a cruel mockery of the idea of papal justice for all time. The papacy had developed a powerful weapon that it used for political aggrandizement. Secular kings and emperors were soon tempted to emulate the pope's diabolical example, and themselves prostituted the religion supposedly based on the concept of a loving God to their own material ends.

One historian, H. C. Lea, was moved to write:

> The judgement of impartial history must be that the
> Inquisition was the monstrous offspring of mistaken zeal, uti-
> lized by the selfish greed and lust of power to smother the
> higher aspirations of humanity and stimulate the baser
> appetites.[7]

Legislation against heresy culminated in the creation of a permanent inquisitorial tribunal endowed with almost limitless authority. These tribunals worked from a fixed base in each district in conjunction with the local bishops and clergy.[8] In 1239, a few years after the establishment of the tribunals, a bishop named Moranis was accused of allowing heretics to live and multiply in his diocese. As a result, a Dominican Inquisitor named Robert de Bougre was sent to the county of Champagne to investigate—a sign that members of Rex Deus far from Languedoc were courting potential disaster. Within a week of the Dominican's arrival, virtually the whole town was on trial. The result was predictable, for, on 29 May, Bishop Moranis and over 180 of his flock were publicly burned as Cathar heretics.[9]

COME ONE, COME ALL!

The Inquisition subjected entire towns, villages, and districts to investigation in a manner designed to inspire widespread, systematic terror. Typically, an announcement was made that the Inquisitors were coming and that a public examination would begin on a fixed date. On that day, and for thirty days thereafter, anyone who voluntarily confessed to heresy would be absolved with minimal punishment—provided, of course, that they incriminated others. People were questioned about their entire lives, from childhood onward. Their associates', friends', and relatives' names were recorded so that they, in turn, could be interrogated at length. Other individuals were arraigned arbitrarily and, while they had a technical right to see a written account of the charges made against them, they had no right to know the names of their accusers or those of any witnesses who were called to testify.[10]

The accused had no right to any form of legal representation, and torture was routinely used from the beginning, although it did not receive formal papal sanction until 1252.[11] This, despite the fact that there was a tradition, dating from the 9th century, that the clergy and the Church were forbidden to shed blood. To draw blood, by lance, sword, or dagger, was traditionally considered un-Christian, so the techniques of the Inquisition were designed to keep actual bloodshed to a minimum. A later pontiff, Pope Alexander IV, authorized Inquisitors to absolve each other for so-called "irregularities," such as the premature death of a victim. In line with the stated policy, however, most forms of torture neatly avoided shedding blood. Methods were devised to cause maximum pain and suffering with a minimum of mess. In fact, the mere sight of the instruments of torture was often enough to extract confessions of heresy. Although references to torture are not common in contemporary documents, it seems that its use was as widespread in late 13th-century Italy and France as it was later in Spain.[12] Of all the methods of torture, the supreme instrument of the Inquisition was fire.[13]

Under preexisting civil law, certain categories of people were theoretically immune from torture, such as doctors, soldiers, knights, and nobles. At first, the Inquisitors themselves were prohibited from administering torture and their role was limited to that of supervisors who instructed the civil executioners and made notes of anything the accused said under duress. In 1252, Pope Innocent IV formally authorized them to administer torture themselves "with restriction that such compulsion should not involve injury to limb or danger of death." The traditional stricture about shedding blood remained in force, so pointed and bladed implements were avoided in favor of the rack, thumbscrews, and devices that caused blood to flow only as a secondary consequence. To tear flesh with pincers would undoubtedly shed blood, unless the pincers were red- or white-hot—in which case, the hot metal cauterized the wound and staunched the bleeding.

The Inquisitors kept meticulous records of their interrogations, which enabled them to continue to harass the descendants of those convicted of heresy. Since the stain of heresy was considered hereditary, the children of heretics could not inherit, and their grandchildren were barred from taking holy orders—unless, of course, they successfully denounced someone.[14] Any failure to go to confession or take communion inevitably aroused suspicion and gave grounds for enemies or commercial rivals to denounce yet another victim to the Inquisitors. Suspects were imprisoned indefinitely or repeatedly summoned and interrogated. The name of the game was to get confessions of heresy at any price. There is not one record of an Inquisitor ever losing a case.

The Church proudly displayed the "Black Book" or *Libero Nero* written by the arch Inquisitor Bernard Gui as a manuscript of instruction for his colleagues. A sample of it reads as follows:

> Either a person confesses and he is proved guilty from his own confession, or he does not confess and is equally guilty on the evidence of witnesses. If a person confesses the whole of what he is accused of, he is unquestionably guilty of the whole; but if he confesses only a part, he still ought to be regarded as guilty of the whole, since what he has confessed proves him to be capable of guilt as to the other points of the accusation....

If, notwithstanding all the means [of torture] employed, the unfortunate wretch still denies his guilt, he is to be considered as a victim of the devil: and, as such, deserves no compassion from the servants of God, nor the pity and indulgence of Holy Mother Church: he is a son of perdition. Let him perish among the damned.[15]

The Inquisitors were paid with the confiscated goods and property of convicted heretics, thus the rich had even more to fear from them than the poor. Various methods were devised for dividing these ill-gotten gains. For example, when the expenses of the scribes and executioners had been paid, half of the remainder went to His Holiness the Pope in Rome; the rest became the personal property of the Inquisitors. While many Inquisitors had a keen eye for the personal profits they could accrue, others operated, questioned, and tortured from a misplaced love of God. These were the "incorruptibles." Furthermore, monetary gain and religious fervor were not the only rewards garnered by these zealous friars; they were also granted the same indulgences as the crusaders.

Over the centuries, the ignominious record of the Inquisition has come to light. The staunchly Catholic historian of Christianity Paul Johnson condemns it vigorously and details its activities and effects with horror.[16] One noted historian, H. C. Lea, described its catalog of crimes as "an infinite series of atrocities."[17] Lord Acton, a Catholic, penned a condemnation, not only of the Inquisition, but also of the Church that spawned it:

Nothing short of religious assassination . . . the principle of the Inquisition was murderous for the popes were not only murderers in the grand style, but they made murder a legal basis of the Christian Church and a condition of salvation.[18]

Even after the Second World War, when all the barbarities of Dachau, Belsen, and Auschwitz, and the horror of the "final solution," had been exposed to the world, one commentator, C. G. Coulson, was still able to claim that the Inquisition was responsible for "the most elaborate, widespread and continuous legal barbarities recorded in civilized history."[19] Rollo Ahmed, the Egyptian scholar of the occult, described the Holy Inquisition as:

> The most pitiless and ferocious institution the world has ever
> known . . . The atrocities the Inquisition committed constitute
> the most blasphemous irony in religious history, defiling the
> Catholic Church with the deaths of innocent victims who were
> burnt to avoid breaking the maxim, *Ecclesia non novit
> sanguinem*—the Church has never shed blood.[20]

The Inquisition still exists under the innocuous name of the
Congregation for the Doctrine of the Faith. Sadly, among some
priests, the thinking that lay behind the Inquisition's foundation was
also alive and well at the beginning of the 20th century when a
Jesuit professor of canon law, Dr. Marianus de Luca stated that the
Holy Roman Catholic Church, "Had the right and the duty to kill
heretics."[21]

Despite the coldblooded efficiency it displayed in its early years
in Languedoc, however, the Inquisition could not completely extin-
guish the Cathar faith. While many perfecti were burned and a vast
number of believers persecuted and punished, some Cathars survived and fled into exile. Others learned the arts of dissembling and
disguise. While the Cathar religion as a visible, coherent entity vanished forever in the 14th century, many individual Cathars survived.
Some sought refuge among the ranks of the warrior-monks who
had refused to play any significant part in the crusade, while others
fled to Tuscany, where their respite was brief. In 1317, the most infamous of Inquisitors, Bernard Gui, was sent by the pope to pacify
northern Italy, which was held to be suffering from a serious infec-
tion of heresy.[22] Other Cathars, so tradition tells us, fled to Scotland
and found a safe haven on the St. Clair estates at Roslin, where they
established a papermaking industry.

CHAPTER 14

THE DECLINE AND FALL OF THE KNIGHTS TEMPLAR

Goethe once said that coming events cast their shadows before them. In other words, significant occurrences do not arise out of some mythical vacuum, unheralded or out of the blue; they are rather the culmination of a series of apparently unrelated circumstances that serve to lay the foundations for the future. With hindsight, we can discern in the historical record a cumulative chain of events that weakened the power of the Knights Templar, deprived them of their bases in the Holy Land and their very reason for existence, and ultimately displayed their vulnerability to apparently inferior forces.

In 1138, the renowned leader who led the armies of Islam to victory over the crusaders, Salah-al-Din Yusuf ibn Ayyub, or Saladin, was born. The son of a skilled general, Najm-al-Din Ayyub, the young Saladin excelled in learning before he took up a military career in the service of the Saracen leader, Nur-el-Din. By 1185, through diplomacy, political realism, and military prowess, he had united the disparate factions of the Muslim world and was ready to act on his lifelong ambition—to wage *jihad*, or holy war, against the Christian forces of the kingdom of Jerusalem.

Saladin's victory at the Horns of Hattin in 1187 not only defeated the largest Christian army ever assembled in the Holy Land; it also set in train the final decline of crusader power in that war-torn country. The fact that the Christian defeat was caused as much by the ill-tempered strategic incompetence of the Templar Grand Master, Gerard de Ridefort, as it was by Saladin's meticulous planning and superb skill does little to mitigate the enormity of the defeat. At the conclusion of the battle, Saladin ordered the execution of all 230 surviving knights of both the Templar and the Hospitaller orders. He is recorded as saying: "I wish to purify the land of these two monstrous orders, whose practices are of no use, who will never renounce their hostility and will render no service as slaves."[1]

Saladin knew that ransom was forbidden for the warrior monks by the rules of both orders. As a result, after each man was offered the opportunity to convert to Islam, which predictably was rejected, he was handed over to the Sufis for beheading. Many people have wondered why the Sufis undertook that grisly task when their beliefs and those of the Templars had so much in common. The answer is simple: The Sufis believed that all warriors who died for their faith went straight to paradise. Furthermore, the Knights Templar and the Hospitallers, as Christian martyrs, knew they would go straight to heaven, so death held no fear for them. The Sufis obeyed orders, like the good soldiers they were, knowing that the victim's instant entry into paradise was a far more noble and merciful fate than a lifetime of slavery.

Saladin's behavior when Jerusalem fell to his army later the same year stood in marked contrast to the bloody day that the holy city was first captured by the Christian armies in 1095. Then there had been a bloodbath, with the crusaders killing everyone in sight—Christian, Jew, and Muslim—until the horses of the conquering knights waded up to their knees in blood. When the forces of Islam recaptured the city, Saladin negotiated a peaceful surrender and its inhabitants were offered the chance to be ransomed and not massacred. After the capture of Jerusalem, the remaining crusader states in the Holy Land lingered for over a century. They were whittled away little by little, until, in 1291 with the fall of Acre, Beirut, and Sidon, the Christian forces lost their last viable foothold in that sacred but blood-soaked country. When this happened, the warrior-monks lost the main justification for their existence.

RESENTMENT AGAINST THE TEMPLARS

Any organization as large and powerful as the Templars that was backed by papal prestige, economic success, and popular esteem derived from its valorous actions in the Holy Land could not help but excite the envy of others. Their very power and independence tended to breed arrogance, and the degree of papal privilege they enjoyed caused lasting resentment among the episcopate and the secular clergy.[2]

Much of this resentment sprang from the fact that the Templars paid no tithes—a situation that resulted in a massive loss of revenue to the local church, for tithes that had been paid into their coffers ceased once lands were donated to the order. The Church also lost valuable revenue in other ways. For example, it would normally have collected considerable income from burials. However, when associate members of the order—the confratres and consores, their relatives, their servants and employees, their craftsmen and their families, or anyone who donated land, goods, or money to the Templars—needed burial, they were interred on Templar lands by the order's own priests and not by the secular clergy. Other important vested interests had their own axes to grind; there was hardly a crowned head in Europe who did not owe money to the warrior-monks.

Matters came to a head with the election of a new Grand Master in 1293. There were allegations of irregularities in this election and it is recorded that, for some inexplicable reason, the Grand Master of the Hospitallers was invited to guide and advise the chapter of their main rivals in this closely fought election.[3] The outcome was that an elderly, and reputedly illiterate, knight from the north of France, Jacques de Molay, was elected as the 23rd Grand Master of the Templar Order. Most accounts of this tragic figure agree that he was brave, strict, and none too bright.

Shortly after the fall of Acre, Pope Nicholas IV died in Rome. His demise ushered in one of the most unedifying episodes in papal history. A succession of popes, all riddled with corruption and tainted by double-dealing and scandal, were elected improperly; forced abdications were followed by elections subject to bribery and violence. Finally, accusations of murder, idolatry, simony, sodomy, and heresy were leveled against Pope Boniface VIII.[4] Eventually, under the malign influence of a cunning and unscrupulous monarch, King Philippe le Bel of France, a French archbishop, Bertrand de Goth, Archbishop of Bordeaux, who was not even a cardinal, was elected to fill the papal throne as Pope Clement V.

Clement became, in effect, a stopgap pope chosen as a supposedly neutral candidate to prevent civil war between the two major contending families in Rome. He distanced himself from the tense situation in the papal city by residing in Avignon, where he reigned in considerable splendor, ruling his flock at the behest of his puppetmaster, King Philippe.

KING PHILIPPE LE BEL

Philippe IV succeeded to the throne of France in October 1285. Although Philippe was of the Capetian line, the Rex Deus traditions had long since died within the royal family of France. Philippe's grandfather, King Louis IX, had been a sincere and zealous Catholic and was canonized as St. Louis for his crusading activities. France itself was now a large kingdom, having gained Normandy, Anjou, Maine, Touraine, the county of Toulouse, and the whole of Languedoc. Despite its size, however, the kingdom was in the grip of acute financial difficulties exacerbated by the costs of the various wars that Philippe had to wage.

In the last decade of the 13th century, Philippe levied a 10 percent tax on the Church and imposed punitive financial measures on Languedoc. Forced loans were frequently imposed from 1294 and 1297 during the war with England, and, between 1295 and 1306, Philippe repeatedly debased the coinage.[5] Ultimately, this provoked riots against the king, who was forced to seek refuge in the Paris temple, the headquarters of the Knights Templar.[6] Lombard bankers to whom he owed over 800,000 livres tournois were despoiled and their assets seized. By this simple expedient, he cancelled his debt and produced considerable income. Throughout the 1290s, Lombard bankers in France were subject to seizures, fines, and expulsions, until, in 1311, all their debts were appropriated and they were imprisoned.[7]

The Jews of France were another obvious target. In 1295, their "usurious profits" were confiscated and they were forced to reveal details of all their financial affairs. In July and August of 1306, all Jewish property throughout France was seized and the penniless, dispossessed owners expelled from the country.[8] Most Jewish families from Languedoc fled for sanctuary to Moorish Spain; Jews from other parts of France fled to Alsace, Burgundy, and northern Italy. A sizable contingent emigrated to the Muslim-controlled Holy Land. No one was safe from the depredations of this desperate and impecunious monarch, especially those to whom he owed large sums of money.

Philippe le Bel had extracted a high price from De Goth for ensuring his election to the papacy. This included his right to retain the tithes collected by the Church in France for a period of five years and a promise that the new pope would reside in Avignon under his watchful eye. Twelve of the king's chosen clergy were made cardinals and, according to some sources, a secret condition was imposed that was never publicly disclosed.[9] In 1306, Clement V wrote letters to the Grand Masters of the Templars and the Hospitallers inviting them to France to discuss their possible amalgamation. They were instructed to "travel as secretly as possible and with a very small train as you will find plenty of your knights on this side of the sea."[10] William de Villaret, the Grand Master of the Knights Hospitaller, declined this invitation, explaining that he was engaged in an assault on the Turkish stronghold of Rhodes. It is clear that both the pope and the king were aware of this, as it was public knowledge. Jacques de Molay had no such ready excuse, however, and, defying the explicit instructions from the pope, sailed for the Templar port of La Rochelle with a fleet of eighteen ships. On board the fleet were sixty senior knights of the order,[11] 150,000 gold florins, and so much silver bullion that it required twelve packhorses to carry it.[12] De Molay knew that he might well have to resort to bribery if reasoned argument against the proposed merger failed. Thus a large train of knights, packhorses, and transport arrived at the temple in Paris, where they were welcomed by the king.[13]

The Grand Master of the Templar Order had, so he believed, prepared his case against amalgamation with some skill. He was prepared to claim that, as both orders had rendered signal service to the Church and the cause of Christianity, there was no rational reason to institute change. He also deployed a spiritual argument: As the members had chosen their respective orders under the guidance of God, it might even be blasphemous to insist that they now join another. He was ready to point out that, as each order owned considerable properties and wealth, any move to amalgamate them might well bring dispute in its train. What he could not disclose to either the king or pope was the central issue that the Order of the Knights Templar was the military creation of descendants of the high priests of the original temple in Jerusalem.

De Molay's preparations were in vain, for the proposed amalgamation of the two military orders was just an excuse used to tempt the Grand Master to exchange the safety of Cyprus for the danger of France. At the funeral of the king's sister-in-law, Catherine de Valois, on Thursday, 12 October 1307, Jacques de Molay occupied the seat of honor near the king.[14] He was to be in a very different position within twenty-four hours.

THE FALL OF THE TEMPLARS

As dawn broke on Friday, 13 October 1307, the king's agents throughout France opened sealed orders that had been distributed nearly one month earlier, on 14 September.[15] Acting on the instructions within them, French soldiers swooped down on every Templar property within the kingdom, arresting the Templar Grand Master, the sixty knights of the inner circle, and all but twenty-four of the members of the order residing in France.[16] Gerard de Villiers, the preceptor of France, was the only leading Templar to escape.

To justify this massive wave of arrests, charges were leveled against the premier warrior order of Christianity that was described as:

> a bitter thing, a lamentable thing, a thing which is horrible to contemplate, terrible to hear of, a detestable crime, an execrable evil, an abominable work, a detestable disgrace, a thing almost inhuman, indeed set apart from all humanity.[17]

The Templars were accused of causing Christ "injuries more terrible than those he endured on the cross,"[18] a comment that echoed the charge against the Cathars that they were more evil than the Saracens. In fact, if one studies the charges brought against heretics throughout European history, there is an appalling sameness about them—as if the accusers, having devoted such thought and effort to devising new methods of torment for their victims, ran out of ideas when it came to framing the charges and simply conformed to tired and formulaic phrases.

King Philippe le Bel was scrupulous in his actions, and extremely careful to explain that he was only acting at the request of Guillaume de Paris,[19] the chief Inquisitor of France, a deputy of the pope and the king's confessor. However, with the king's hold over Clement V and his relationship with Guillaume, it is obvious that Philippe was the prime mover in the whole affair and that, in this instance, the Inquisition was acting as an arm of the state and not at the behest of the pope. It is plain that, although Philippe and Clement may have discussed these matters prior to 13 October, the king had neither sought the pope's consent for the arrests nor informed him of them until after the event.[20]

The Inquisitors subjected many of the knights to threats and acts of torture long before their first interrogation. The Inquisitors were at least consistent with their own established, if somewhat dubious, standards in that, after each victim's deposition was taken it was duly recorded that the accused had "told the pure and entire truth for the safety of his soul" and not because he had been subjected to intimidation and torture.[21] Of the 138 depositions from those hearings in Paris in October 1307, which included those of Jacques de Molay and his leading knights, only four record that men were able to withstand the horrors to which they were subjected.

The results in other parts of France were comparable. The inquisitorial records disclose that, as usual, the Inquisitors were scrupulous in keeping within their papal policy of *ecclesia non novit sanguinem*— the Church shall not shed blood—and that, therefore, the tortures applied to the Templars were the standard ones that had proved so effective over the years. Although the English authors Knight and Lomas allege that the Inquisition crucified Jacques de Molay, there is not one shred of credible evidence that the Inquisition ever used crucifixion on any of its victims at any time in its long and bloody history. To crucify anyone would have been considered the ultimate blasphemy by the fanatical Dominicans.

TROUBLE AT THE TOP

Although King Philippe had outwardly conformed to established procedures by using the Inquisition, Pope Clement V was outraged at this apparent usurpation of his own prerogative. It was particularly galling for him, as the Templars were responsible to the pope and the pope alone. However, Clement lacked both the power and the will to halt the proceedings. In a vain attempt to regain some semblance of control over the situation, he issued a papal directive, dated 22 November 1307, ordering all Christian rulers in Europe to arrest all the Templars[22] in their domains and confiscate their properties in the name of the pope.[23]

This missive was not received with universal acclaim or agreement. The king of England had previously refused to give "easy credence" to the charges against the Templars and had written as much to the pope. He had also written to the kings of Portugal, Castile, Aragon, and Naples in terms that left no doubt that he supported the maligned order. The terms of the papal directive, however, left him no choice, and he replied that he would initiate action against the order "in the quickest and best way."

His actions were somewhat different from those taken by the king of France, however, in that very few knights were actually arrested and imprisoned; most were allowed to stay in their preceptories and, as torture was forbidden under English law, no one confessed to heresy when interrogated. Proceedings in England were, therefore, unproductive, until June 1311, when one knight, Stephen de Stapelbrugge, confessed to denying Christ and claimed that homosexuality had been encouraged within the order. This was after papal pressure had resulted in the full application of ecclesiastical law and the use of torture had at last been sanctioned, a situation that resulted in further confessions.[24]

In Portugal, the trial of the order resulted in a verdict of not guilty, and in Scotland, the trial of the Templars, conducted by William de Lamberton, bishop of St. Andrews, brought in, under his explicit direction, the old Scottish verdict of "not proven, despite the best efforts of the prosecutor," John Solario, the papal legate.[25] Lamberton was a close associate of Baron Henry St. Clair of Roslin, and was also the leader of a shadowy group responsible for organizing support for Robert the Bruce in his struggle to gain the throne of Scotland.

The archbishop of Compostela wrote to the pope pleading that the Templars be acquitted, especially as their skills and resources were desperately needed in the wars against the Moorish forces in Spain.[26] The rulers of Lombardy, the Rex Deus family of the House of Savoy, ensured that most of the bishops in their realm supported the Templar cause and those bishops issued a statement claiming that they could find no incriminating evidence against the order. Others were less favorable, and did bring in convictions; in Germany and in Greece the results were equally mixed. In France, however, the agony of the Templars continued until it reached its fiery finale in 1314.

The Death of Jacques de Molay

On 18 March 1314, the archbishop of Sens, accompanied by three papal commissioners, took their places on a stage erected outside the west front of the cathedral of Notre Dame de Paris. The archbishop was hardly a disinterested party, for he had already supervised the burning of fifty-four Templar knights in 1310.[27] The bishop of Alba read out to the assembled crowd the confessions that had been extracted from the tortured knights and sentenced them all to perpetual imprisonment.

At this point, the inept and illiterate Jacques de Molay redeemed himself by an act of calculated bravery that will never be forgotten. This tortured wreck of a once-great warrior, now seventy years of age and physically and mentally scarred by seven years in the care of the Inquisition, indicated that he wished to speak. The assembled bishops, under the impression that De Molay wished to confess, graciously granted him leave to address the crowd. The Grand Master then made a speech that ensured his immortality:

> It is just that, in so terrible a day, and in the last moments of my
> life, I should discover all the iniquity of falsehood, and make the
> truth triumph. I declare, then, in the face of heaven and earth,
> and acknowledge, though to my eternal shame, that I have
> committed the greatest of crimes but . . . it has been the
> acknowledging of those which have been so foully charged on

the order. I attest—and truth obliges me to attest—that it is innocent! I made the contrary declaration only to suspend the excessive pains of torture, and to mollify those who made me endure them. I know the punishments which have been inflicted on all the knights who had the courage to revoke a similar confession; but the dreadful spectacle which is presented to me is not able to make me confirm one lie by another. The life offered me on such infamous terms I abandon without regret.[28]

De Molay's refutation of his previous confession was greeted with roars of support from the assembled crowd. Geoffroi de Charney moved to stand beside his Grand Master as a sign of total support for his statement and spoke in similar terms, asserting the sanctity of the Templar order. He, too, revoked his previous confession.[29]

The clergy immediately suspended the proceedings, cleared the square, and reported the events to the king. He solved the matter once and for all by sentencing the two brave knights to a slow and lingering death. The execution took place on the evening of the same day on the Isle des Javiaux. A slow, hot, and smokeless fire was prepared to ensure that the Templars' agony would be as prolonged as possible, and both Jacques de Molay and Geoffroi de Charnay were slowly cooked to death. Legend claims that, before being placed on the fire, Jacques de Molay cursed Pope Clement V and King Philippe le Bel and called upon them both to appear before God in heaven within the year.[30] If the legend is true, then it must be said that both the accursed king and the pope heeded that prophetic call: Pope Clement, who had suffered from chronic ill health for many years, died on 20 April, and King Philippe IV of France followed him to the grave on 29 November the same year.

THE ACCUSATIONS

The list of formal accusations made against the Knights Templar was considerable—denial of Christ and defiling the cross, adoration of an idol's head (Baphomet), ritual murder and a ritual kiss, wearing a cord of heretical significance, alteration of the Mass, an unorthodox form of absolution, homosexual aberration, and treachery to other

Christian forces.[31] As the vast majority of the Templars were devout Christians, these charges were mostly without foundation. For the inner circle of Rex Deus nobles who actually controlled the order, nobles who were undoubtedly heretics in the true meaning of the word, the accusations were also largely fabricated. Despite the fact that they believed Jesus had come to reveal rather than redeem, they were under an obligation from their own secret traditions to follow the outward form of the prevailing religion, namely Christianity. Thus most of these charges were unfounded. The last, however, may seem to be justified, although it probably arose from strategic incompetence rather than any collusion with the Muslims. Homosexuality and sexual immorality were charges that were traditionally levelled against anyone accused of heresy. The wearing of a cord of heretical significance does have the ring of truth, for in the initiation ceremonies they used a cable-tow noose just as the modern craft of Freemasonry does today.

The most credible charge against the order was that of idolatry—adoring the bearded head of the idol, Baphomet. Their veneration of one bearded head in particular is established beyond all doubt, for the cathedral of Amiens was founded to house one object of veneration that was of supreme importance to the Templars—the reliquary reputed to hold the severed head of St. John the Baptist. Other depictions of bearded heads have been found on Templar property, such as the large painting of a head discovered at the English holding at Templecombe in Somerset.

The French scholar J-A Durbec lists among the symbols that he claims are indicative of Templar influence the "Mandylion, a depiction of a bearded head on a cloth, much like the Veil of Veronica or the Turin shroud.[32] The English scholar and historian Noel Currer-Briggs suggests that there is a considerable body of evidence that the Shroud of Turin was the original used to design the head at Templecombe and that the inner circle of the Templar order used it.[33] This may yet prove to be the case, since an internationally renowned microbiologist, Dr. Leonicio Garza-Valdes, has now discredited the carbon dating of the Shroud of Turin on purely scientific grounds.[34]

At first glance, the most absurd charge was that of ritual murder. However this may have some tenuous basis in Templar ritual. It is highly probable that the initiation ceremonies of the medieval Knights

Templar had much in common with those of the Children of Solomon. Moreover, it is not unreasonable to suggest that they included a reenactment of the murder of Hiram Abif, much as modern Freemasons use today. This may have led to the making of this otherwise inexplicable charge.

PAPAL SUPPRESSION OF THE ORDER

Whatever the truth or falsehood of the charges, the Templars were never, as an organization, convicted of any of them. Yet the decision to suppress the order was announced in a papal bull, *vox in excelso*, issued on 22 March 1312. The wording of the document is revealing, since, in effect, the pope suppressed the order without actually condemning it:

> ... considering, moreover, the grave scandal which has arisen
> from these things against the Order, which it did not seem
> could be checked while this Order remained in being ... even
> without blame being attached to the brothers ... not by judicial
> sentence, but by way of provision, or apostolic ordinance, we
> abolish the aforesaid Order of the Temple ... and we subject it
> to perpetual prohibition. ... Which if anyone acts against this,
> he will incur the sentence of excommunication *ipso facto*.[35]

The next problem was what to do with the order's vast estates, financial assets, and other possessions. Clement was opposed by most of his own clergy in his plan to transfer all Templar assets to the rival Order of the Knights Hospitaller. However, he got his own way and, in another bull, announced the confiscation and transfer. The only exceptions he allowed were Templar properties in the kingdoms of Castile, Aragon, Portugal, and Majorca. In France, however, certain deductions were authorized in favor of King Philippe before any such transfer could take place. These covered the costs of the interim administration of these properties since the time of the original arrests, and the expenses incurred by the imprisonment and interrogation of the knights of the order. The Knights Templar thus were made to pay for their own imprisonment and torture.

The fate of the treasure that the king of France saw during his stay in the Paris temple and the considerable sums he observed being carried into the temple when Jacques de Molay and his large train arrived from La Rochelle is a mystery that still provokes intense speculation. When, after the initial arrests, the king's seneschals raided the temple, the treasure had vanished, and, by the time his troops reached La Rochelle, the Templar's Atlantic fleet, along with the eighteen ships that had carried Jacques de Molay and his retinue from Cyprus, had disappeared, its destination unknown.

A variety of explanations have been proposed for the mysterious disappearance of both the Templar treasure and the fleet. One story, so far uncorroborated, claims that an unspecified sum was transported northward to Belgium in a cart covered by hay. The historians Stephen Dafoe and Alan Butler claim that much of the Templar treasure was secretly transported eastward to Switzerland, where the Templars owned considerable property. They suggest that the Templar knights then went underground and used their financial assets and skills to found that country's banking system.[36] Did the rise of Swiss banking owe its origin to the Knights Templar? No one can as yet be certain, but it is a line of inquiry worth following.

These theories are not mutually exclusive, nor do they negate the third hypothesis, which at least has the merit of plausibility and, more important perhaps, is substantiated by considerable circumstantial evidence. To understand this third theory, however, we must first examine the fate of the surviving members of the newly suppressed order.

THE FATE OF THE SURVIVING KNIGHTS

After the suppression of the order, individual Templar knights fled throughout Europe. The fate of many of them is hardly mysterious and can easily be established—they joined other warrior orders. Some joined the Teutonic Knights, who were carving out their own fief on the shores of the Baltic; many more joined the Order of Calatrava in the kingdom of Aragon; others, equally interested in fighting the infidels, joined either the Knights of Alcantara or the Knights of Santiago and continued their service in Spain.

The Knights of Santiago, also known as the Knights of the Sword, actually became affiliated with the Knights Hospitaller to ensure their survival, proving that they had learned a lesson from the persecution of the Templars. They, too, became immensely powerful and, by the end of the 15th century, controlled over 200 commanderies throughout Spain.[37] In Portugal, the order changed its name to the Knights of Christ and continued to administer the old Templar properties. It also switched its previous allegiance and obedience from the pope to the Portuguese king and carried on much as before. Many fleeing knights joined this renamed order, but soon, the rule of the Order of the Knights of Christ was changed to accept only those born in Portugal.

In England, many knights were granted a small pension and others simply ended their days in other monastic orders. Some fled for sanctuary to Lombardy, where many Cathars had sought refuge before them. Lombardy was renowned, not only for its tolerance, but as a center of banking that certainly enjoyed a measure of resurgence after the suppression of the Templars. However, it would be wise not to place too much emphasis on Templar exiles as the source of this renewed activity, for, with the suppression of the Templar order, the Lombard's main competitor in financial services was destroyed. Many more Templars simply seemed to vanish.[38]

TEMPLARS IN SCOTLAND

There was one safe haven in Europe where the pope's writ simply did not run—Scotland. The kingdom of the Scots was riven by civil war precipitated by a bitter conflict for the crown. The main contender, Robert the Bruce, was excommunicated for the ritual murder of one of his rivals, John Comyn, on Church premises. The papal decree against Robert the Bruce was ignored by his nobles, and they too were excommunicated. That, too, was ignored and the pope, in an act of total desperation, excommunicated the entire country.

Many Templars fled by sea to this Celtic refuge and, along with those who came on foot over the border from England and the Templars who were stationed in Scotland, offered their assistance to Robert the Bruce. At the battle that finally secured the throne for the Bruce and completely vanquished the English invader, the Battle of Bannockburn, 432 Templar knights, including Sir Henry St. Clair, Baron of Roslin, and his sons, William and Henry, took part in the final charge that routed the English army and preserved Scottish independence.[39] Rex Deus tradition recounts that, after Bannockburn, as an act of gratitude and recognition, King Robert the Bruce became the Sovereign Grand Master of the Templar Order.[40]

The king was, above all, a pragmatist; he knew that, in order for his new realm to survive, he would have to live in the medieval world as it really was, and that meant making peace with the pope in Rome. Accordingly, he warned the Templars in Scotland to go underground—a feat that, with the assistance of the many Rex Deus and Templar families, was accomplished in a manner that ensured the long-term survival of Templar traditions. Templar property in Scotland passed to the Knights Hospitaller. The manner in which those holdings were administered in Bruce's realm was, however, very different from their administration in the rest of Europe. In most countries, Templar holdings were absorbed into the itineraries of the Hospitallers. In Scotland, they were accounted for separately, as though they were being "held in trust" and might be restored to their rightful owners at some time in the future.

But what of the vanished treasure? Nothing can be proven, but French Masonic tradition recounts that it was destined for Scotland. The fortunes of the leading Scottish Templar family, the St. Clairs of Roslin, underwent a dramatic improvement from that time forward. The St. Clairs, who were already wealthy, suddenly became what, in modern parlance, we call "super-rich." A later St. Clair Baron of Roslin who became the third Earl of Orkney, William St. Clair, was renowned for his incredible wealth.[41] Earl William was the architect and builder of Rosslyn Chapel, a unique library in stone of arcane symbolism, a superbly carved reliquary of the Holy Grail, a memorial of Templar beliefs, and the core church of Freemasonry. He was also known as "one of the Illuminati" and was initiated into some of the leading chivalric orders in Europe.

CHAPTER 15

SURVIVAL AND RESURGENCE

The elimination of Jewish power in Septimania, the destruction of the Cathar Church, the earlier disintegration of the Norman kingdom of Sicily, the reconquest of the Holy Land by the Saracens, and finally, the brutal suppression of the Knights Templar should have ensured the total elimination of Rex Deus influence and the end of their particular heresy. Was the influence of those who knew the truth—the subversive and secretive families who had been enemies of the Church from the very beginning—now destroyed? Had the families who carried their traditions forward as a vibrant and effective spiritual path that survived the Exodus, the Babylonian Exile, the destruction of Jerusalem by the Romans, and all the vicissitudes and persecutions by the Christian Church finally been silenced? Or did they have means to survive and spread their message? And what does the historical record hold as evidence of either their inaction or their success?

The total number of Templars arrested in France on Friday, 13 October 1307 was only 620, and not all of these were knights. Yet, according to most historians, the number of Templar personnel in the country leading up to that date probably numbered over 3,000. If only one in five was arrested, what befell the others? One survivor, who was eventually detained in Paris in November of 1309,[1] admitted that he fled from his base more than fifteen days before the initial wave of arrests. Moreover, the proportion of Templars apprehended in other countries was even lower than in France. It is reasonable to assume, therefore, that some prior warning of the French king's intention must have leaked out.

The fate of many one-time Templar knights can be found in the archives containing the records of the pensions paid to them in various countries. Some became involved in scandal or crime, and their actions, too, are a matter of record. Most, as mentioned earlier, joined other orders—among them, many from the Rex Deus families and the inner circles of the Templar hierarchy. Thus the descendants of the twenty-four ma'madot were able to turn adversity to advantage and spread their influence into military orders in which, because of their talent and bravery, they gained positions of power and influence far greater than their numbers may suggest.

The heretical families' experience in founding the Knights Templar had demonstrated both the benefits and the risks of having a military arm within their movement. Rex Deus learned from its earlier mistakes and, like a many-headed hydra, regrouped and redeployed by infiltrating other military and chivalric organizations. They had also learned the advantages that could accrue to their cause from having a well-disciplined executive arm positioned close to the seat of political power. However, this time they took great care to ensure that their new creations and affiliations differed from those of the Templars of old. Any newly founded orders would own no property or derive any income from their own resources. Outwardly, these new orders lacked autonomy and were ostensibly attached to one king or another who was responsible for financing their activities. They gave the illusion of being more interested in prestige than real power, and became vehicles of royal patronage staffed by courtiers rather than military officers. They used the Templar tradition as a model, however, in the creation of their rites and rituals, and in the mystique they wished to project.[2]

It is not surprising that the leading order among these new creations was the brainchild of certain familiar Scottish families with a long history of Templar involvement. What is surprising, however, is that this new order was deliberately created to serve the royal house responsible for the arrest of their noble predecessors.

REX DEUS IN SCOTLAND

The tightly knit group of families in Scotland who were linked by Cohenite ties of intermarriage acted as a vibrant repository of Rex Deus tradition and teaching. They also acted as a conduit for its transmission in a variety of highly effective forms that, in one way or another, still exert considerable influence in the modern world. Some years after the fall of the Templars, this group gave birth to a new military organization that Michael Baigent and Richard Leigh describe as, "Perhaps the most genuinely neo-Templar institution of them all."[3] This new order fit neatly into the context of a recently initiated Franco-Scottish military sphere of cooperation, known today as "the auld alliance," created by a treaty between Robert the Bruce and Charles IV of France in 1326.

The auld alliance played a vital role in the Hundred Years War and for many centuries afterward, and is still remembered with affection in the 21st century. Scottish troops played a significant role at the siege of Orleans during the campaigns led by Joan of Arc, in which three Scottish commanders—the two Douglas brothers and Sir John Stewart—distinguished themselves. Scotland's ties with France were strong during that era, for John Kirkmichael became bishop of Orleans. Indeed, the celebrated white banner that was the rallying point for the French army was reputedly painted by a Scot.[4]

Although French forces were victorious in this campaign, in the immediate aftermath, the country was in a state of turmoil, the countryside ravaged by bands of demobilized and impoverished soldiers. The new king, Charles VII, created a standing army to restore order and maintain his hold on the kingdom. This was the first standing army in Europe since the suppression of the Knights Templar and the first national one since the fall of the Roman Empire.[5] Fifteen *compagnies d'ordonnance* of 600 men each comprised this new force; of these, the elite regiment was the *compagnie des gendarmes Ecossais*. This signal honor was awarded to the Scottish regiment in recognition of over 100 years of distinguished service rendered by them to the French crown. The outstanding bravery of this unit and its unequivocal commitment to the French king was demonstrated at the Battle of Vermeuil in 1424, where the Scots company, led by John Stewart, the Earl of Buchan, and his senior officers, Alexander Lindsay, Sir

William Seton, and the Earls of Douglas, Murray and Mar, was almost annihilated.[6]

THE SCOTS GUARD

In recognition of this supreme act of gallantry, a special unit of Scots troops was established and given the honor of rendering personal service to the king of France. The company of thirteen knights was assisted by twenty archers and divided into two sections—the *garde du roi*, or the king's guard, and the *garde du corps du roi*, the king's bodyguard.[7] The king's bodyguard were in constant attendance, with some even sleeping in the his bedchamber. In 1445, the number of Scots Guards was increased to 67 men and their commander in the king's guard, and 25 men and their commander in the bodyguard. All officers were honored with initiation into the Order of St. Michael; a branch of this prestigious order was later established in Scotland.[8]

Unlike purely chivalric and honorary orders like the Knights of the Garter, the Order of the Bath in England, or the Order of the Golden Fleece in Burgundy, the Scots Guard was an active military order that underwent military training and was often given the opportunity to test themselves in battle, thus gaining all the rights and privileges of elite professional soldiers. Despite their small numbers, the Scots Guard was powerful enough to play a decisive role in the wars of that era. They professed no particular religious belief and their allegiance was to the king of France, not to the pope. Drawn from the leading families of Scotland—the Setons, St. Clairs, Stewarts, Montgomerys (who still take a particular pride today in their family's long association with the Scots Guard), and Hamiltons, all names familiar to the study of Rex Deus—the Guard became "a special vehicle whereby they [the young Scots Nobles] were initiated into martial skills, politics, court affairs, foreign manners and mores and, it would appear, some species of ritualistic rite as well."[9] The Scots Guard enjoyed immense status in France for over 150 years, and their officers were used as emissaries and couriers in matters of importance and delicacy in both the political and diplomatic fields. The commander of the Guard often also discharged the function of royal chamberlain.

The Scots Guard owed their allegiance to the ruling house of France, the Valois dynasty, whose right to rule was under almost constant threat from the House of Guise, a cadet branch of the House of Lorraine. This was not mere political or dynastic rivalry; it was a truly murderous quarrel. No less than five French kings are alleged to have died either by violence or poison, and many members of both the Guise and Lorraine families were assassinated. The Scots Guard was now in an almost impossible and ambivalent position, for the family of Guise were Rex Deus. Moreover, in 1538, Mary of Guise married King James V of Scotland, thereby uniting two of the leading families within the secretive group. Because of this marital bond, and despite being granted a considerable increase in salary by Henry II of France in 1547, the Guard often acted on behalf of the rival House of Guise.

Matters came to a head in June 1559, when a captain of the Guard, Gabriel Montgomery, caused the death of King Henry II during a jousting tournament by striking the king's head with a broken lance. A splinter from the lance pierced the king's skull above the right eye and he died from his wounds eleven days later. It has been alleged that this was no accident, but part of a plot to benefit the family of Guise.[10] From that time on, the fortunes of the Scots Guard declined appreciably. Despite the troubling events that led to their eclipse, however, the Guard were a major conduit for Rex Deus traditions for three centuries and became the vehicle whereby their secret teachings were refreshed, renewed, and reimplanted in French society. They also acted as a conduit through which Rex Deus ideas and traditions flowed from the French families to their Scot counterparts, with insights derived from the families of Lorraine, Guise, Savoy, and the House of Burgundy.

OTHER CHIVALRIC ORDERS

The Knights of Santiago, who provided a haven for fleeing Templars in Spain, carried Templar traditions and practices throughout the Spanish-speaking world for centuries. Over time, with the reconquest of Spain by the forces of Christendom, the order developed a "chivalric" nature and welcomed into its ranks leading members of Rex Deus families from all over Europe, including William St. Clair, Earl of Orkney and Baron of Roslin.[11] Owing allegiance, as they did, to the kings of Spain and having established their orthodox credentials by playing a crucial role in the *Reconquista*—the expulsion of the Moors from Spain—the Knights of Santiago became an ideal vehicle for Rex Deus purposes. The order's mixed membership (only a select but influential few were members of the secretive family group) proved a perfect disguise for the actions of the Rex Deus members attempting to reestablish themselves without risking exposure. Thus the Rex Desu families were able to use the order for their own purposes, secure behind the respectable façade of a group whose members were drawn from a wide variety of families committed to the church/state establishment.

Similar orders were also infiltrated by Templar knights: the Knights of Alcantara and the Knights of Calatrava, for example. Bernard of Clairvaux played some mysterious role in the foundation of both these orders of Spanish knighthood,[12] and it is reasonable to speculate that, from the very first, they were designed to provide some sort of fall-back position in the event the Templars were destroyed—a reasonable precaution to take to provide alternative means of transmission for the Rex Deus message. We have also wondered if a similar approach had been taken in respect to the Scottish members of the Knights Hospitaller, for their actions after the suppression of the Templars, in accounting for Templar lands as though they were separate resources held in trust, may indicate that Rex Deus influence was a major factor in this order in Scotland as well for many centuries.

In 1430, Philip the Good, Duke of Burgundy,[13] founded the Order of the Golden Fleece, whose membership was restricted to twenty-four knights carefully chosen from the best families in Europe who were all senior members of Rex Deus. They were described by Pope Eugenius IV as "Maccabeans resurrected"[14]—a telling phrase that contained more truth than the pope could ever know! This chivalric order was of such standing that expulsion from it, or any deviation from its high sense of purpose, cast dishonor on the name of the family concerned for all time. A black shield carved above the seat of the Count of Nevers in a church in Bruges is a lasting testament to the shame he incurred by his exclusion from the order.[15]

The number twenty-four has deep symbolic significance to the families of Rex Deus, for it is the number of hereditary families of the ma'madot, the hereditary high priests of the temple in Jerusalem. It is also the number of knights permitted in another chivalric order founded by the king of Hungary in 1408. The founding members were pledged to practice "true and pure fraternity," and were granted the right to wear armorial bearings emblazoned with a dragon encurved upon a circle and decorated with a red cross. When the founder, King Sigismund, became Holy Roman Emperor, the order became known as the Imperial and Royal Court of the Dragon.[16] Its membership was drawn from both the nobility and the royal houses of Europe, and included the Duke of Lithuania, the King of Poland, and the King of Aragon. Over the next two centuries, autonomous branches of the order were founded in Bulgaria, Bosnia, Arcadia, Italy, and France.

RENÉ D'ANJOU

Another restricted order was the Order of the Croissant, founded at Angers in 1448 by a leading Rex Deus member, René d'Anjou. Only knights of noble birth and absolutely unblemished character were eligible for membership. The rule of the order required that its members live in harmony and by the principles of fraternal love founded upon the precepts of religion, courtesy, and charity. No impious oath or indecent jest was to pass their lips, and their integrity must be of such a high standard that women and children could be committed to their care without reservation. They were particularly enjoined to use their best offices in aiding the poor.

René d'Anjou, who fought bravely for France under the leadership of Joan of Arc, was the titular King of Jerusalem, King of the Two Sicilies, Aragon, Valencia, Majorca, Sardinia, and Corsica. He was also Count of Provence, Forcalquier, and Piedmont, Prince of Gerona, Duke of Calabria, Lord of Genoa, and the Count of Guise.[17] Many strands of Rex Deus ancestry were united in this one man. His mother was Yolande of Aragon and his wife was Isobel of Lorraine, the daughter of Charles II of Lorraine and Margaret, daughter of Emperor Robert III of Bavaria. Yolande was the eldest daughter of Duke Robert I of Bar and Princess Marie of France. René's marriage was arranged by his granduncle, Cardinal Louis de Bar.

René d'Anjou was not merely highborn, but a most accomplished man in his own right. He was a scholar of international repute and a regular correspondent with Earl William St. Clair. Like Earl William, he collected original manuscripts in Hebrew, Greek, Arabic, Turkish, and Latin. He was famous for organizing jousts and festivals, usually centered on themes drawn from the Grail romances. His Order of the Croissant merged many years later with another order of Rex Deus creation to form the Order of the Fleur de Lys, which adopted a four-barred cross as its symbol—each bar was of equal length to distinguish it from the cross of Golgotha, and each was topped with the emblem of the fleur de lys. This emblem, *La Croix Fleury*, is still worn with pride by members of the Order in the 21st century. Membership is strictly by invitation or by right of birth into certain families, and only families from the Rex Deus tradition are allowed to hold office.

According to our first Rex Deus informant, Michael, the Order of the Bath in England may well have been another "cover" for Rex Deus activities at the time of its original foundation. Therefore, a comparative study of the membership lists of these various orders could give great insight into the members of this proud and secretive tradition, which has reached out over the millennia, from ancient Egypt to the present. Membership of the families within these various orders also tends to explain certain differences in ritual that exist between the various Rex Deus traditions. We were quite surprised to discover, when we introduced our first informant to another self-declared Rex Deus member who holds high rank within the Order of the Fleur de Lys, that while they were each able to fill in gaps in the knowledge and understanding of the other, certain distinct differences in their traditional rituals did exist. Developing and constantly evolving traditions within the differing chivalric orders used by the families readily explains this. The use of so many orders also gives us an insight into the wisdom of these families, who, after the suppression of the Knights Templar, were not about to risk the failure of their divinely inspired mission by putting all their eggs in one basket. That had nearly led to ruin in the past and they were not about to let it happen again.

This raises a question, however, that we cannot answer: For safety reasons, had the Rex Deus families now split into two or more completely separate groups that began to operate without knowledge of each other? The promulgation of the Grail sagas had begun to spread the benefits of initiatory spirituality far beyond the ever-widening ranks of the Rex Deus group. Now was the time to build on this quiet but sustained success story and spread the net far wider to include as many curious seekers-after-truth as possible.

CHAPTER 16

RE-AUTHENTICATION
OF A FAMOUS "FAKE"

When ex-King Umberto of Italy died in 1983, an internationally renowned holy relic that had been in the possession of his family for centuries was bequeathed to the Catholic Church—the Shroud of Turin. This relic, which had generated considerable controversy from the time of its first public exhibition in the early 14th century until the Vatican inherited it, was now to be subjected to radiocarbon dating in an attempt to establish its true age and provenance in hopes of ending the controversy. Three highly reputable laboratories were involved in the actual testing: the University of Arizona in Tucson, the Swiss Federal Institute of Technology in Zurich, and the Oxford Research Laboratory. The whole process was conducted under the eagle eye of Dr. Tite of the British Museum Research Laboratory, who had accepted overall responsibility for its supervision.

Samples from the shroud were taken in private, with only Church hierarchy and members of staff drawn from each of the laboratories present. The entire process was recorded on videotape. A seven-centimeter sample was cut from one corner and, under observation, divided into three parts. One piece of the sample was sealed in an appropriate container for each of the testing laboratories.

The bombshell of the results exploded on the world stage with an announcement by Cardinal Ballestrero in Turin on 13 October 1988. His announcement was confirmed later the same day by Dr. Tite in England. Ballestro stated that it was now 99.9 percent certain that the Shroud of Turin was manufactured somewhere between 1000 and 1500 C.E. and, furthermore, that it was 95 percent certain that it dated from between 1260 and 1390.[1] The Christian world was in a state of shock and outrage, for this widely venerated relic, supposedly the burial cloth of Jesus, had apparently been scientifically proven to be of medieval manufacture. The Shroud of Turin was a fake! Catholics were outraged; Protestants were puzzled. Holy Mother the Church quickly distanced itself in an ambivalent way when Professor Luigi Gonella, the Vatican's scientific advisor, stated: "The tests were not commissioned by the Church and we are not bound by the results."

Conspiracy theorists, journalists, and fantasists had a field day; articles on the reputed provenance of the shroud were sunk beneath a flood of verbiage claiming that the tests had been tainted by conspiracy. The right-wing luminary of *La Contre Réforme Catholique au XXme Siècle*, Brother Bruno Bonnet-Eymard, accused Dr. Michael Tite of switching the samples with those taken earlier from a 13th-century cope, alleging that Dr. Tite was rewarded for his duplicity by the granting of a professorship. This spokesman for divinely revealed truth not only slandered Dr. Tite, but also claimed that the results were "fixed as part of a deliberate plot by the scientific community to undermine Christianity."[2] Professor Werner Bulst stated that a Masonic anti-Catholic plot was responsible, making his accusation on television.[3]

Two German authors wrote a best-selling book that took a very different approach, however. Holger Kirsten and Elmar Gruber alleged that the carbon-dating results were rigged by the scientists acting in collusion with the Church, and went on to suggest that the video cameras were switched off during the sampling procedure. In this manner, the authors claimed, the samples were, in fact, switched, as alleged by the right-wing cleric Bonnet-Eymard. They further suggested that there were considerable discrepancies between the description of the samples taken from the shroud and those received by the testing laboratories. The motive they ascribe to this bizarre conspiracy theory is rather interesting; they assert that the Church had a strong vested interest in discrediting the shroud, as the forensic evidence from it proves beyond all doubt that Jesus was alive when taken down from the cross. In other words, the Church's central belief, that Jesus' redemptive death on the cross saved us from sin, was, apparently, disproved by one of Christianity's most holy relics—if, that is, it had been authenticated by the tests.[4]

THE THEORIES PROLIFERATE

The English authors Lyn Picknett and Clive Prince came up with another theory—one that, in some respects at least, has a degree of plausibility. They pointed the finger of suspicion at the one figure in the late medieval era who just might have had the ability to fake an artefact such as the Shroud of Turin, namely the Renaissance giant Leonardo da Vinci. However, for reasons that will become apparent, we have reason to believe that they were, nonetheless, very wide of the mark.

Two other noted English writers in the field of speculative history, Robert Lomas and Chris Knight, also joined the mad scramble to "use" the carbon dating to promote their own theories on the origin of the shroud. They claimed that it was the cloth used to wrap the body of Jacques de Molay after he was crucified by the Inquisition—a claim we dismissed earlier. They also stated categorically that the cloth of the shroud, a three-to-one twill linen weave, was extremely common in 14th-century Europe. This unsupported statement is a complete fabrication, for Dr. Tite, with all the resources of the British Museum and other leading European museums at his disposal, could not find a single piece of three-to-one twill weave from that era to use as a control for the radiocarbon dating tests.

So what is the present situation regarding the provenance of the shroud? And what message does it contain—genuine or fake—that so worries the Church? To answer these questions, we must examine the circumstances of the relic's first documented exhibition, as well as its subsequent history both prior to and after the tests.

EARLY EVIDENCE OF THE SHROUD

In 1203, Robert de Clari, a French crusader, described an object he had seen exhibited in the church of My Lady Saint Mary of Blachernae at Constantinople:

... where was kept the sidoine in which Our Lord had been
wrapped, which stood up straight every Friday so that the *figure*
of Our Lord could plainly be seen there ... no one, either
Greek or French ever knew what became of this sidoine after
the city was taken.[5]

The translation of the key word, figure, caused some confusion,
as it could mean face, using the modern French translation into
English, or a full-length drawing. Some historians claim that, folded
and framed, the shroud may have been the object exhibited as the
Mandylion, the "face on the cloth," which one legend recounts was
sent by Jesus to King Abgar of Edessa. Another claims the figure was
imprinted on the veil of Veronica as Jesus walked to Calvary.

Two other traditions link the Mandylion and the Shroud of
Turin. The first is the persistent legend that neither image was "made
by the hand of man"; the other is that the known and provable history of the Mandylion matches, with only one short gap, the earlier
missing history of the shroud.[6] The question posed by Ian Wilson
was: "Are they one and the same?"

Templar links to the shroud can be traced as a result of its first
provable public exhibition at a small church in Lirey in France in
the mid-14th century. Henry, Bishop of Troyes, wrote of it:

Many theologians and otherwise persons [have stated] that this
could not be the real Shroud of Our Lord having the Saviour's
likeness thus imprinted upon it, since the holy Gospels made
no mention of such imprint, while, if it had been true, it was
quite unlikely that the holy Evangelists would have omitted to
record it, or that the fact should have remained hidden until the
present time.[7]

So right from the beginning, the provenance of the shroud was
the center of a dispute. There were, of course, many possible reasons
for this. Reasoned scepticism in an age renowned for the manufacture of holy relics is one. Another is the fact that the relic was first
exhibited in the diocese of Troyes, an area of one-time Templar influence. Yet another arises from the Templar connections with its owners,
the de Charney family. Geoffrey de Charney, who died in 1356, was
the nephew of Geoffroi de Charney,[8] who was martyred with Jacques

de Molay on the Isle des Javiaux in 1314. The family were also intimately connected with the families of Brienne, De Joinville, D'Anjou, and the House of Burgundy. The English genealogist Noel Currer-Briggs has traced many of these families' involvement in the sack of Constantinople,[9] which may link the shroud with the relic described by Robert de Clari cited above. We have suggested in an earlier work that this group of Rex Deus families preserved the shroud because of the heretical message it contained, and that they knew, in one way or another, it would play its part in disclosing that Jesus came to reveal and not to redeem, as claimed by the Church.[10]

Papal Authentication of the Shroud

At age seventy-two, Marguerite de Charney was childless and the last of the de Charney line. In 1453, she was gifted the Castle of Varanbon and the income from estates at Miribel by Duke Louis of Savoy, the ruler of a large part of Lombardy and another Rex Deus member. These generous donations were in return for certain valuable services to the House of Savoy that included the gift of the shroud. Both of Marguerite's husbands, Geoffrey II and Humbert de Villersexel, had been created knights of the Order of the Collar of Savoy by earlier dukes.[11]

In the 15th century, the Church began to refer to this relic as the burial shroud of Jesus. Francesco della Rovere, a theologian, wrote in 1464: "This is now preserved with great devotion by the dukes of Savoy, and is coloured with the blood of Christ."[12] Five years later, Francesco della Rovere became Pope Sixtus IV. In his treatise, *On the Blood of Christ*, the shroud was not merely given papal recognition and approval, but was also awarded its own feast day on 7 May.[13] The shroud was damaged by fire at least twice during the 16th century and, after the fire of 1532, was repaired by the addition of fourteen large and eight small triangular patches, all made from an altar cloth. It was also backed with a simple piece of Holland cloth.[14]

In 1578, the Duke of Savoy had the shroud brought to Turin, the city that has been its home ever since. A later duke commissioned the architect Guarino Guarini to design a magnificent Baroque cathedral dedicated to St. John the Baptist in which to house the shroud. The relic took up its new abode on 1 June 1694, when it was carried into the building and locked behind a cast-iron grille situated in the place of honor above the high altar. From that time onward, the shroud was only exhibited to the public on carefully selected occasions such as papal visits, special feast days, or important weddings of local nobility.

Forensic Examination of the Relic

The relic measures fourteen feet three inches (4.36 meters) long by three feet seven inches (1.1 meters) wide. It is composed of a single piece of material, with the addition of a full-length strip 3.5 inches (8.5 centimeters) wide joined to the main body of the cloth by a seam on the left-hand side. The monochrome image on the cloth is almost pure sepia in color and very subtle; under normal viewing conditions, it is very difficult to discern. Yet there is sufficient detail in the faded bloodlike image to have convinced generations of the devout that it is, indeed, the burial shroud of Jesus.

A local amateur photographer, Secondo Pia, photographed the shroud in 1898. As the image of the figure developed on the photographic plates, Secondo felt a considerable degree of relief that soon changed to amazement. He expected to see a poor negative image of the same indistinct figure he had seen when he took his photographs; instead he saw developing before his eyes a highly detailed photographic likeness with such a contrast between the light and shade that it appeared almost three-dimensional. Bloodflows from the head, hands, and feet showed up with a nearly magic realism.[15] The figure that appeared on the plate was of a tall, well-developed man with a startlingly lifelike bearded face.

The publication of the photographs caused a worldwide sensation and stimulated the in-depth investigations that continued until their apparent culmination in the radiocarbon dating tests. The shroud was not photographed again until 1931, this time by a professional photographer whose results were even more remarkable. Since then, as far as we are aware, it has only been photographed twice—in 1969 and 1973.

Forensic tests on the shroud were made after its public exposition in November 1973. Professor Gilbert Raes of the Ghent Institute of Textile Technology examined several threads taken from the cloth and the cloth itself. The cloth was woven in a three-to-one herring-bone twill pattern that was common at the time of Jesus, but more usually found in silk than linen. Examination under polarized light convinced Raes that the material was, in fact, linen. Further microscopic examination of the strands, however, showed that there were traces of cotton of a variety known as *gossypium hebaceum*, a plant native to the eastern Mediterranean region. Raes concluded that the fabric had been woven in the Middle East on a loom that had previously been used to manufacture cotton cloth.[16]

Dr. Max Frei, a leading Swiss criminologist, took samples of particles adhering to the shroud and identified among them particles of mineral, fragments of human hair, fibers of plant origin, bacterial spores, spores from varieties of moss and fungi, and pollen grains from several types of plants. Among the pollen samples were examples from desert varieties of *tamarix*, *suaeda*, and *artemesia* that only grow around the shores of the Dead Sea.[17] Frei's comments included the following observation:

> These plants are of great diagnostic value for our geographical studies as identical plants are missing from all the other countries where the Shroud is believed to have been exposed in the open air. Consequently, a forgery, produced somewhere in France during the Middle Ages, in a country lacking these typical halophytes could not contain such characteristic pollen grains from the deserts of Palestine.[18]

In all, there were six different varieties of pollen from plants native to Palestine found on the surface of the shroud. In addition, there were pollens consistent with its alleged exposure in Turkey, France, and Italy.

Samples of dust taken from near the imprint of the feet were analyzed and found to be limestone. Dr. Ricardo Levi-Setti, of the Enrico Fermi Institute at the University of Chicago, conducted comparative tests with samples taken from limestone tombs in the Jerusalem area. These tests showed an almost identical match. The limestone particles were quite specific—primarily travertine aragonite and not the more common calcite.[19] Travertine aragonite is a relatively rare form of limestone that is common in tombs in the vicinity of Jerusalem.

From the time of the publication of Secondo Pia's first photographs until the announcement of the carbon-dating results, scientific and forensic interest in the shroud continued unabated. Each technological advance relevant to the investigation was applied to the shroud and to the analysis of the figure depicted on it almost as soon as the techniques were developed. The results of these prolonged inquiries were of such magnitude that even the arch-skeptic, Bishop John Robinson of "Honest to God" fame, was moved to remark that the burden of proof had shifted and it was now up to those who doubted the relic's authenticity to prove their case rather than the reverse.[20] To his intense surprise, and to the grave disappointment of millions of believers from every nook and corner of Christendom, it would appear that was exactly what happened with the announcement of the carbon-dating results.

True or False?

In theory, the carbon-dating results, which invalidated the shroud as a true relic, should have put an end to the controversy over the shroud, with the possible exception of the conspiracy theories we have already mentioned. Now it was perfectly reasonable to dismiss the relic as a fake and face up to some fascinating, if unanswerable, questions. Who could have made it? And, perhaps more important, how had they made it? Before either of these questions could be answered, however, an internationally famous American microbiologist made a discovery that irrevocably invalidates the 1988 radiocarbon dating results. His discovery not only reopened the question of the relic's provenance, but may also provide proof that it is an artefact of the 1st century.

Carbon-dating techniques are not as infallible as the general public believes. Porous substances like mortar, for instance, are most unsuitable for testing, as they continue to exchange carbon dioxide with the atmosphere, which skews the results to the extent that they are completely unreliable.[21] Tests of all materials are subject to massive distortion by extremely small amounts of contamination, which is why samples used for dating the shroud were cleansed by the most reliable techniques then known. Yet, despite all the precautions taken, the tests on the shroud were rendered highly inaccurate by a form of contamination that was unknown at the time and that arose from the very nature of the cloth being tested.[22]

The English author Ian Wilson described the relic as having "a damask-like sheen."[23] This shiny appearance has recently been discovered to result from a growth of microbiological organisms that completely envelop each constituent thread of the cloth. The extent of this contamination, which proved to be completely resistant to the cleansing methods used by the laboratories concerned, is such that what was, in fact, being tested was slightly less than 40 percent shroud material and more than 60 percent living organism.[24] Furthermore, tests have shown that the cleansing agents used were not only ineffective in removing the microbiological organisms, but also tended to dissolve part of the cellulose from the strands of the material itself, thus heightening the inaccuracy of the test results already created by the microbiological coating.[25] As a result of such a gross distortion of the test results, the whole question of the age and authenticity of this controversial relic is still wide open.

THE BIOPLASTIC COATING

The presence of a microbiological coating formed of living organisms has been demonstrated on jade carvings, Mayan stone carvings, and ancient Egyptian linen mummy wrappings. An American microbiologist, Dr. Leoncio A. Garza-Valdes, who was Professor of Microbiology at the Health Sciences Center of the University of Texas, first described this type of contamination. A keen collector of Mayan carvings, he noticed that many of them had a peculiar lustrous sheen caused by a layer formed partly of bacteria and partly of fungi. He called this bacterial and fungal layer "bioplastic coating."[26] He found similar coatings on cotton threads joining jade plates that formed pectorals. Examination by electron microscope and by an industrial analysis laboratory in San Antonio confirmed that these coatings were organic and not man-made.

Garza-Valdes then examined the wrappings on two very different Egyptian mummies. The first was that of a thirteen-year-old girl discovered by Sir Flinders Petrie that now rests in the Egyptology section of Manchester Museum in England. Both the mummy and its wrappings were carbon dated by Manchester University with somewhat disturbing results. The girl's bones were dated to 1510 B.C.E., but her wrappings to only 225 C.E., a discrepancy of over 1,700 years.[27] Similar tests performed by Garza-Valdes on a mummified ibis in his own collection revealed a discrepancy between the mummy and the wrappings of between 400 and 700 years. In January 1996, Garza-Valdes found that the flax fibers of the cloth on the Manchester mummy all carried a thick bioplastic coating similar to those he had found on other old textiles. Intrigued by these findings and anxious to see if they might apply in a similar manner to the Shroud of Turin, he traveled to Italy.

As a devout Catholic, Dr. Garza-Valdes naively believed that his news would be welcomed by the Church authorities and result in permission to examine the Shroud of Turin. To his surprise, his news was about as welcome as a cobra at a cocktail party, and the hierarchy took no action whatever to order a retest. However, Garza-Valdes had a personal introduction to Professor Giovanni Riggi Numana, who had cut the original samples for the carbon-dating tests in 1988. The professor showed him a small, unopened packet that contained tiny fragments of the original shroud samples, authenticated by the unbroken seal of Cardinal Balestrero. Professor Riggi also showed him pieces of Scotch tape that had been used to remove blood samples from the back of the head of the image on the shroud. Opening the sealed packet, Professor Riggi removed one thread from the original sample, which Dr. Garza-Valdes then placed under the microscope. The American microbiologist was immediately able to discern that a bioplastic coating completely covered the fibers of the thread.[28] This coating was later cultured and found to be composed of living organisms that were still absorbing carbon from the atmosphere. Consequently, Dr. Garza-Valdes formed the reasonable opinion that, if the shroud were retested using the same cleansing techniques applied in 1988, the new results would indicate an even later date, because the bacteria would have multiplied considerably in the intervening years, increasing the proportion of living organism to thread.

The American did not restrict his examination to the threads alone; he also rigorously examined the pieces of Scotch tape and the so-called "blood" samples adhering to them. Bloodlike samples from the shroud had been examined over the years by a variety of scientists and had produced conflicting results. Prior to the radiocarbon dating, an Italian scientist, Dr. Bauma-Bollone, had claimed that these stains were human blood, type AB.[29] Drs. Adler and Heller, examining similar tapes, agreed with their Italian colleague's findings.[30]

Dr. Garza-Valdes' examination of the samples given to him by Professor Riggi again proved the presence of type AB human blood—the most common blood group found in the Jewish community. He was also able to state that, due to the amount of degeneration he found in the sample, the bloodstains were of ancient origin.[31] He methodically examined everything he found on the piece of tape provided by Professor Riggi and, in the sample taken from the occipital area, he found several microscopic tubules of wood that proved to be oak.[32] These, if the shroud does prove to be authentic, could only have come from the cross on which Jesus was crucified.

Dr. Garza-Valdes published the results of his tests on the shroud material in an article that placed them in the context of his earlier discoveries of bioplastic coatings on other artefacts. The cover of the journal carried an image of the face of Jesus taken from the shroud, captioned: "Secrets of the Shroud—Microbiologists Discover How the Shroud Hides Its True Age." The article concluded that the shroud is many centuries older than the radiocarbon dating suggested. The reaction from the scientific community was largely supportive of this provocative thesis. Dr. Harry Gove of Rochester University, the principal developer of the method used to carbon-date the shroud, said: "This is not a crazy idea." As the carbon dating has now been discredited until such time, if ever, that the papacy allows a retest using appropriate cleansing techniques, any reasonable assessment of the shroud's true provenance must be based upon the results of the many earlier scientific examinations.

EARLIER FORENSIC EVIDENCE

In 1902, in Paris, Professor Yves Delage claimed that the wounds and anatomical data recorded in the image on the Shroud of Turin were so accurate that it was impossible that they could be the work of an artist. Furthermore, he went on to comment on the near impossibility of any artist replicating the detail so accurately in the form of a negative image.[33] In the 1930s, the anatomist Dr. Pierre Barbet of St. Joseph's Hospital in Paris, conducted a series of experiments on human cadavers and amputated limbs that led him to the conclusion that the wounds depicted on the shroud were genuinely those of a crucified man.[34]

Dr. Barbet is of the opinion that the men who conducted the crucifixion were extremely experienced and knew their anatomy. Using a recently amputated arm, Barbet experimented with nailing at the wrists as depicted in the shroud. The nail passed through a gap in the wrist bones known as "the space of destot" in a manner that would have supported the weight of a crucified man.[35] Furthermore, in these experiments, the thumb on the affected hand contracted as a result of the nail passing through the median nerve. Consulting photographs of the shroud image, he found that no thumb was discernible on either hand. He then posed the question: "Could any forger have imagined this?" The answer is obviously, no!

Barbet used similar experimental techniques on the feet, emulating the nailing depicted on the shroud. The nail passed easily between the second and third metatarsals and he concluded that a single nail impaling both feet could have adequately supported the weight of a crucified body.[36] The radiologist Professor Hermann Moedder of Cologne[37] and Dr. Judica-Cordiglia, professor of Forensic Medicine at the University of Milan, confirmed these conclusions. Further study was made of the bloodstains by Dr. Anthony Sava of Brooklyn and Dr. Robert Bucklin, now of California.

Modern technological advances were used by British photographer Leo Vala to produce a life-size, three-dimensional model of the head of the figure shown on the shroud.[38] Ethnology Professor Coon of Harvard examined photographs of this model and described the face as being "of a physical type found in modern times among Sephardic Jews and noble Arabs."[39] Dr. David Willis stated that the wounds depicted on the head of the image were incapable of any valid description except in the context described in the Gospels.[40] The wound marks on both the back and front of the image that are seen in groups of three from the shoulder level downward have been classified by several doctors as physiologically accurate depictions of wounds caused by flogging. Bruising on the shoulders that is consistent with carrying a heavy crossbeam have also been described, and Professor Judica-Cordiglia has analyzed the wounds on the knees as being consistent with those arising from repeated falls.[41]

The blood-flow depicted on the shroud is fascinating for two reasons: First, it is completely consistent with what one would expect from a crucifixion, and, second, it is so profuse that it can only be explained by the fact that it continued for some time after the body was wrapped in the cloth. The blood flowing from the wound in the left wrist indicates that the arm must have been raised at an angle of between fifty-five and sixty-five degrees from the vertical for some considerable time.[42] There is also an obvious wound between the fifth and sixth ribs on the left side of the image that, allowing for mirror image reversal, would have been on the right side of the victim. The broken blood flow from this wound indicates that the "clear" areas are made by a mixture of clear liquid with the blood[43] and that the wound was inflicted when the victim was in a nearly erect position. According to the German radiologist, Professor Moedder, the clear fluid in the breaks originated from the pleural sac. Dr. Anthony Sava, who noted that there is often an accumulation of fluid in the pleural cavity following prolonged and sustained physical injury, confirmed this. Dr. Sava suggested that the scourging that caused the wounds on the upper body was the most likely cause of this pleurisy, exacerbated by the actual crucifixion.[44]

Jewish Burial Practice

Jewish burial custom and practice of that time would have demanded that Jesus' body be laid out full-length in the tomb, with his hands crossed over the pelvic area. This position is identical to those of other corpses examined by Father de Vaux of the Ecole Biblique during his excavation of the Essene graveyard at Qumran.[45] His discovery is ironic, in that Fr. de Vaux spent most of his time and energy at Qumran trying to deny any connection between Jesus and the Essenes. The details shown on the shroud also indicate that, in complete contradiction to established Jewish burial practice in the Holy Land during the 1st century, the body wrapped in the shroud had not been washed, but had been anointed with a large quantity of ointment before being wrapped in the cloth. This bears out the account found in the Gospel of John, where it is written:

> . . .so Joseph came and took the body away. He was joined by
> Nicodemus (the man who first visited Jesus by night) who

brought with him a mixture of myrrh and aloes, more than half
a hundredweight. They then took the body of Jesus and
wrapped it in the linen cloth according to Jewish burial customs. (John 19:38–41)

Not only was this procedure contrary to Jewish burial customs
in that the body was not washed, but custom decreed that women
handle corpses, not men. Had the men even touched a dead body,
they would not have had the time to go through the ritual purification procedures before the feast of Passover. Furthermore, myrrh
and aloe are expensive healing ointments; they would not have been
wasted on a mere corpse.

Summary of the Evidence

As the 1988 carbon dating of the shroud is now invalidated pend-
ing a retest, we have to evaluate the age and origin of this controversial relic by assessing the forensic and scientific evidence available.
According to Professor Delage in 1902, the shroud depicts wounds
and anatomical detail of a crucified man that would be impossible
for any forger to create. Dr. Barbet's studies of the nailing and the
anatomical consequences that would be created by this are such that
the image is definitely a crucified man. Moedder, Judica-Cordiglia,
and Bucklin have confirmed his views. Professor Coon's comments
on the probable ethnicity of the face on the shroud places its origin
firmly in the Middle East. The weave of the cloth again indicates
Middle Eastern origin, as do the pollen analysis and the examination
of the dust particles. We believe that, judged on the balance of prob-
abilities, the scientific evidence clearly demonstrates that this disputed artefact may indeed be the cloth used to envelop the body of
Jesus the Nazorean when he was taken down from the cross. So
what was its importance to the members of Rex Deus and the
Knights Templar?

The use of such massive quantities of expensive healing ointments ensured that Jesus gained the maximum chance of recovery
after the debilitating trauma he had suffered. Death by crucifixion
results from the massive secretion of pleural fluids that create sufficient pressure on the lungs to bring about asphyxiation. The spear

thrust into Jesus' side relieved that pressure by draining the fluid in the pleural sac, thereby saving his life—and not, as the Gospel account would have it, proving he was dead. Persistent stories that have circulated for over 2,000 years tell us that Jesus survived his ordeal at Golgotha. One early father of the church, Iraneus, the Bishop of Lyon, attests to this and mentions that Jesus lived to a great age and traveled to the East with St. John.[46]

Two places claim to house Jesus' tomb and both are in the East—one in Kashmir and the other in Japan. It is recorded in *The Lost Gospel According to St. Peter* that Jesus was seen leaving the tomb supported by two members of the Essenes. In one of the Stations of the Cross at the Church of the Magdalene in Rennes-le-Chateau in Languedoc, Jesus is shown leaving the tomb by moonlight. Baigent, Leigh, and Lincoln record that an Anglican priest informed them that Jesus was alive as late as 45 C.E.

Rex Deus teaching, the long-standing traditions of Jesus' survival from his ordeal on the cross, and the message preserved in the image on the Shroud of Turin all point to the fact that the central belief of the Christian Church—that Jesus died on the cross as a sacrifice for our sins—is untrue. St. Paul, the first "Christian" heretic, was the man responsible for deifying Jesus and promulgating the blasphemous doctrine: "He died for us." This man, who was described by the Ebionites as "the spouter of lies and the distorter of the true teachings of Jesus," became, albeit unknowingly, the founder of the most cruel and repressive society in history, the Christian Church. Now, after more than 2,000 years of burnings, torture, and repression, the truth is finally being made public—Jesus came to reveal and not to redeem.

CHAPTER 17

SPREADING THE LIGHT FROM LOMBARDY

The Cathars who fled from Languedoc sought sanctuary in two principal locations: Scotland and Lombardy. Some years later, many knights of the persecuted Templar order did the same, because they knew, as did the Cathars, that lands ruled by Rex Deus nobility offered some semblance of safety and toleration. In time, both sites developed into important centers for the propagation of Rex Deus beliefs—beliefs that, albeit in very different ways, still touch our lives in the 21st century.

Italy was far from a unified country at that time, composed of a large number of city-states in the north, the Papal States in the center, and the kingdoms of Naples and Sicily in the south. In west Lombardy, or Piedmont, the Rex Deus counts of Savoy had created a state that was only outshone in power and ambition by the Visconti domains to the east—a state that was soon to become the most powerful in Italy. The mild Azzo Visconti (1329–1339) began to enlarge the family domain and, with considerable skill and foresight, his successor and uncle, the Archbishop Giovanni (1339–1354), ruled a vast area that ranged from the Apennines to the Alps. He overran Bologna and even threatened the independence of the proud city-state of Florence. Only determined efforts by the pope and his allies served to check Giovanni's progress.[1]

The traditional rivalry between Venice and Milan was the principal factor in the struggle for power between the various city-states of northern Italy. Venice had already amassed enormous wealth by trading with the East and from its great overseas empire. Milan had achieved greatness from its rich agricultural hinterland by breeding incomparable horses and by the manufacture of silks and embroideries. Its superb geographic position gave it a frontier at the base of the great commercial routes across the Alps, and the city eventually developed an industry in arms and armaments that were sold to fighting men throughout the world, regardless of their race, creed or color. Any ruler blessed by resources and opportunities such as these was destined to become the richest man in Europe—which is what happened when a family originating from lowly knights in the service of the Carolingians, who later took part in the Crusades before becoming mercenary soldiers, took control of Milan and began to absorb adjoining states into their territory. The Viscontis of Milan became the richest family in Europe. Over time, they intermarried with the royal houses of Valois, Hapsburg, Tudor, Stuart, and Hanover,[2] as well as with the Bourbons, who later became the kings of France.[3]

The strength and success of the Visconti rulers in central Lombardy continued after the death of Archbishop Giovanni. Although his estates were divided among his three nephews (soon reduced to two), and they were repeatedly under attack by the papacy and its allies, they lost little save Genoa and Bologna. Gian Galeazzo Visconti reunited the Visconti lands and was the most astute and ambitious ruler of his day. His farsighted ambition was to establish a united kingdom of Italy, even though that entailed attacking the Papal States. He actually managed to extend his rule to include the chief cities of Tuscany, with the notable exception of Florence, and purchased the title of Duke of Milan from Wenceslaus, king of the Romans.[4]

The despots who ruled the northern city-states of Italy, despite activities that were often marred by the cruelty, craft, and caprice all too common in that era, were tolerant of those who fled oppression elsewhere and certainly did nothing to stunt the free expression of the human spirit among their own people. Nor did they attempt to introduce habits of servility and abasement. Their rule spawned one of Europe's greatest flowerings of human genius—the Renaissance. During this productive era, there was a massive explosion of creative talent and the energy of the popular will was unimpaired and forceful. The rulers who were most successful were those who, like the Medici of Florence, knew their people and under-stood and catered to their needs.[5] An indication of the tolerant and heretical nature of one ruler's thinking manifested itself in a strange form of artistic expression—the tarot trumps. According to the Catholic theologian Margaret Starbird, the tarot was "a virtual cat-echism for the suppressed beliefs of the alternative Christian Church, the 'Church of the Holy Grail,' whose articles of faith included the partnership of Christ and his bride, the woman whom the Gospels called the Magdalene."[6]

THE TAROT

Needless to say, Holy Mother the Church viewed these cards with grave suspicion, branding them as both dangerous and heretical. According to one monk at the time, the tarot trumps were "rungs on a ladder that leads straight to hell."[7] Other priests described the cards more simply as the devil's breviary.[8] It is rare for someone as well versed in Scripture as Margaret Starbird to make a serious study of the hidden meaning of the tarot trumps. Yet she interprets them using scriptural references to the dynasty of Israel's rulers, the House of David, and the medieval heresy of the blood royal—*the sang real*—which she claims leads us to their secret meaning.[9]

The origins of the tarot are disputed. Some believe it originated only in medieval times from the areas of Provence and northern Italy. Others claim it came to the West via the crusaders and that the original eastern packs were transformed by influences traceable to the Cathars, the Gypsies, the Knights Templar, the Kabbala, and ancient Greek hermetic thought.[10] The English Grail scholar Malcolm Godwin believes: "It is possible that the Templars learnt their use from their Saracen rivals."[11] He is also of the opinion that the overt references to the Holy Grail and the obvious gnostic content of the tarot was the principal reason for the Church's hostile attitude toward it. The Church had good cause to be uneasy, for the use of the tarot as a system of visual teaching, either as "flash cards" or as a pocket-sized teaching board, was very much in the Templar tradition—a tradition that was continued into the 21st century by the world-wide fraternity of Freemasonry and the modern Templar orders.

Margaret Starbird's astute analysis was based on the historical evidence found within the actual designs on the cards. She correctly places their origin in the late medieval period and bases this on the fashionable costumes and symbols used within the early packs, which she claims "are directly and irrefutably related to the Church of Amor and the medieval heresy of the Holy Grail."[12] With unerring insight, and despite being completely unaware of the Rex Deus tradition at the time she wrote her book, she states without fear of contradiction that all four suits of the handsome, vividly hand-painted 15th-century decks produced in Provence and northern Italy were clearly associated with the medieval heresy surrounding surviving descendants of the Holy Grail.[13] She again unknowingly reinforces the validity of the Rex Deus tradition by stating:

> The very elaborate cup symbol found on some of the early fif-
> teenth-century decks—the Visconti-Sforza (usually dated
> between 1440–1480) packs named for the artist's patrons—is
> very similar to numerous medieval images of the Holy Grail.
> And it is precisely the noble families of Provence and Northern
> Italy, the allied ducal families of Anjou and Milan, who were
> connected by ties of friendship and even related by blood and
> marriage to the *sang real*. The trump cards in the fifteenth-cen-
> tury tarot decks belonging to the Visconti family of Milan
> appear to be among the earliest in existence . . .[14]

Certainly the tarot teaches a form of spirituality very different from that of the Catholic Church, touching on heretical themes such as reincarnation, renewal or spiritual rebirth, and transforma-tion.[15] In the tarot, the goddess Isis, the seat of wisdom venerated by the Templars as the Black Madonna, is depicted in the card known as Temperance. Perceval, the hero of Wolfram von Eschenbach's Grail saga, is represented symbolically on the bottom left of this card as a valley between two peaks—Perce a Val. The pack is a symbolic depic-tion of a form of Grail quest in which an innocent pilgrim under-goes initiatory trials, including a symbolic death to this world and resurrection to spiritual gnosis, before he meets the goddess. The card known as the Fool is Parzival; the Hermit represents the Grail hermit; the Fisher king is depicted as the Hanged Man, although this is also a reference to the tortured Templars; the Tower is a symbolic representation of the Magdalene; the Moon is the Grail bearer.[16] One suit is held to represent the House of Pendragon, a reference to the Arthurian legends; another, the South, or the House of the Spear, refers to the St. Clair family as the House of Lothian and Orkney, for the St. Clairs were Lords of Roslin in Lothian and also the Earls of Orkney.

The families of the hidden tradition were both wise and circumspect in their use of myth, legend, and allegory to spread their heretical message. The Grail sagas took a hold on European consciousness that they have never lost in the intervening centuries, and the tarot, in its many forms, is far more widespread in its use today than ever before. However, this was not the only form of artistic expression spawned by the Renaissance that promulgated the spiritual message of hope and love. As the Church lost its monopoly on commissioning paintings and sculpture, patronage passed from the priesthood to the newly rich merchant classes and the ruling nobility. Both of these media were employed by the families of Rex Deus to pass their liberating message to the general public, carefully encoded in great works of art.

THE MEDICI OF FLORENCE

As the impracticality of the Visconti dream of a united kingdom of Italy became apparent, the pressing need for a truly equitable balance of power among the northern city-states became ever more obvious. The man who did most to bring this about was Cosimo de' Medici, a clever political manipulator who converted the Florentine republic into a concealed tyranny. It was almost absurdly easy for Cosimo, the wealthiest banker in Europe, to assume his traditional leadership of the smaller traders and artisans, a role that brought with it considerable influence in the affairs of Florence. The adroit use of his European banking business and his innate skill in foreign policy based on sound commercial principles were the twin pillars of his power.

When the last Visconti duke of Milan died, Cosimo made an alliance with the new Duke Sforza to maintain the balance of power in northern Italy.[17] When Francesco Sforza consolidated his hold on Milan after many years of fighting against the traditional enemy,

Venice, the maritime city was faced with an enemy who made his predecessors look like infants in matters of subtlety, strategy, and force of arms.[18] Thus the Medici's alliance with Sforza of Milan made an enormous contribution to political stability in Italy and was a considerable check on the ambitions of Venice.[19] It was also an alliance between two of the secret families, the Medici and the Sforza, whose Rex Deus antecedents are indicated by the fact that he married the daughter of the last Visconti duke of Milan and was initiated into René d'Anjou's prestigious Order of the Croissant.[20]

JEWISH SETTLERS IN ITALY

Like so many areas under the rule of the Rex Deus nobility, northern Italy, despite its almost incessant internecine strife, became not only a haven for religious dissidents such as the Cathars and the Templars, but also a refuge for the Jews fleeing persecution in other parts of Europe. The assets and financial acumen of these Jewish exiles did a great deal to enhance and accelerate the established trend toward commercial success resulting from the northern city-states geographical advantages. These self-governing states began to attract Jewish financiers from lands beyond the Alps at the end of the 13th century, when there was already a flourishing and well-established Jewish community in the Papal States in Rome. By the second half of the 14th century, Jews from Rome moved to the Po valley just as large numbers of Jews crossed the Alps into northern Italy from Germany. These new immigrants, fleeing pogroms and persecution, sought sanctuary in an area renowned for its tolerance, relative security, and economic opportunity. A third wave, smaller in number, arrived after being expelled from France in 1396 and settled mainly in Piedmont and Savoy.

Throughout northern Italy, the most prosperous period for Jews was the Renaissance, when their communities reached their zenith.[21] The immigration of Jewish bankers to the northern Italian city-states gave a great impetus to Jewish settlement throughout this prosperous region and greatly assisted in the development of town and rural centers. Their settlement received legal foundation when the founders of banks were granted a *condotta* (privilege), giving them residential rights for long enough to establish a stable and self-supporting community.[22] In this manner, the Ashkenazi Jews from northern Europe established themselves in northern Italy between 1350 and 1420.[23]

In 1438, the Pisa Bank, the largest Jewish bank in Renaissance Italy, was founded in Florence. Thus the Medici were just as tolerant of the persecuted, but financially astute, Jewish community as their forefathers in Carolingian times had been. This policy flourished, both in the territories controlled by the Medici family and in those under the sway of the Sforzas. In consequence, when the Jews were expelled from Spain and the Spanish territories of Naples and Sicily, they were encouraged to settle in Piedmont, Milan, Ravenna, Pisa, Genoa, Livorno, and Florence.[24]

THE RENAISSANCE

René d'Anjou, the esotericist who founded the Order of the Croissant, was one major figure who acted as a catalyst to the Renaissance. He spent several years in Italy, where he had many possessions, and, through his intimate friendship with the ruling Sforza family of Milan, he was put in contact with their allies, the Medici of Florence. René's influence was a major factor in Cosimo de' Medici's decision to embark on a series of projects that, ultimately, transformed Western civilization. In 1439, Cosimo sent agents all over the Mediterranean world in a quest for ancient manuscripts. In 1444, he founded the Library of San Marco, Christian Europe's first public library—an institution that challenged the Church's stranglehold on learning. Later, Cosimo ordered the University of Florence to teach ancient Greek for the first time in seven centuries.[25]

The study of the classical literature, philosophy, and science of ancient Greece flourished and became the pivotal focus of the intellectual spirit of inquiry that triggered the new artistic, intellectual, and spiritual Renaissance. Under the leadership of two Florentines, Petrarch (1304–1374) and Boccaccio (1313–1375), these studies were pursued with an understanding and appreciation not seen before in medieval Europe. Petrarch and Boccaccio searched for and rehabilitated classical works lying disregarded in the monastic libraries of Christian Europe and elsewhere.[26] After the Reconquista, much of the learning of Hellenic times was transmitted to Florence from the Muslim Libraries of Granada and Toledo.[27]

Predictably, the papacy did not view this outburst of creative activity and intellectual freedom with approval. And now papal power was brought to bear against the Rex Deus nobility in the north. The assassination of Galezzeo Maria Sforza in 1476 resulted from a papal plot, as did the Pazzi conspiracy that cost Guliano de' Medici his life in 1478.[28] Despite these predictable attempts to stultify, halt, or even reverse the new spirit of intellectual inquiry and progress, Lorenzo de' Medici, known as Lorenzo the Magnificent, consolidated his family's power in Florence within a short time and surrounded himself with scholars imbued with the mysticism of Egypt and the wisdom of Greece. Devotional literature, philosophy, and science flourished, and artists of immense stature—among them Botticelli, Michelangelo, Verroccio, and Ghirlandaio—worked under his generous patronage.[29]

LEONARDO DA VINCI

Of this galaxy of artistic and creative talent, few were as influential as Leonardo da Vinci (1452–1519), who made his mark, not only on his time, but on all subsequent centuries. Da Vinci's visionary genius and insight foresaw the machine age and technologies that only came to fruition the 19th century. He was an avid reader and translator of Euclid, Vitruvius, Pliny, Ptolomy, Celsius, as well as of Arab authors; he amassed, as did his associate Piccolo della Mirandola, a range of scientific, anatomical, and medical knowledge unequalled for centuries.[30]

Leonardo worked, at first, as a painter in Florence and then, in 1483, at the age of thirty, he went to Milan where he enjoyed the patronage of Duke Ludovico Sforza, known as Il Moro because of his dark complexion. He returned to Tuscany for a short while, then went back to Milan and, later, on to Rome, before finally being welcomed by Francis I at Amboise in 1515, where he stayed until his death.

In his paintings, da Vinci ceaselessly pursued both the visible form and the symbols that reveal the invisible spirit and the cosmos, including some that teach subtle forms of heresy in the guise of straight, Catholic devotional paintings.[31] Despite his reputation among his contemporaries as having "a somewhat heretical turn of mind," however, Leonardo's genius and the apparently unassailable power of his patrons protected him from the unwelcome attentions of the Inquisition. He was brought to Milan to create a mounted statue of the first Sforza duke of Milan that was never, in fact, completed. However, during his prolonged stay in the city, he created three works of towering genius and sublime artistry that are still regarded by the Church as supreme examples of Christian devotional art. These paintings comprise two different versions of *The Virgin of the Rocks* and one work that is the basis for the most commonly reproduced work of art in the Western world—the painting known as *L'Ultima Cena*, or *The Last Supper*.

This huge fresco covers an entire wall in the refectory of the Convent of Santa Maria della Grazie in Milan and shows Jesus and the disciples having dinner on the eve of his arrest. It is, without doubt, the best-known piece of Christian iconography in the world; copies of it hang in churches, chapels, schools, offices, and private homes, both Catholic and Protestant. To the vast majority of Christians, it is the ultimate reminder of the original communion service and the sacred, but mistaken, belief that Jesus died for us as our saviour. Yet, in reality, the symbolism subtly coded within it preaches outright heresy that contradicts some of the Catholic Church's most cherished doctrines.

All great art is ambivalent at many interlocking levels; the representation of three-dimensional scenes on a two-dimensional plane is, to start with, unreal; the use of perspective creates an illusion of distance, a lie used to convey truth. Moreover, each era has its own fashions and conventions within which the artist operates. A true artist also uses ambivalence to provoke us into perceiving familiar scenes in a distinctly different manner than we usually do. As in all art, it is sometimes difficult to know which is paramount—the insight of the artist or that of the patron.

During the Renaissance, the instructions of the patron were paramount and were laid out in precise detail in contracts drawn up before work commenced. Thus we can discern the precise intentions of the patrons concerned. In the case of painters and sculptors of genius, such as Leonardo da Vinci, we must also consider how the technical skill, spiritual insight, and outright genius of the artist enhance the patron's vision.

L'Ultima Cena—THE LAST SUPPER

The vast fresco of The Last Supper, the lowest borders of which are at shoulder level of the viewer, combines the art of perspective with a subtle distortion of visual reality in a way that is so inspired, the average viewer is not aware that he or she is being inherently misled. Despite the fact that the bulk of the painting is above eye level, the artist persuades viewers that their heads are almost on a level with that of the central figure. Viewers have a sense of looking down onto the surface of the dining table, seeing through the window at the rear of the supper room, and observing the horizon just below the midpoint of the windows. The view through this window demonstrates that it is bright daylight outside. Yet the painting is supposed to represent the Last Supper, an evening meal.

Jesus, the central figure, sits with his hands and arms outstretched, flanked by two groups of three disciples. Reading from the viewer's left to right, the figures in the first group are Bartholomew, James the Righteous (the brother of Jesus), and Andrew, all of whom are looking in the direction of Jesus. The next group of three is comprised of the leaning figure of Peter, whose left hand touches the shoulder of John, the beloved disciple, whose head is inclined as if listening to Peter. In front of and between these two is the half-turned figure of Judas. Jesus, in isolation, holds center stage. In the third group, Thomas, Jesus' twin brother, sits with the upraised index finger of his right hand gesturing at Jesus angrily and threateningly. Immediately in front of Thomas is James the Great, strangely represented almost as Jesus' double. Half leaning over James and looking sorrowfully at Jesus is Philip. The final threesome contains two men, Matthew and Thaddeus, facing away from Jesus, but gesturing emphatically in his direction in a state of some perturbation and Simon sitting at the end of the table facing Jesus, but with his face slightly averted in the direction of Thaddeus.

There is obviously some form of dispute in progress. A discussion centered on the issue of who will be in charge after Jesus dies is given considerable prominence in the Gospel accounts of the Last Supper. We submit that this heated argument is precisely what is portrayed in the painting. Furthermore, Peter's apparently secretive conversational pose, whispering in the ear of John, is counterbalanced by his almost disembodied right hand appearing from behind Judas, clutching a knife that points straight at James the Righteous, as if he were saying to John: "No, it is not I who is to be the new leader, but him!"—a simple reflection of historical truth that is heretical in the extreme.

Judas, clutching a well-filled leather purse in his right hand, has just knocked over a container of salt that has spilled across the table— a small nod in the direction of an age-old superstition and a delightful example of Leonardo's ability to make the smallest detail count. The various hand gestures of the disciples are also important, but deserve a far more detailed discussion than we can give in this work.

Most recent works on the fresco have focused on the figure of St. John, who, according to Picknett and Prince, is not a man at all, but a distinctly female figure whom they claim to be Mary Magdalene. We think that, although this may be remotely possible, it is unlikely. The most probable explanation for this distinctly effeminate figure is similar to that given for the equally ambivalent sexuality of the figure of the archangel Uriel in another of Leonardo's paintings, The Virgin of the Rocks. In esoteric tradition, the truly enlightened initiate becomes a hermaphrodite—that unique balance between the primal Adam and Eve of mankind's legendary origins. John, renowned as the supreme Christian initiate, is the "Beloved Disciple" to whom Jesus passed his secret teachings. John, along with John the Baptist, another biblical figure painted frequently by Leonardo, was revered by the Rex Deus families, the Knights Templar, and the Cathars.

The Last Supper occupies almost the entire expanse of the wall of the refectory of Santa Maria della Grazie. Immediately opposite it, in a sort of entrance hall at the other end of the refectory, is another painting—The Crucifixion by Giovanni Donato Montofano. Both artists were at work at the same time; therefore, each knew both the relative positions of the finished works and their subject matter. The obvious theological bridge between the events depicted is the institution of the sacrament of Holy Communion. Leonardo's masterpiece does show bread and wine, but the bread is ordinary leavened bread and none of it appears to be broken. The plates, rolls of bread, and the wine glasses are all placed in a highly formalized manner that bears no recognizable relationship to the diners at the table. It is definitely a ritualized and sacramental pattern that was acceptable to the Church hierarchy, and yet we sense instinctively that something important is going on here that can only be recognized by the initiated.

The whole table is arranged in undisturbed order, with the exception of the spill of salt near Judas's elbow. None of the wine glasses are prominent and there is nothing remotely resembling a chalice that would have been the most obvious and easily recognizable symbolic representation of the first communion cup. Jesus sits with open arms, left hand facing upward, right hand almost palm down. He looks as if he is being remonstrated by Thomas, James the Great, and a worried Philip. The only argument likely to have provoked this animated discussion that we can read in the Gospels is over the future leadership. Peter's denial of the role ascribed to him by the Church has been mentioned, and the symbolism used to depict John tells us that he is to be the main carrier of the teachings revealed by Jesus. The close resemblance between the figures of Jesus and James the Great is a direct reference to another heresy—that of the Holy Twins, or the two Jesuses, who are referred to in at least two other paintings by Leonardo.

The Virgin of the Rocks

There are two versions of the painting known as The Virgin of the Rocks, both by Leonardo da Vinci. Their layout and overall design are very similar, the differences being mainly in detail and color. The first of these was commissioned by the confraternity of San Francesco Grande in Milan as the centerpiece above the altar in one of the chapels. The exact size was specified in the contract drawn up before work began, which also gave details of the positioning of the figures. The figures are painted in a grotto, with the Virgin seated almost in the center with her right arm and hand around the shoulder of a baby boy. Her left hand is outstretched protectively over the head of another small child seated in front and to her left. An angelic figure seated beside the second child is pointing directly at the figure of the baby beside the Virgin. The child with the Virgin's hand on his shoulder is kneeling with his hands clasped in a prayerful attitude looking at the other, who has his fingers raised in blessing. This version now hangs in the Louvre in Paris. The second and later version is, broadly speaking, the same with only minor, but important, differences of posture and emphasis with the angel sits slightly behind the second child, looking adoringly at him. This painting now hangs in the National Gallery in London.

The average devout Christian seeing either of these paintings for the first time naturally assumes that the child with the Virgin's arm around his shoulders is Jesus. To their eyes, Jesus is praying to John the Baptist, who is blessing the so-called Son of God. This is, in fact, erroneous, for the child beside the Virgin is not Jesus, but John the Baptist, while the one giving the blessing is Jesus. We can only assume that whoever was responsible for drawing up the tight and precise contract was a heretic within the priesthood, because, when Leonardo followed his instructions to the letter, the result was wide open for misinterpretation on a grand scale. The paintings appear absolutely innocent to anyone unaware of the contractual instructions of the priests and their explanation of the scene.

At some stage in the painting's history, the dangerous degree of confusion over the relative identities of the two children must have become apparent, so steps were taken to clarify the matter. After all, no devout Catholic could condone any artwork that implied, even by misinterpretation, that, right from the start, John the Baptist was more important than Jesus. Another artist was employed to make additions to the work that is now in London; distinctive halos for each child were added and the identifying mark of a long-stemmed cross for the infant John the Baptist. That should, of course, have settled the matter. However, to the initiated, we have here two glorious examples of hidden references to the heresy of the holy twins: two depictions of the even more heretical concept of the two Jesuses. No wonder there are two nearly identical paintings of this scene by the towering genius Leonardo. However, these were not the only artistic references to these explosive heresies created in the late 15th century; there were others in Scotland.

CHAPTER 18

The St. Clairs of Roslin and the Foundation of Freemasonry

The Cathars and the Knights Templar who fled to Scotland found refuge and sanctuary principally in the lands of the St. Clairs of Roslin, a dynasty whose continuous and unbroken record of service, loyalty, and courage earned them the name of The Lordly Line of the High St. Clairs. The first member of the family to come to Roslin, William the Seemly St. Clair, arrived in Scotland in 1057 with the knight Bartholomew Ladislaus Leslyn, escorting Princess Margaret, who later married King Malcolm Canmore.[1] The first St. Clair born in Scotland, Henri de St. Clair, fought under Godfroi de Bouillon in the Holy Land in 1096 and was present at the siege of Jerusalem,[2] accompanied by members of eleven other leading Scottish aristocratic families.

Representatives of all twelve families met regularly prior to the crusade and continued to meet at Roslin until the late 18th century, by which time all hopes of a Stuart restoration had died. The families in the group—which included the Stuarts, Montgomerys, Setons, Douglases, Dalhousies, Ramseys, Leslies, and Lindsays, as well as the St. Clairs—were linked by marriage and shared beliefs, were all involved with the Templars, and continued to propagate Templar traditions after the order's suppression. They all played a part in the foundation of Freemasonry in Scotland and supported the Stuart cause.

In *The Bloodline of the Holy Grail*, Laurence Gardner validates one important aspect of the Rex Deus legend, claiming that the

Stuarts were descended from leading families among the hierarchy in biblical Israel at the time of Jesus—dynastic roots similar to those shared by the families who met so regularly at Roslin.

EARL WILLIAM ST. CLAIR

The figure who did the most to preserve and propagate Rex Deus traditions was Earl William St. Clair, who lived in the 15th century. He was not only the Lord of Roslin, but also the third St. Clair Earl of Orkney. His description as a Knight of the Cockle and Golden Fleece[3] indicates his membership in two different orders mentioned earlier—the Knights of Santiago,[4] represented by the Cockle, and the Order of the Golden Fleece, founded by the Duke of Burgundy. Earl William was also described as "one of the Illuminati, a nobleman with singular talents" and as "a man of exceptional talents much given to policy, such as buildings of Castles, Palaces and Churches."[5] He was a patron of craftmasonry throughout Europe, "a Grand Master and an adept of the highest degree."[6] Scottish records confirm that he was not only hereditary Grand Master of the craftmasons, but also of all the hard and soft guilds in Scotland,[7] such as the shipwrights, papermakers, tanners, and foresters.[8]

William, a true son of the Renaissance, lived at the same time as René d'Anjou and corresponded with him. Like Cosimo de' Medici, he was an obsessive collector of original manuscripts and acquired a vast library that he housed at Roslin Castle. The respect accorded to this collection by Earl William is recorded by a family historian:

> About this time (1447) there was a fire in the square keep by occasion of which the occupants were forced to flee the building. The Prince's chaplain seeing this, and remembering all of his master's writings, passed to the head of the dungeon where they all were, and threw out four great trunks where they were. The news of the fire coming to the Prince through the lamentable cries of the ladies and gentlewomen, and the sight thereof coming to his view in the place where he stood upon College Hill, he was sorry for nothing but the loss of his Charters and other writings; but when the chaplain who had saved himself by coming down the bell rope tied to a beam, declared how his

Charters and Writs were all saved, he became cheerful and went
to recomfort his Princess and the Ladys.[9]

The importance of these documents reinforces the fact that spiritual insight runs like a river through the history of the St. Clairs.
Earl William was described in his own day as one of the Illuminati,
which gives a strong indication of the respect in which he was held—
for what are the qualities of "the enlightened ones" except those of
deep and abiding spiritual knowledge and perception? Indeed,
according to Tessa Ransford, a director of the Scottish Poetry Library,
the name Roslin translates from Scottish Gaelic as "ancient knowledge passed down the generations."[10]

The St. Clairs of Roslin were the guardians of the divinely
inspired gnosis that was the true treasure of the Knights Templar.
Earl William preserved this heritage for all time by encoding it within
the carvings of Rosslyn Chapel.

ROSSLYN CHAPEL

Earl William is best remembered for his most lasting and enigmatic
legacy, the mystical shrine of Rosslyn Chapel. Originally planned
as a large collegiate church, the chapel's foundations were laid between
1446 and 1450. To build this church, William brought skilled and
experienced master masons from every part of Europe[11] and considerably enlarged Roslin village in order to accommodate them.
In fact, Roslin grew at such a pace that it began to rival nearby
Haddington and even Edinburgh in size; it was given its royal char-
ter in 1456 by King James II.

The master masons were paid £40 per year, an enormous amount
for a time when ordinary masons drew only £10 per year. As architect, patron, and designer of the chapel, Earl William exercised total
control over every aspect of its construction. Nothing was left to
chance and, like patrons of the artists in Renaissance Italy, he outlined his instructions with such precision that they became the stuff
of legend. Before any carving was made in stone, a model was carved
in wood and submitted to the earl for approval. Only then did the
stone carving begin. Thus the essential, symphonic harmony of
design in Rosslyn Chapel is the cumulative result of several factors:

a plan drawn up by a remarkable and supremely gifted man who exerted absolute control over design, quality, and construction; a comparatively rapid rate of building that left no time for contamination of the original conception; and a band of highly skilled masons who worked continuously and without a break on the same project, a rare occurrence in church building in that era.

Trevor Ravenscroft wrote: "The sculptures in Rosslyn are magnificent manifestations of spiritual insight or vision, given substance in stone." In an article published in 1982, Douglas Sutherland described the chapel thus: "A medieval masterpiece of masonry, containing some of the most exquisite carvings ever fashioned in stone, Rosslyn Chapel may now be half-forgotten but it is still very memorable."[12]

No realistic analysis of the meaning of the spiritual and artistic content of the carvings in this unique building can be made unless it is conducted in the light of the family history and complex character of its founder. Considered on their own, the carvings are simply beautiful and mysterious manifestations of Masonic art that are susceptible to gross misinterpretation. Part of the puzzle of Rosslyn Chapel is that, in this late-medieval, supposedly Christian church, we find a multitude of symbolic references in stone to every initiatory spiritual tradition that can be found in the history of mankind before its construction: a carving of the head of Hermes Trismegistos, the reputed author of the Emerald Tablets who is so often equated with the Egyptian god Thoth; prolific carvings of the green man that commemorate the principle of spiritual death and rebirth central to all initiatory paths; carvings of rosettes and five-pointed stars that once decorated the temples dedicated to Ishtar and Tammuz in ancient Babylonia, 2,500 years before the birth of Jesus.

TEMPLAR SYMBOLISM IN ROSSLYN CHAPEL

Symbolism intimately associated with the Knights Templar is also found throughout the chapel. French scholar J-A Durbec lists the signs and seals that validate the Templar attribution of any building as follows:

1. Carvings of a five-pointed star, *L'étoile*.
2. Two brothers on one horse, *deux frères sur un seule cheval*.

Badly weathered head of Hermes
Trismegistos on the east wall of Rosslyn Chapel.

3. The seal known as the Agnus Dei, also known as the Templar seal, *un agneau pascal (nimbé ou non) tenant une croix patté au-dessus de lui.*

4. A stylized representation of the head of Jesus, like that represented in the Shroud of Turin or on the Veil of Veronica, known as the Mandylion.

5. A dove in flight carrying an olive branch. *Une colombe tenant en son bec une branche d'olivier.*

6. A form of oriental cross known as the floriated cross.[13]

In making any attribution to the Templars, we must proceed with caution, however, for the symbols listed by Durbec are, of course, all well-known items of standard Christian iconography. However, when we find two or more of them in combination within the same building, this suggests strong Templar influence. When they all occur together prior to the suppression of the order, we know we have a genuine Templar edifice.[14] In the case of Rosslyn Chapel, which was founded over a century after the suppression of the Templars, we have something of a mystery. The sacred geometry within its architecture contains all the signs of true Templar construction. Moreover, within the iconography, indications of Templar influence are not restricted to the diagnostic symbols already listed; they occur in one form or another at almost every turn.

In the vault of each bay in the aisles and arching across the roof of the crypt are carvings of the engrailed cross of the St. Clairs. At the junction of the arms of each of these crosses, subtly but distinctly delineated in each case, is a variant on the *croix patté* of the Knights Templar known as the cross of universal knowledge. Nor is it mere coincidence that the heraldic colors of the St. Clair family are argent and sable, the same as those sported by the Sforzas of Milan and proudly carried on the battle flag of the Templar order, the Beauseant.

Two Templar burial stones from local graveyards reside in the chapel—one in the crypt, adjoining a 17th-century guild stone depicting the King of Terrors, the other in the north aisle of the chapel, engraved with the name William de Sinncler and surmounted by a floriated cross. The Templar seal of the Agnus Dei appears on a pillar on the north wall; a similar pillar on the south wall bears the Veil of Veronica. The superb carving of the dove in flight carrying an

Badly weathered carving of a Knights Templar
initiation on the south wall of Rosslyn Chapel.

olive branch in its beak adorns the western section of the roof in a sea of five-pointed stars.

The St. Clair family of Roslin was intimately connected with the Templar order from the very beginning. They were members of Rex Deus who founded the order, and the family castle was the ultimate destination of Hughes de Payen when he returned from the Holy Land in 1127. The grave-marker within the chapel that is so beautifully decorated with Templar symbolism—the floriated cross—is a memorial to the man who led the Templar charge at Bannockburn in 1314, the charge that preserved the independence of Scotland and secured the crown for Robert the Bruce.[15]

Viewing the Templar symbolism within Rosslyn Chapel in the light of St. Clair history leads to one inevitable conclusion: the chapel, whose design and content was so strictly supervised by Earl William, was created as a lasting memorial to the much-maligned heretical Order of the Knights Templar and as a means of transmission of their ideals and beliefs to future generations. That is why Earl William used the skills of his Masonic colleagues to such good effect in celebrating every known initiatory spiritual pathway that contributed, in one way or another, to the sacred gnosis preserved at such cost by the descendants of the twenty-four ma'madot of Israel.

This form of lasting celebration was not the only means used by Earl William to ensure the preservation of these initiatory rites. In fact, there are more clues and signposts in the chapel to his plans for the future. These symbolic representations of sacred principles central to the Rex Deus tradition have been used for over 500 years by a fraternity founded by Earl William, for he used the construction of this holy shrine as the first step in creating an organization that would treasure and guard these secrets, and pass them on to future generations throughout the world—the craft of Freemasonry. This organization's members have used their spiritual insight to transcend the geographic, cultural, and religious barriers that normally impede the progress of man.

THE FOUNDATION OF FREEMASONRY

The mystery that surrounds the foundation of Freemasonry has been further clouded by the secrecy adopted by the craft itself in its rela-

Death mask of King Robert the Bruce on
the east wall of the retro-choir, Rosslyn Chapel.

Detail of the Apprentice Pillar at Rosslyn Chapel
showing Rex Deus symbolism of the Staffordshire knot.

tionship with the general public. The original craft guilds of medieval masons throughout Europe had their own, sometimes very different, foundation myths, traditions, and initiation rituals. Somehow and somewhere, the craftmasons were transformed into the precursors of modern Freemasonry. The debate about how, where, and when this happened has been prolonged and bitter. The innate habit of secrecy adopted by the early Masonic brethren has made it incredibly difficult for historians to document the precise development of Freemasonry, and has complicated rational study of this issue.

The debate over Masonic origins often degenerates into a modern version of *odium theologicum*, in which the character of the proponent is questioned more vigorously than his or her theories. However, open-minded researchers from both sides of the argument are pursuing their various theories in a manner that will eventually resolve the issue. We believe that one family above all others had the means, the motive, and the opportunity to exert a transformative effect on the medieval craft guilds of operative masons and used it to such good effect that they developed into the modern craft of Speculative Freemasonry. This belief will not silence those who vociferously defend their pro- or anti-Templar theories of origin, but it will, eventually, provide keys that can resolve this historical conundrum for all time.

Here, we will describe certain aspects of the history of operative masonry, demonstrate how various members of Masonic guilds were brought together in one place, and how, under the guidance of the St. Clairs of Roslin, they began their transformation into the modern speculative craft. Further proof of the Rex Deus origins of the craft can be deduced from certain ancient rituals.

EARLY ORIGINS OF THE CRAFT

According to English poet and mythologist Robert Graves, Freemasonry began as a Sufi society. It first reached England during the reign of King Athelstan (924–939) and was later introduced into Scotland as a craft guild. Graves describes the Sufic origins of the craftmasons, the important role played by the Templars, and the much later transformation of the operative craft guilds into Freemasonry. He places the origins of the Sufis long before the foundation of Islam:

> An ancient spiritual freemasonry whose origins have never been traced or dated although the characteristic Sufic signature is found in widely dispersed literature from at least the second millennium B.C.E.[16]

He also recounts how their hidden wisdom was passed down through the generations, from master to pupil, as in so many other initiatory orders.[17]

Graves stresses the role played by Sufi masters in the building of Solomon's Temple. We know that there is a strong connection with the Hebrew people, for the Sufis' legendary mystical teacher, *el Khidir*, or the Verdant One, is an amalgam of two prophetic figures of biblical Israel—Elijah and John the Baptist. The question thus arises: From where did they get their ancient knowledge? The answer can be found in ancient Egypt in the era the Pyramid Texts describe as the First Time.

We have already described the level of sophistication and insight achieved by the three main branches of the Compagnonnage in early medieval France. Similar craft guilds operated in Germany, Spain, and Italy, and those who built in the Gothic style had a particularly close relationship with the Templar order. Thus, when the historian John Robinson describes how the fleeing Templar knights were aided in their escape by lodges of craftmasons, our only unresolved question is: Were these particular lodges that gave shelter and passage in this manner the Children of Master Jacques, who later gained the name of *les Compagnons Passants*?

In Portugal, the refugees joined the Order of the Knights of Christ; in the Baltic States they joined the Teutonic Knights; in Lombardy, aided by the Cathars who had preceded them, they used their skills to strengthen the emergent banking system. In Scotland, however, the story was very different. Warned to go underground by King Robert the Bruce, the Templars nonetheless kept their traditions alive. We submit that, under the protection of the St. Clairs of Roslin, Templar tradition and the craftmason's gnosis were given an opportunity to merge, to their mutual benefit.

MASONIC GNOSIS

The gifted and insightful master masons who created Rosslyn Chapel took it for granted that their artwork should be beautiful. Mere beauty, however, was not enough. There had to be meaning—not merely meaning in the storytelling sense, although this was often an essential ingredient, but a deeper and more spiritual meaning. Remember that, for the medieval craftmasons, *ars sina scienta nihil est*—art without knowledge is nothing. In this context, the knowledge referred to is "gnosis"—spiritual knowledge or mystical insight.

The people of the medieval and Renaissance eras for whom the artwork was designed would have found themselves more deeply moved and far more involved in the symbolism of the art than any modern observer, however learned. In that creative era, carvings, paintings, and even buildings were deliberately designed for men and women for whom symbolism was the breath of spiritual life—a spiritual life, moreover, that was startlingly different from that taught by the Church.

> For occultists, or medieval man, symbols have a real meaning. A symbol that is merely a symbol, merely a copy or an image, has no meaning; there is only significance in that which can become a reality, in what can become a vibrant force. If a symbol acts upon the spirit of humanity in such a way that intuitive forces are set free, then and only then are we dealing with a true symbol.[18]

Earl William had planned a new reality for coming generations, an organization of like-minded men who, from its inception, were, trained to learn by means of ritual, symbolism, and allegory. For them, symbolism became the mainspring of true inspiration. This means of progressive involvement in the spiritual world, achieved through ascending degrees of initiation, brought the gnostic realities preserved by the families of the hidden tradition to a far wider audience.

THE APPRENTICE PILLAR

Of all the mysteries and legends that envelop Rosslyn Chapel, few are as well known as that surrounding the most puzzling and beautiful of its artistic gems—the Apprentice Pillar. The story of the murdered apprentice, with its obvious reference to the initiation rituals of both the medieval guilds of craftmasons and the far older legend of Hiram Abif, master Mason at the building of King Solomon's Temple, has immense symbolic, spiritual, and ritual resonance for the worldwide brotherhood of Freemasonry.

The pillar is a representation of the Tree of Life so central to the study of the Kabbala; it also represents the Yggdrasil tree of Norse mythology—the World Ash that binds together heaven and hell. It is another example of artistic and spiritual ambivalence that can be understood by Christians, pagans, and Jewish Kabbalists in a manner that transcends all petty religious divisions.

The Apprentice Pillar is one of three that separate the retro-choir from the main body of the chapel. Next to it is the Journeyman's Pillar, and then the sublime carving of the Master Mason's Pillar. According to Masonic tradition, every true lodge must be supported by three grand pillars of deep symbolic significance. The Master Mason's Pillar represents wisdom or sacred gnosis; the Journeyman's Pillar symbolizes strength; the Apprentice Pillar signifies beauty. In the architectural terms pertinent to Masonic tradition, wisdom constructs, strength supports, and beauty is designed to adorn. Furthermore, wisdom is ordained to discover, strength is made to bear and sustain, while beauty is made to attract.

Yet all is for naught unless these pillars are erected upon the same rock or foundation—the one named Truth and Justice. These qualities reflect those aspired to by the humble initiate of any valid spiritual path:

> He who is as wise as a Perfect Master will not be easily injured by
> his own actions. Hath a person the strength which a Senior
> Warden represents he will bear and overcome every obstacle in
> life. He who is adorned like a Junior Warden with humility of
> spirit approaches nearer to the similitude of God than any other.[19]

Rosslyn Chapel was founded in 1446 and Freemasonry some centuries later. Yet within the confines of the chapel, symbolic references to Masonic ritual, belief, and practice abound—to such a degree that there are few Masons in the world today who do not regard this place of beauty and spiritual enlightenment as the unof-

Apprentice Pillar, Rosslyn Chapel.

Master Mason's Pillar, Rosslyn Chapel.

ficial core church of the worldwide craft. There are symbolic references within the chapel to the Hiram Abif legend; the maul-marked face of the murdered apprentice gazes fixedly across the chapel at the contorted features of the Master Mason who reputedly killed him.

One strange anomaly arose when plaster casts of the carvings were taken some years ago as an aid to the restoration process. It was discovered that the head of the apprentice had been substantially altered—at one time, his face had sported a full beard that was chiseled off. We have reason to believe that this alteration occurred because Earl William had gone too far in his depiction of heresy, and that the two bearded faces were originally designed to show the heresy of the holy twins and the secret legend of the two Jesuses. Nearby, on the south wall of the clerestory, is the carved face of the grieving widow and the phrase: "Who will come to the aid of the son of the widow?" This is one phrase that has held particular resonance for members of the Masonic crafts and guilds from the times of ancient Egypt down to the present. *Memento mori* proliferate, perhaps the finest example being the superb carving of *la danse macabre*, the dance of death, on the ribbed vaulting of the retro-choir.

Head of the murdered apprentice with the
maul mark on the right temple, Rosslyn Chapel.

Head of the Master Mason, Rosslyn Chapel.

Head of the grieving widow, south clerestory, Rosslyn Chapel.

Long before the foundation of Rosslyn Chapel, and acting under the guidance of the St. Clairs, certain members of the inner circle of the Templar order were carefully selected from operative craft guilds for instruction in sacred knowledge. The subjects of instruction included science, geometry, history, philosophy, and the contents of the documents recovered by the Templars during their excavations in Jerusalem.[20] As a result, after the suppression of the Templars, Scotland in general and Midlothian in particular became beacons of enlightenment. This new brotherhood of speculative "free" masons created charitable institutions to support the poorer members of society, and their respective guilds also set money aside for the benefit of their less fortunate neighbors. According to Prince Michael of Albany, these were not only the first charitable institutions to be established in Scotland that were outside the control of the Church, they may well have been the first such organizations anywhere in Europe.[21]

The foundation of Rosslyn Chapel, the assemblage of such a large group of skilled and influential masons from every part of Europe, and the creation of their own community to house them gave Earl William the opportunity to extend and develop this type of organization. He knew that he was taking enormous risks, for the days of persecution and burning at the stake were far from over. In creating the arcane library in stone that is Rosslyn Chapel, however, and in stimulating and strengthening the new speculative "free" Masonic orders, he left us a lasting legacy that ensured that he, like his illustrious grandfather, Earl Henry St. Clair, richly deserved the title of "worthy of immortal memory."

Earl William's position as hereditary Grand Master of all the hard and soft guilds in Scotland, his authority over the Masonic court at Kilwinning, his Templar antecedents, the Masonic symbolism within Rosslyn Chapel, and his position as a scholar of esotericism all combine to demonstrate that he had the means, the motive, and the opportunity to play an active role in transforming the ancient craft guilds into the modern speculative fraternity. The new Freemasonry recognized no barriers of class and eventually included King James VI of Scotland, who was initiated into the craft at the Lodge of Perth and Scone in 1601.[22] When he became King James I of England two years later, he needed influential allies as a counterweight to the greed of the self-serving British aristocracy. He found them among the members of the trade and craft guilds of England and introduced them on an informal basis to Freemasonry.[23] The first documentary proof of inductions into English Freemasonry dates from 1640, during the reign of James' son, Charles I. In this era of repression, bloodshed, and war fought in the name of religion, the new fraternity wisely decided to be secretive from the start.

This secrecy makes it extremely difficult to evaluate the full spectrum of esoteric streams that coalesced to form the order, and to understand the different circumstances in each country that influenced local and national developments. In Scotland, the craft had a democratic appeal from the beginning, and has continued in this manner ever since. There, the tradition of preserving the sacred gnosis in an ascending hierarchy of degrees was kept almost intact and developed a high degree of sophistication and complexity. This led, ultimately, to the development of the Royal Arch degrees of Scottish Freemasonry and Scottish Rite Freemasonry, which is still preserved in a relatively unpolluted form in parts of continental Europe and the United States. In Europe, Freemasonry developed an innate anticlerical and anti-Catholic bias and, for the first two or three centuries, maintained close links with its Scottish brethren, both those at home and those in exile.

This long-term association is recorded in the Rite of Strict Observance, where we discover that Masons from operative lodges of the Compagnonnage in France visited a lodge in Aberdeen in 1361, beginning a relationship that continued for several hundred years. To this day, French lodges take particular pains to preserve, as far as possible, the original esoteric teaching of the craft. In England, the anticlerical bias was not so pronounced, and English Freemasonry became an integral part of the church/state establishment. After substantial alterations to its rituals and beliefs, it became a major support for the House of Hanover following the expulsion of the Stuart line.

The inherently democratic traditions of the Scottish craft that were the principal influence on the development of American Freemasonry may explain the high quality of the attainments of members on the new continent. These supremely gifted men possessed great spiritual insight and a moral force that left a lasting imprint on the emerging American nation, primarily in the form of the Constitution of the United States, a ringing endorsement of

freedom, democracy, and the rights of man that is the lasting spiri-
tual legacy of this branch of Freemasonry.[24] A large number of those
who created and signed the American Constitution were either
Freemasons or Rosicrucians,[25] including such figures as George
Washington, Benjamin Franklin, Thomas Jefferson, John Adams, and
Charles Thompson.

Medieval alchemical symbolism became enshrined in the American
way of life with symbols such as the eagle, olive branch, arrows, and
pentagrams, while the truncated pyramid and the all-seeing eye that
decorate American banknotes, buildings, and monuments all point to
the influence of the mystical past of Freemasonry on American life.

Rex Deus in Masonic Ritual

The knowledge of Freemasonry and its internal workings that is accessible in the public domain is limited to what has been published by
the craft, and is further circumscribed by vows of secrecy taken by individual members. Thus, what we reveal here is presented in the certain
knowledge that it represents only the tip of an iceberg. Nonetheless,
there are certain correspondences between Masonic ritual and Rex
Deus tradition that are readily identifiable. For example, the Rex Deus
oath of secrecy, "Lest my throat be cut or my tongue cut out," has a
parallel in the ritual of the first craft degree of Freemasonry:

> These several points I solemnly swear to observe, without eva-
> sion, equivocation or mental reservation of any kind under no
> less a penalty than to have my throat cut across, my tongue torn
> out by the root and my body buried in the rough sands of the
> sea at low water mark ...

The phrase, "Lest my heart be torn or cut out of my chest,"
which is the second part of the penalty of the Rex Deus oath, has
its equivalent in Freemasonry's second degree:

> ... under no less a penalty than to have my left breast cut open,
> my heart torn there from, and given to the ravenous birds of
> the air, or to the devouring beasts of the field as prey.

Two other replications of the Rex Deus oath are found in
Masonic ritual: "Lest my eyes be plucked out" is rendered in the

ritual of the Knight White Eagle as ". . . under the penalty of forever remaining in perpetual darkness." While the use of a knife as a
threat in the oath is replicated in the penalties listed for the Past
Master degree.

> . . . having my hands lopped off at the wrist and my arms struck
> from my body and both hung at my breast suspended at the
> neck as a sign of infamy till time and putridity consume the
> same.

The charge of idolatry in the form of the worship of a head that
was leveled at the Knights Templar, as well as their ritual use of skulls,
also finds echoes within Freemasonry. The Masonic historians Knight
and Lomas recount that, "Freemasonry around the world probably
possesses some 50,000 skulls!"

The support of English Freemasonry for the Hanoverian dynasty
led to a bizarre attitude adopted by the United Grand Lodge of
England, which actively discourages serious investigation into the
origins of the craft, as they wish to expunge from the record any
reference to Scottish origins and its earlier alliance with the Stuart
cause. As a result, there was a thorough purging of Scottish rituals
from English Masonic practice. Thanks to the dedicated work of the
Masonic scholar Dimitrije Mitrinovic in the early years of the 20th
century, however, we are able to trace a high level of Rex Deus influence in some of these purged rituals.

Mitrinovic's library contains one book that records that the
fourth degree—that of the Secret Master—is concerned with mourn-
ing someone who remains anonymous.[26] The ritual of this degree
commemorates a time when the building of the temple was brought
to a halt due to a tragedy. For this ceremony, the lodge is draped in
black and white and illuminated by the light of eighty-one candles.
The jewel of the degree is inscribed with the letter "z," which refers
to Zadok.[27] The Dead Sea Scrolls record that the sons of Zadok were
the descendants of the high priests of the temple who were known
as the Righteous Seed and the Sons of Dawn. This connection to
James the Just, who succeeded Jesus in the position of the Zadok, or
Teacher of Righteousness, is part of the ancient Jewish tradition of
the hereditary transmission of holiness preserved by the Rex Deus
families.

HIRAM ABIF

Freemasonic tradition and ritual claim that the craft arose at the time
of Hiram Abif, who was killed by a blow to the temple for his refusal
to betray a secret. This creates an inescapable parallel with the recorded
details of the death of James the Just. Hiram was killed immediately
prior to the completion of Solomon's Temple and, almost 1,000
years later, when work on the Herodian Temple was nearing completion, building was brought to a temporary standstill as a mark of
respect for James, the brother of Jesus, who had just been ritually
murdered. In the opinion of Chris Knight and Robert Lomas, the
tradition concerning the death of Hiram Abif is used as an allegory
to mask the ritual commemoration of the murder of James the Just.
Thus, when Freemasons celebrate the ritual death of Hiram Abif,
they are commemorating one of the founders of Rex Deus.[28]

Another of the suppressed degrees—that of the Perfect Master—
supposedly commemorates the reburial of the corpse of Hiram Abif.
In this ritual, the lodge is lit by four groups of four candles, each
placed at the cardinal points of the compass. The ritual recounts that
King Solomon ordered Adoniram to build a tomb for Hiram Abif
in the form of an obelisk of black-and-white marble. The entrance
to the tomb, which was completed in nine days, was set between
two pillars supporting a square lintel engraved with the letter "j."
Thus is the association between this degree and the death of James
the Just made explicit. In this degree, the lodge is draped in green;
green and gold are the heraldic colors of the royal house of David.
Green and gold again occur as part of the 15th degree—that of the
Knight of the Sword and the Knight of the East—which celebrates
the building of Zerubbabel's Temple. We have always been puzzled
that, at Rosslyn, a place of such importance to Freemasonry, while
the building of Zerubbabel's Temple is commemorated on a lintel
near the retro-choir, there is no direct reference to Solomon's Temple,
only individual carvings of Solomonic interest.

The founding of the Knights Templar is also recorded in a suppressed degree of Masonic ritual, the Knight of the East and West.
This ritual states that the degree was first created in 1118 when
eleven knights took vows of secrecy, fraternity, and discretion under
the eagle of the patriarch of Jerusalem. These knights include all

Retro-choir, Rosslyn Chapel.

nine founders of the Knights Templar, with the addition of Count Fulk d'Anjou and Count Hughes I of Champagne. In this rite, the presiding officer is known as the Most Equitable Most Sovereign Prince Master, and the High Priest supports him. Knight and Lomas suggest that the Most Equitable Sovereign Prince Master was originally King Baldwin II of Jerusalem, and that the High Priest was most probably the Grand Master of the Templar order.

We suggest that it is far more likely that the High Priest in this ritual represents the patriarch of Jerusalem. During this ritual, a large Bible hung with seven seals is placed upon a pedestal. A floor display accompanies it consisting of a heptagon within a circle, in the center of which is a figure of a white-bearded, white-cloaked man with a golden girdle around his waist. The figure's extended hand holds seven stars that represent friendship, union, submission, discretion, fidelity, prudence, and temperance. This strange figure has a halo around his head, a two-edged sword issuing from his mouth, and is surrounded by seven candlesticks.[29] The seven seals dangling from the Bible and the seven stars are part of the principle of seven-foldness found in the Revelation of St. John the Divine, one of the two St. John's so revered by the Templars.

Another suppressed degree—the 20th degree, that of Grand Master—describes the terrible destruction of the second temple in Jerusalem by the Romans in 70 C.E. Its ritual tells of the grief experienced by the brethren who were in the Holy Land and how they had to flee from their homeland with the intention of erecting a third temple that would be a spiritual rather than a physical edifice.

Creation of this new spiritual temple of God on Earth became a sacred duty. The story describes how they divided themselves into a number of lodges before scattering throughout the length and breadth of Europe. One of these lodges came to Scotland, established itself at Kilwinning, and was charged with the sacred duty of keeping the records of their order. Thus the distinct outline of the story of the original Rex Deus families is described in this degree. As we have seen, another records the founding of the Knights Templar, while a third commemorates the death of James the Just.

Enshrining Rex Deus secrets in a variety of degrees within the complex symbolism of Freemasonry is akin to a man on the run seeking refuge in a large and crowded city. It is similar to the device used by Earl William in randomly hiding a plethora of Templar and Rex Deus symbolism among the crowded and apparently confused collection of carvings in Rosslyn Chapel. Despite the vigorous attempts of the Hanoverian censors, the rituals used in these degrees have been recorded for posterity and may well still be in use in France and America.

Not only did the spiritual inspiration of Freemasonry give us the gift of the American Constitution, but it also contributed a great deal to the establishment of the principles of *liberté, égalité, et fraternité* that inspired the French Revolution and, ultimately, the transformation of despotism into democracy. Freemasonry also played a major role in the campaign for the reunification of Italy through its influence on the Carbonari; both of the principal leaders of this revolutionary movement, Garibaldi and Mazzini, were active Freemasons. When their armies liberated Rome from the tyranny of the papacy and gave a vibrant new reality to the old Visconti dream of a united kingdom of Italy, Pope Pius IX, stripped of all temporal power, began his lifelong exile in his self-imposed prison of the Vatican.

The pope freely acknowledged the Freemasons as the true authors of his debasement and fulminated furiously against them in a series of encyclicals, papal bulls, and allocutions. Unlike many Masonic historians within the craft today, this aged pope was under no illusions as to the true origins of the diabolical organization that had stripped him of all earthly power. For him, Freemasonry derived directly from the heretical Order of the Knights Templar, whom he describes as being gnostic from their inception and followers of the Johannite Heresy. Nor was Pius under any illusions as to the true purpose of the Masonic fraternity, for, according to him, their aim was to destroy Holy Mother the Church. For him, there was little difference between the true aim of the Rex Deus families—that of reforming the Church around what they knew to be the true teachings of Jesus—and the destruction of the Church that had propelled him to the dizzy heights of the papacy. Should we doubt his views? Surely not, for this was Pius IX, who first promulgated the doctrine of Papal Infallibility.

CHAPTER 19

Spiritual Awakening in the 21st Century

In the first nineteen centuries of Christianity, which were largely dominated by a repressive Church that sought perpetual control over the spirits, hearts, and minds of its flock, the hidden streams of Rex Deus did their work well. They preserved, sometimes at horrendous cost, the true teachings of Jesus and the spiritual path that was his lasting legacy—a path founded on the ancient, tried, and tested principles of initiation and completely free from restrictive and misleading dogma. This experiential path revealed to novices the steps to take to reunite their individual and innate "divine spark" with almighty God and thus attain enlightenment.

This was no mere exercise to be followed out of fear of eternal hellfire and damnation, but a dedicated search for truth, undertaken as an act of gratitude for the wonderful gift of life. The dissemination of Rex Deus traditions using the Grail sagas, the tarot, and Freemasonry, and its many offshoots and imitators bore fruit in the esoteric revival that occurred toward the end of the 19th century when the Catholic Church was visibly losing its grip. Thus began a process that is only now approaching its culmination.

HIDDEN STREAMS OF SPIRITUALITY

By the end of the 19th century, the world had grown dissatisfied with the tired, outworn, and empty dogma of the Church—dogma perceived as increasingly irrelevant to the modern world. For a time at least, the allure of science and the temptations of the postwar consumer society seemed set to replace religion as the main focus of life. This illusion did not last, however. Spiritual curiosity grew steadily and cumulatively throughout the 20th century and crystallized around a growing core of deep dissatisfaction with modern materialism.

The horrors of scientific discovery began to outweigh its benefits in a way that instilled fear among people of all nations and stimulated a profound distrust of political and scientific "experts," whose pronouncements appeared to dominate our lives. One American writer voiced this sense of unease along with a glimmer of realistic hope:

> The evolution of consciousness has given us not only the
> Cheops Pyramid, the Brandenburg Concertos, and the Theory
> of Relativity, but also the burning of witches, the Holocaust,
> and the bombing of Hiroshima. But that same evolution of
> consciousness gives us the potential to live peacefully and in
> harmony with the natural world in the future. Our evolution
> continues to offer us freedom of choice. We can consciously
> alter our behavior by changing our values and attitudes to
> regain the spirituality and ecological awareness we have lost.[1]

He was far from alone, for under the pressures of the crises confronting mankind during the last half of the 20th century, people were thinking deeply, critically reevaluating old conceptions, and beginning to view the world with new eyes. In the 1950s, P. W. Martin predicted that:

> For the first time in history, the scientific spirit of inquiry is being
> turned upon the other side of consciousness. There is a good
> prospect that the discoveries can be held this time and so become
> no longer the lost secret, but the living heritage of man.[2]

Curiosity about ancient systems of meditation grew apace, and the study and spiritual discipline of the initiatory tradition came into the open at last.

The social activism of the 1960s and the consciousness revolution of the early 1970s combined to create a new and historic synthesis that revealed the possibility of a revolutionary and outward transformation of society arising from a multiplicity of individual spiritual forms of internal transformation. This new awareness has continued to grow and now inspires an ever-expanding group of spiritually inspired people who, individually and collectively, form a growing pool of consciousness that carries with it potential benefits for all mankind.

The gentle and courageous man, Archbishop Desmond Tutu, outlined the nature of the problems we face:

> We find that we are placed in a delicate framework of vital relationships with the divine, with fellow human beings, and with the rest of creation. We violate nature only at our peril, and are meant to live as members of one family. This is the law of our being, and when we break this law things go disastrously wrong.[3]

The answers can be found on the initiatory path in all the traditions:

> We are in pursuit of an extensive and perfect freedom at its highest level. Perfect freedom is what we seek now—not in the future. Civilization is neither to have electric lights nor aeroplanes, nor to produce nuclear bombs. Civilization is to hold mutual affection and to respect each other.
> Nichidatsu Fujii, Founder, Nipponzan Myohoji
> Buddhist order[4]

To create this civilization, we need to learn to let go of our dogmatic attitudes in religion, politics, economics, and philosophy, and escape the complex web of human relationships that these disciplines sustain. In the words of Meister Eckhart, "Only those who dare to let go can dare to re-enter."[5]

AN APPARENT MULTITUDE OF CHOICES

The rich tapestry of worldwide mystical traditions has now become available to entire populations, both in their original form and in contemporary commentaries. Mystical literature is available in bookshops, at airport newsstands, in hardback erudite editions, and in paperback. Courses offering instruction in a wide range of meditative and contemplative techniques are easily accessible; university extension courses, weekend seminars, Buddhist centers, and Hindu ashrams abound; Theosophists and anthroposophists thrive, lecture, and publish. Highly effective and valid initiatory schools and colleges, like the Ramtha School of Ancient Wisdom in America and Beshara, the Sufi center in Scotland, help people connect to both new and traditional sources of spiritual change, personal transformation, and integration. This all contributes to a growing sense of harmony and unity.

The modern information age also plays a role in this transformative process, which is accelerating exponentially with the development of the Internet. This explosion of interest in spiritual matters, however, can sometimes be hindered or even impeded by the non-stop flood of information that assails us from every side. Thus the crucial problem that faces any earnest seeker of spiritual growth now is one of discernment. How can we decide what is true and what is false? By what standards can we judge the vast variety of options that are on offer? We find the answer in the words of Jesus the Nazorean: "By their fruits shall ye know them."

The tidal wave of interest in so-called New Age philosophy and lifestyle has spawned a vast range of publishing and a proliferation of courses, workshops, and seminars that seem to offer an instant "cure-all" for the ills of the modern world. Many of the books and courses on offer are variants on techniques and pathways, old and new, valid and spurious. Some are led by teachers of great insight and ability, others by plausible rogues whose intent is focused more on the engraving on a dollar bill than on the Holy Grail. Navigating this maze of options is not easy without effective criteria by which to assess them.

All valid spiritual paths, regardless of the culture from which they spring or the technical jargon in which they are dressed, have certain principles and values in common. First, they are not "instant" in their effects; they require humility, patience, perseverance, and dedicated work. They are experiential rather than informational in content. All are based on revealing to the novice that which is already within him or her, recognition of the divine spark within all of creation. The spiritual quality described by the gifted Jesuit, Pierre Teilhard de Chardin, as "the withiness of all things" is the same as the force that links the Sufis to all of creation so that they can recognize the divine unity within the diversity of people or species. The true spiritual path or Way leads seekers into the path of service to the community within which they move, as it did the initiates of the Egyptian temple mysteries of ancient times, the Templar Knights and Sufis of the medieval era, or the mystics of more recent times such as Mother Teresa.

True travelers on the Way no longer simply believe in God; they know that God is and, furthermore, that God is within us all. Thus, by serving others, they serve God. The overwhelming need for this type of transformation, and the comforting fact that a massive change in consciousness is taking place among us now, was voiced by M. C. Richards:

> Human consciousness is crossing a threshold as mighty as the one from the Middle Ages to the Renaissance. People are hungering and thirsting after experience that feels true to them on the inside, after so much hard work mapping the outer spaces of the physical world. They are gaining courage to ask for what they need; living interconnections, a sense of individual worth, shared opportunities. . . . New symbols are rising: pictures of wholeness. Freedom sings within us as well as outside us. . . . Sages seem to have foretold this "second coming." People don't want to feel stuck, they want to be able to change."[6]

Mysticism in the Church

Rejection of the outworn strictures of dogma should not blind us to the fact that mysticism and initiation have played an important role in all of the major monotheistic religions. The works of medieval Christian mystics like Hildegarde von Bingen, Mechtilde of Magdeburg, Julian of Norwich, and the sublime Meister Eckhart brought a penetrating spiritual insight into the problems of their day. Now, because of their supreme relevance to the modern era, they are again being studied by millions of people across the world. However, their insight and humility posed enormous problems to the rigid and corrupt Church in the Middle Ages, and they suffered for it. Meister Eckhart is still on the condemned list of the Catholic Church.

Study of a Christianized form of the Kabbala became popular in Europe from the 13th century onward and this spiritual path still exerts an appeal in the modern era that transcends all religious denominations. The Kabbala has been one of the main pillars of faith for the Hasidim in Orthodox Jewry for nearly three centuries. The Sufi initiatory tradition still flourishes within Islam. Sufi teaching began to fascinate Western devotees from the earliest years of the 20th century, and one respected esoteric school in Scotland, the Beshara School, founded on the teachings of Bulent Rauf, exists to promote an important aspect of this respected initiatory path.

We have chosen the examples given above for good reason—they are all establishments or esoteric systems that can be assessed by the lifestyle and insight displayed by their adherents. Moreover, they hold irrevocably to the essential truth of all being—that God is all in all— and their teaching inevitably results in a life dedicated to service, love, and harmony. We chose them because their aims and methodology display the essentials of the one true path preserved by the Rex Deus families despite appalling persecution. There is but one truth; valid paths to that truth only appear to differ in language and cultural aspects. The discipline, dedication, and experience they entail remain the same. The experiential manner of learning means that initiates use their spiritual gnosis as the mainspring of action in the temporal world. This ability differs markedly from mainstream religious experience.

There is, of course, a wonderful uniformity of principle found in all the great faiths, for they share a common spiritual source for all their teachings. This manifests itself in a surprising degree of unanimity between them on moral issues. However, these religious moral principles have not failed because they have been tried and found wanting; they have almost always been regarded as too difficult to achieve, or as ideals that are frankly simply beyond our reach. In the Talmud is the simple instruction: "What is hateful to you, do not to your fellow men. That is the entire law, all the rest is commentary." Buddhism teaches us: "Hurt not others with that which pains yourself." In Zoroastrianism, we find: "That nature only is good when it shall not do unto another whatever is not good for its own self." In the Gospel of St. Matthew, it is written: "All things whatsoever ye would that men should do to you, do ye even so unto them; for this is the law of the prophets." Islam teaches simply: "No one of you is a believer until he desires for his brother that which he desires for himself." In the Hindu *Mahabharata*, it is written, "This is the sum of duty: do naught to others which if done to thee would cause thee pain." Yet despite this unanimity of ideals, Aristotle's sad comment, "It is more difficult to organise peace than to win a war," written more than 2,000 years ago, is just as true today.

There is an urgent need to go beyond religious ritual observance and access the world of the spirit that will enable us to act on
our principles, not merely pay lip service to them. The changing
spiritual perspective that can bring this about was mentioned by the
Catholic theologian Anthony Padovano, when he addressed a con-
ference on meditation in 1976:

> The religious response that has occurred in the Western
> world—a revolution that has made us more sensitive to the
> religions of the Orient—is an understanding that whatever
> answers there are must come from ourselves. The spirit
> demanding interiority causes the great turmoil in the religions.
> Faith is not dying in the West, it is merely moving inside.[7]

In 1968, Professor Joseph Campbell, argued that:

> The only possibility for our time is the free association of men
> and women of like spirit ... not a handful but a thousand
> heroes, ten thousand heroes, who will create a future image of
> what humankind will be.[8]

Thoreau, writing more than 140 years ago, stated simply: "Live
your beliefs and you can turn the world around." The Nobel laureate
Ilya Prigogin believes: "We are in a very exiting moment in history,
perhaps a turning point. Stress and perturbation can thrust us into a
new and higher order ... Science is proving the reality of a deep cultural vision."[9] At our last meeting with the French mystic and initiate
Frederic Lionel in Paris in 1997, he made the following statement:

> You are writing of matters that are known to very few. You have
> a sacred duty, you must continue, there is not much time.

For if our world cannot be transformed into a global, just, and
equitable society, stripped of violence, greed, and poverty, why should
it survive? We can find the answers to these problems in the hidden
wisdom preserved by the Rex Deus families and those who followed
the tried and trusted initiatory paths of other great faiths. The question is: Have we the wit, the humility, and the courage to apply them?

We live in a world of turmoil, a world of war, famine, and injustice,
but we can change this if we seek the means to do so. Recent events in
Northern Ireland, the peaceful transition of power in South Africa, the

massive outpourings of aid in the face of natural disasters such as famine and earthquake all demonstrate that, in our hearts, we have the will. The custodians of truth throughout the ages have preserved for our benefit the spiritual engine that can drive us to transform our world as it transforms our own inner and outer lives. That can provide the way.

The new Aquarian age is prophesied to be one in which science will be harnessed to the service of humanity—an age of increasing international harmony within which mankind can apply warmhearted generosity to practical and humanitarian ends. Only we, and others like us, can ensure that this will come to pass by creating an environment wherein true fraternity, compassion, and justice are realities and not simply ideals. We must utilize this spiritual awareness as the motor for action in the temporal world. Action is indeed the magic word!

Thank God our time is now
When wrong comes up to meet us everywhere
Never to leave us 'till we take
The greatest stride of soul
Man ever took.
Affairs are now soul size
The enterprise
Is Exploration unto God.
Where are you making for?
It takes so many thousand years to wake.
But will you wake
For pity's sake

"A Sleep of Prisoners," Christopher Fry

For:

There is only one religion,
the religion of Love.
There is only one language,
the language of the heart.
There is only one God
he is omnipresent.
There is only one caste,
the caste of humanity.

Sathya Sai Baba

NOTES

INTRODUCTION

1. Published in London by Jonathan Cape in 1982.
2. Broadcast in the Timewatch series.
3. *The Woman with the Alabaster Jar* (Rochester, VT: Bear & Co., 1993).
4. See Lawrence Gardner, *Bloodline of the Holy Grail* (Shaftsbury, UK: Element Books, 1995) and HRH Prince Michael of Albany, *The Lost Monarchy of Scotland* (Shaftsbury, UK: Element Books, 1998).

CHAPTER I

1. Colin Wilson, *From Atlantis to the Sphinx* (London: Virgin Books, 1997), p. 81.
2. Bauval Robert and Gilbert Adrian, *The Orion Mystery* (London: Heinemann, 1994), p. 58.
3. I. E. S. Edwards, *The Pyramids of Egypt* (London: Pelican Books, 1947), p. 150.
4. Robert Bauval and Adrian Gilbert, *The Orion Mystery* (London: Heinemann, 1994), p. 59.
5. Gaston Maspero, *Recueil des Travaux Relatifs a la Philologie et l'Archaéologie Égyptiennes et Assyriennes III* (Cairo: Institut d'Égypte, 1887), p. 179.
6. J. H. Breasted, *Development of Religion and Thought in Ancient Egypt* (Philadelphia: University of Pennsylvania Press, 1972), p. 102.
7. Bauval, *The Orion Mystery*, p. 63.
8. Bauval, *The Orion Mystery*, p. 63.
9. Edwards, *The Pyramids of Egypt*, p. 151.
10. R. O. Faulkner, *The Ancient Egyptian Pyramid Texts* (Warminster: Aris & Philips, 1993), p. v.
11. John Anthony West, *Serpent in the Sky* (Wheaton, IL: Quest Books, 1993), p. 1.
12. David Rohl, *Legend: the Genesis of Civilisation* (London: Century, 1998), p. 310.
13. M. Rice, *Egypt's Making: The Origins of Ancient Egypt 5000–2000 BC* (London: Routledge, 1990), p. 33.
14. H. J. Kantor, "The Relative Chronology of Egypt and its Foreign

Correlations Before the Late Bronze Age," published in *Chronologies in Old World Archaeology*, p. 6.

15. Rohl, *Genesis of Civilisation*, p. 316.

16. D. E. Derry, "The Dynastic Race in Egypt," *Journal of Egyptian Archaeology*: 42 (1956), pp. 80–85.

17. H. Frankfort, *Kingship and the Gods* (Chicago: University of Chicago Press, 1948), p. 101.

18. A. E. P. Weighall, *Travels in the Upper Egyptian Desert* (London, 1909).

19. H. Winkler, *Rock Drawings of Southern Upper Egypt* (Oxford: Oxford University Press, 1938–9).

20. Rohl, *Genesis of Civilisation*, p. 274.

21. Rohl, *Genesis of Civilisation*, p. 316.

22. Rohl, *Genesis of Civilisation*, p. 265.

23. Bauval and Hancock, *Keeper of Genesis* (London: William Heineman, 1996), p. 203.

24. Bauval and Hancock, *Keeper of Genesis*, p. 193.

25. G. Goyon, *Le Secret des Batisseurs des Grandes Pyramides: Kheops* (Paris: Pygmalion, 1991).

26. Bauval and Hancock, *Keeper of Genesis*, p. 154.

27. Aristotle, *De Caelo II*.

28. Proclus Diodachus (5th cent. A.D.) *Commentaries on the Timaeus*.

29. Bauval and Hancock, *Keeper of Genesis*, p. 154.

30. Edwards, *The Pyramids of Egypt*, pp. 284–286.

31. Wilson, *From Atlantis to the Sphinx*, p. 21.

32. Bauval and Hancock, *Keeper of Genesis*, p. 228.

33. E. A. E. Reymond, *Mythical Origins of the Egyptian Temple* (Manchester: Manchester University Press, 1969), p. 273.

34. André Vanden Broeck, *Al-Kemi* (New York: Lindisfarne Press, 1987).

35. Wilson, *From Atlantis to the Sphinx*, p. 32.

36. René Schwaller de Lubicz, *Sacred Science* (Rochester, VT: Inner Traditions, 1998).

37. Wilson, *From Atlantis to the Sphinx*, p. 14.

38. Louis Pauwels and Jacques Bergier, *The Dawn of Magic* (London: Panther, 1964), p. 247.

39. Rohl, *Genesis of Civilisation*, p. 381.

40. Rohl, *Genesis of Civilisation*, p. 381.

CHAPTER 2

1. Rachi, *Pentatuque selon Rachi, La Genèse* (Paris: Samule et Odette Levy, 1993), p. 251.

2. *Sepher Hajashar*, ch. 26 (Prague: 1840).

3. "Have you seen the old man and woman who brought a foundling from the street and now claim him as their son?" Isadore Epstein, *The Babylonian Talmud* (London: Socino Press, 1952).

4. *The Koran* (The Prophets), Sura 21.72; also cited by Ahmed Osman, *Out of Egypt* (London: Century, 1998), p. 12.

5. See Genesis 14:19.

6. See *Midrash Bereshith Rabba*, p. 44.

7. Sigmund Freud, *Moses and Monotheism* (Paris: Gallimard, 1939).

8. E. Sellin, *Moses and His Significance for Israelite-Jewish History* (N.p., n.d.).

9. Osman, *Out of Egypt*, pp. 10, 12, 16.

10. A. Osman, *Stranger in the Valley of the Kings* (London: HarperCollins, 1998).

11. A. Weighall, *The Life and Times of Akenhaten* (New York: Cooper Square Publishers, 2000).

12. T. Davis, *The Tomb of Iouiya and Touiya* (London, 1907).

13. *Imago*, 1:1912, pp. 346–347.

14. R. Feather, *The Copper Scroll Decoded* (London: Thorsons, 1999), p. 34. Also confirmed by Joseph Popper-Linkeus in *Der Sohn des Konigs von Egypten. Phantasieen eines Realisten* (N.p.: Carl Resiner, 1899).

15. Osman, *Moses: Pharaoh of Egypt*.

16. Osman, *Moses: Pharaoh of Egypt*, p. 13.

17. M. Cotterell, *The Tutenkhamun Prophecies* (London: Headline, 1999), p. 335.

18. Sigmund Freud, *Moses and Monotheism* (Paris: Gallimard, 1939).

19. Freud, *Moses and Monotheism*.

20. Cited by Feather, *The Copper Scroll Decoded*, p. 36.

21. F. Petrie, *The Religion of Ancient Egypt* (Belle-Fourche, SD: Kessinger, 2003)

22. M. and R. Sabbah, *Les Secrets de L'Exode* (Paris: Godefroy, 2000), p. 99.

23. Osman, *Moses Pharaoh of Egypt*, pp. 172–173.

24. Faulkner, *Book of the Dead*, p. 29.

25. Geddes and Grosset, *Ancient Egypt Myth and History* (New Lanark: Geddes & Grosset Ltd., 1997), p. 268.

26. A. F. D'Olivet, *La Langue Hébraïque restitué* (Paris: L'Age d'Homme, 1991).

27. Sabbah, *Les Secrets de l'Exode*.

28. Sabbah, *Les Secrets de l'Exode*.

29. Sabbah, *Les Secrets de l'Exode*.

30. David M. Rohl, *A Test of Time* (London: Century, 1995), p. 284.

31. Sabbah, *Les Secrets de l'Exode*, p. 7.

32. Rachi, *Pentatuque selon Rach l'Exode* (Paris: Samuel et Odette Levy, 1993).

33. M. C. Betro: *Hieroglyphes, Les Mysteres de l'ecriture* (Paris: Flammarion, 1995), p. 22.

34. Freud, *Moses and Monotheism*.

35. Sabbah, *Les Secrets de l'Exode*, p. 6.

36. Sabbah, *Les Secrets de l'Exode*.

37. Feather, *The Copper Scroll Decoded*, p. 123.

38. Sabbah, *Les Secrets de l'Exode*, p. 112.

CHAPTER 3

1. Sigmund Freud, *Moses and Monotheism* (Paris: Gallimard, 1939).

2. J. M. Allegro, *The Dead Sea Scrolls and the Christian Myth* (London: Abacus, 1981), p. 65.

3. N. Cantor, *The Sacred Chain—a history of the Jews* (London: Fontana, 1996), p. 7.

4. Cantor, *The Sacred Chain*, p. 11.

5. P. Johnson, *A History of the Jews* (London: Orion Books, 1993), p. 42.

6. Allegro, J. M., *The Dead Sea Scrolls and the Christian Myth* (London: Abacus, 1981), p. 40.

7. Allegro, *The Dead Sea Scrolls*, p. 173.

8. Allegro, *The Dead Sea Scrolls*, p. 174.

9. *The Wisdom of Solomon* ch. 10, v. 17 in the Apocryphal books of the Old Testament.

10. K. Armstrong, *A History of God* (London: Mandarin, 1994), p. 82.

11. Josephus, *Antiquities of the Jews*, bk. 3, ii, 3, 49 (Edinburgh: Nimmo, 1869).

12. W. Keller *The Bible as History* (London: Hodder & Stoughton, 1956).

13. Cantor, *The Sacred Chain*.

14. R. Lane Fox, *The Unauthorised Version: Truth and Fiction in the Bible* (London: Penguin, 1991), pp. 225–233.

15. Ammon Ben Tor (ed.), *The Archaeology of Ancient Israel*, R. Greenberg (trans.) (New Haven, CT: Yale University Press, 1992).

16. Johnson, *A History of the Jews*, p. 43.

17. Armstrong, *A History of God*, p. 19.

18. Rachi, *Pentatuque selon Rachi, l'Exode* (Paris: Samuel et Odette Levy, 1993).

19. Johnson, *A History of the Jews*, p. 45.

20. Armstrong, *A History of Jerusalem*, p. 27.

21. Armstrong, *A History of Jerusalem*, p. 30; Allegro, *The Dead Sea Scrolls*, p. 61.

22. Armstrong, *A History of Jerusalem*, p. 30.

23. A. Baring and J. Cashford, *The Myth of the Goddess* (London: Penguin, 1991), p. 454.

24. *Jerusalem Bible* (London: Eyre & Spottiswoode, 1968), p. 419. The *Jerusalem Bible* has been translated directly from Hebrew and not via Greek. See also I. M. Zeitlin, *Ancient Judaism* (Cambridge: Polity Press, 1992), p. 173; G. Hancock, *The Sign & the Seal* (London: Mandarin, 1993), pp. 419–420.

25. A. E. Cowley, *Aramaic Papyri of the Fifth Century BC* (Oxford: Oxford University Press, 1923).

26. Feather, *The Copper Scroll Decoded*, pp. 255–256.

27. Cowley, *Aramaic Papyri*.

28. Armstrong, *A History of Jerusalem*, p. 59.

29. Armstrong, *A History of Jerusalem*, p. 40.

30. D. Ussishkin, "King Solomon's Palaces," *Biblical Archaeologist* 35:1973.

31. Armstrong, *A History of Jerusalem*, p. 34.

32. S. Sanmell, *Judaism and Christian Beginnings* (Oxford: Oxford University Press, 1978), p. 22.

33. Aristobulus, *Fragment 5* (cited in Eusebius, *Preparatio Evangelica* 13.12.11).

34. J. Pritchard, (ed.), *Solomon and Sheba* (London: Phaidon, n.d.), p. 13.

35. Pritchard, *Solomon and Sheba*, p. 48.

36. Pritchard, *Solomon and Sheba*, in a chapter by Edward Ullendorff, p. 104.

37. E. A. Wallis Budge, *The Queen of Sheba and her only son Menelik being the 'Book of the Glory of Kings' (Kebra Nagast)* (London: Research Associates School Times Publications, 2000).

38. J. Doresse, *Ancient Cities and Temples of Ethiopia* (London: Elek Books, 1959), p. 21.

39. Graham Phillips, *The Moses Legacy* (London: Sidgewick & Jackson, 2002), p. 52.

40. Isadore Epstein, *Judaism* (London: Pelican, 1964), p. 37.

CHAPTER 4

1. Cited in *The Historical Atlas of the Jewish People*, Eli Barnavi (ed.) (London: Hutchinson, 1992), p. 22.

2. Paul Johnson, *A History of the Jews* (London: Orion, 1993), p. 82.

3. Isadore Epstein, *Judaism* (Harmondsworth: Pelican, 1964), p. 83.

4. Robin Lane Fox, *The Unauthorised Version* (London: Penguin, 1992), p. 53.

5. Dan Cohn-Sherbok, *A Concise Encyclopedia of Judaism* (Oxford: Oneworld, 1998), pp. 61–62.

6. Cohn-Sherbok, *A Concise Encyclopedia of Judaism*, pp. 43–44.

7. Fox, *The Unauthorised Version*, p. 72.

8. Armstrong, *A History of God* (London: Mandarin, 1994), p. 79.

9. Norman Cantor, *The Sacred Chain* (London: Fontana, 1996), p. 29. Also cited in B. S. J. Isserlin *The Israelites* (London: Thames and Hudson, 1998), p. 204.

10. M. and R. Sabbah, *Les Secrets de L'Exode* (Paris: Godfroy, 2000), p. 6. See also Sigmund Freud, *Moses and Monotheism* (Paris: Gallimard, 1939), pp. 96, 123.

11. Cantor, *The Sacred Chain*, p. 29.

12. Armstrong, *A History of Jerusalem*, p. 86.

13. Armstrong, *A History of Jerusalem*, p. 87.

14. Armstrong, *A History of God*, p. 75.

15. Armstrong, *A History of Jerusalem*, p. 96.

16. Epstein, *Judaism*, p. 85.

17. Epstein, *Judaism*, p. 91.

CHAPTER 5

1. Josephus, *Antiquities of the Jews,* bk. 18, ch. 1, 2–6 (Edinburgh: Nimmo, 1868).

2. Armstrong, *A History of Jerusalem* (London: Mandarin, 1994), p. 121.

3. Josephus, *Antiquities*, bk. 18, ch. 1, v 5.

4. Josephus, *Antiquities*, bk. 18, ch. 1, v. 5.

5. Epstein, *Judaism*, p. 112.

6. Johnson, *A History of Christianity*, pp. 15–16.

7. Epstein, *Judaism*, p. 97.

8. Robert Eisenman, *The Dead Sea Scrolls and the First Christians* (Shaftsbury, UK: Element Books, 1996), p. 227.

9. Epstein, *Judaism*, p. 97.

10. Josephus, *Antiquities*, bk. 18, v. 6.

11. Geza Vermes, *Jesus the Jew* (London: HarperCollins, 1973), p. 79

12. Armstrong, *A History of Jerusalem*, p. 116.

13. Eisenman, *James the Brother of Jesus*, p. 200.

14. Eisenman, *James the Brother of Jesus*, p. 133.

15. Zohar 59b on "Noah."

16. Epstein, *Judaism*, p. 103.

17. Epstein, *Judaism*, p. 105.

18. *Jerusalem Talmud*, Sanhedrin, X, 5.

19. Johnson, *A History of Christianity*, p. 10.
20. Strabo, *Geographica*, 16. 2. 46.
21. Peter Richardson, *Herod: King of the Jews and Friend of the Romans* (Columbia, SC: University of South Carolina Press, 1996), pp. 184–185.
22. Josephus, *The Wars of the Jews*, bk. 1, 4, 22; *Antiquities*, bk. 16, 1, 47.
23. Josephus, *Wars*, 1.4.24; *Antiquities*, 16.1.47.
24. Josephus, *Antiquities*, 15.2. 59–65.
25. Macrobius, *Saturnalia*, 2.4.1.
26. Josephus, *Wars*, 1.6.48–55; *Antiquities*, 17.1.49–67.
27. Trevor Ravenscroft and Tim Wallace-Murphy, *The Mark of the Beast*, (London: Sphere, 1990), p. 113.
28. Epstein, *Judaism*, p. 106.
29. Josephus, *Antiquities*, bk. 17, ch. 10, 9; Josephus, *Wars*, bk. 2, ch. 5, 1.
30. Jospehus, *Antiquities*, bk. 17, ch. 10, 10; *Wars*, bk. 2, ch. 5, 2.
31. Eisenman, *James the Brother of Jesus*, p. xxi.
32. Josephus, *Wars*, 1.1.
33. Mark Allen Powell, *The Jesus Debate* (London: Lion, 1998), p. 30.
34. Hugh Schonfield, *The Essene Odyssey* (Shaftsbury, UK: Element Books, 1985), p. 39.
35. Johnson, *A History of Christianity*, pp. 19–20.
36. Josephus, *Antiquities*, bk. 18, ch. 5, v. 2.
37. John Dominic Crossan, *Jesus: A Revolutionary Biography* (San Francisco: HarperSanFrancisco, 1994), p. 34.
38. Joan E. Taylor, *The Immerser: John the Baptist in Second Temple Judaism* (Cambridge: Wm. B. Eerdmans—Lightning Source, 1997), p. 278.
39. A. N. Wilson, *Jesus* (London: HarperCollins, 1993), p. xvi.
40. Armstrong, *A History of Jerusalem*, p. 145.
41. James Robinson (ed.), "Gospel of Thomas," in *The Nag Hammadi Library* (London: HarperCollins, 1990), p. 108.
42. Morton Smith, *The Secret Gospel* (Wellingborough, UK: Aquarian Press, 1985).
43. See Matthew 21:1–11; Mark 11:1–11; Luke 19:28–44; John 12:12–19.
44. See Matthew 21:12; Mark 11:15; Luke 19:45.
45. Philo of Alexandria, *De Legatione ad Gaium*, p. 301; Epstein, *Judaism*, p. 106; Wilson, *Paul: The Mind of the Apostle*, p. 56.
46. Wilson, *Paul: The Mind of the Apostle*, p. 107.
47. Tacitus, *Annals*, 15, 44.

CHAPTER 6

1. James Robinson (ed.), "Gospel of Thomas," v. 12, in *The Nag Hammadi Library* (London: HarperCollins, 1990).
2. *Pseudo-Clementine Recognitions*, 1, 4.
3. Epiphanius, *Against Heresies*, 78.7.7.
4. Robert Eisenman, *James the Brother of Jesus* (London: Faber & Faber, 1997), p. xx.
5. Eusabius, *Ecclesiastical History*, 2, 234–235; Epiphanius, *Against Heresies*, 78, 14, 1–2.

6. In a series on St. Paul on BBC Radio 4 broadcast.

7. A. N. Wilson, *Jesus* (London: HarperCollins, 1993), p. 101.

8. Fida Hassnain, *A Search for the Historical Jesus* (Bath: Gateway Books, 1994) p. 84.

9. Hassnain, *A Search for the Historical Jesus*, p. 84.

10. Published in Rochester, VT, by Bear & Co., 1993.

11. See Matthew 26:7; also described in Mark 14:3

12. Margaret Starbird, *The Woman with the Alabaster Jar* (Rochester, VT: Bear and Co., 1993), p. 36.

13. Andrew Welburn, *The Beginnings of Christianity* (Edinburgh: Floris Books, 1991), p. 55.

14. Eisenman, *James the Brother of Jesus*, p. xix.

15. Epiphanius, *Against Heresies*, A29.4.1.

16. Eisenman, *James the Brother of Jesus*, p. 79.

17. Eisenman, *The Dead Sea Scrolls*, p. 340.

18. Eisenman, *The Dead Sea Scrolls*, p. 146

19. The Community Rule, viii, 20ff., from the original Dead Sea Scrolls.

20. Johnson, *A History of Christianity*, p. 41.

21. Tim Wallace-Murphy and Marilyn Hopkins, *Rosslyn: Guardian of the Secrets of the Holy Grail* (Shaftsbury, UK: Element Books, 1999), p. 67.

22. Cited by Laurence Gardner in *The Bloodline of the Holy Grail* (Shaftsbury, UK: Element Books, 1995), p. 154.

23. Robert Eisenman devotes an entire chapter to Paul's attack on James, citing a variety of sources in chapter 16 of *James the Brother of Jesus*. See also the *Pseudo-Clementine Recognitions.*

24. A glossed-over account of this can be read in Acts 21:33.

25. Wilson, *Paul: The Mind of the Apostle*, p. 54.

26. Josephus, *Antiquities*, bk. 14, ch. 8, v.3.

27. Eisenman, *The Dead Sea Scrolls,* p. 230.

28. B. San. 81b–82b in the *Mishna Sanhedrin.*

29. Armstrong, *A History of Jerusalem*, p. 151.

30. Jerome, *Lives of Illustrious Men* 2.

31. Eisenman, *The Dead Sea Scrolls,* p. 262.

32. Armstrong, *A History of Jerusalem*, p. 151.

33. Ute Ranke-Heinemann, *Putting Away Childish Things* (San Francisco: HarperSanFrancisco, 1995), p. 173.

34. Josephus, *Wars*, bk. 2, ch. 17, v. 4.

35. Josephus, *Wars*, bk. 2, ch. 20, v. 1.

Chapter 7

1. Neil Faulkner, *Apocalypse: The Great Jewish Revolt against Rome* (Stroud, Gloucestershire: Tempus, 2002), p. 276.

2. Robert Eisenman, *James the Brother of Jesus* (London: Faber & Faber, 1997), p. xxi.

3. Karen Armstrong, *A History of Jerusalem* (London: Mandarin, 1996), p. 156.

4. Sifre on Leviticus 19:8

5. Armstrong, *A History of Jerusalem*, pp. 168–169.

6. Eusabius, *Ecclesiastical History*, IV, v.

7. Eusabius, *Ecclesiastical History*, III, xi; see also Armstrong, *A History of Jerusalem*, p. 153.

8. Fida Hassnain, *A Search for the Historical Jesus* (Bath: Gateway, 1994), p. 55–60.

9. Marilyn Hopkins, G. Simmans, and Tim Wallace-Murphy, *Rex Deus* (Shaftsbury, UK: Element Books, 2000), p. 79.

10. *Guidebook to Les Saintes Maries de la Mer*, p. 3.

11. Andrew Welburn, *The Beginnings of Christianity* (Edinburgh: Floris Books, 1991), p. 87.

12. Armstrong, *A History of Jerusalem*, p. 155.

13. Ralph Ellis, *Jesus: Last of the Pharaohs* (Dorset: EDFU Books, 1991), p. 208.

14. Mark Allen Powell, *The Jesus Debate* (Oxford: Lion, 1998), p. 41.

15. Eisenman, *James the Brother of Jesus*, p. 54.

16. Hugh Schonfield, *Those Incredible Christians* (London: Hutchinson, 1968), p. 56.

17. Burton L. Mack, *The Lost Gospel* (Shaftsbury, UK: Element Books, 1993), p. 2.

18. Mack, *The Lost Gospel*, p. 4.

19. Schonfield Hugh, *Those Incredible Christians*, p. 48

CHAPTER 8

1. *De Trinitate*, 7.7.10.

2. Matthew Fox, *The Coming of the Cosmic Christ* (San Francisco: HarperSanFrancisco, 1998), pp. 31–32.

3. R. I. Moore, *The Formation of a Persecuting Society* (Oxford: Basil Blackwell & Co., 1990), p. 12.

4. Moore, *The Formation of a Persecuting Society*, p. 12.

5. Paul Johnson, *A History of Christianity* (Weidenfeld & Nicolson, 1978), p. 87.

6. Trevor Ravenscroft and Tim Wallace-Murphy, *The Mark of the Beast* (London: Sphere, 1990), p. 124.

7. David Christie-Murray, *A History of Heresy* (Oxford: Oxford University Press, 1989), p. 1.

8. Johnson, *A History of Christianity*, p. 117.

9. Johnson, *A History of Christianity*, pp. 116–117.

10. Cardinal Ratzinger speaking in 1990, cited in Baigent and Leigh's *The Dead Sea Scrolls Deception* (London: Corgi, 1992), p. 191.

11. Hopkins, Simmans, and Wallace-Murphy, *Rex Deus*, p. 100.

12. Ravenscroft and Wallace-Murphy, *The Mark of the Beast*, p. 79.

13. Tim Wallace-Murphy, *The Templar Legacy and the Masonic Inheritance within Rosslyn Chapel* (London: Friends of Rosslyn, 1994), p.12.

14. Johnson, *A History of Christianity*, p. 135–138.

15. Wallace-Murphy, *The Templar Legacy and the Masonic Inheritance*, p.13.

16. Bede, *A History of the English Church and People* (London: Penguin, 1978), p. 66.

17. *Trias Thermaturga*, p. 156b.

18. Isabel Hill Elder *Celt, Druid & Culdee* (London: Covenant, 1994).

19. HRH Prince Michael of Albany, *The Forgotten Monarchy of Scotland* (Shaftsbury, UK: Element Books, 1998), p. 30.

20. HRH Prince Michael, *The Forgotten Monarchy of Scotland*, p. 19.
21. Elder, *Celt, Druid & Culdee*, pp. 131–132, 134.
22. Barry Dunford, *The Holy Land of Scotland* (Aberfeldy, Perthshire, UK: Brigadoon Books, 1996).
23. Wallace-Murphy and Hopkins, *Rosslyn: Guardian of the Secrets of the Holy Grail* (Shaftsbury, UK: Element Books, 1998), p. 83.
24. Ravenscroft and Wallace-Murphy, *The Mark of the Beast*, p. 132.
25. George Holmes (ed.), *The Oxford Illustrated History of Medieval Europe* (Oxford: Oxford University Press, n.d.), p. 4.
26. Marcus Hattstein and Peter Delius (eds.), *Islam Art & Architecture* (Cologne: Konemann, 2000), p. 211.
27. Godfrey Goodwin, *Islamic Spain* (San Francisco: Chronicle Books, 1990), pp. 8–9.
28. Karen Armstrong, *Muhammad* (San Francisco: HarperSanFrancisco, 1993), pp. 23–24.
29. Armstrong, *Muhammad*, p. 22.
30. Holmes, *The Oxford Illustrated History of Medieval Europe*, p. 15.
31. Goodwin, *Islamic Spain*, p. 5.
32. S. W. Ahmed Akbar, *Discovering Islam*, (New York: Routledge, 2002), p. 4.
33. Goodwin, *Islamic Spain*, p. 43.
34. Alfred Guillaume, *Islam* (Edinburgh: Penguin, 1956), p. 84.
35. Hattstein and Delius, *Islam Art & Architecture*, p. 210.
36. Goodwin, *Islamic Spain*, p. 10.
37. Holmes, *The Oxford Illustrated History of Medieval Europe*, pp. 57, 59.
38. Holmes, *The Oxford Illustrated History of Medieval Europe*, p. 32.
39. Goodwin, *Islamic Spain*, p. 12.
40. Goodwin, *Islamic Spain*, pp. 42–43.
41. Holmes, *The Oxford Illustrated History of Medieval Europe*, p. 61.
42. Ravenscroft and Wallace-Murphy, *The Mark of the Beast*, p. 125.
43. Holmes, *The Oxford Illustrated History of Medieval Europe*, p. 208.
44. Holmes, *The Oxford Illustrated History of Medieval Europe*, pp. 207–208.
45. Armstrong, *Muhammad*, p. 29.
46. Hattstein and Delius, *Islam Art & Architecture*, p. 12.
47. Hattstein and Delius, *Islam Art & Architecture*, p. 14.
48. Hattstein and Delius, *Islam Art & Architecture*, p. 16.

Chapter 9

1. Marilyn Hopkins, G. Simmans, and Tim Wallace-Murphy, *Rex Deus* (Shaftsbury, UK: Element Books, 2000), p. 105.
2. Hopkins, Simmans and Wallace-Murphy, *Rex Deus*, p. 105.
3. Trevor Ravenscroft, *The Spear of Destiny* (York Beach, ME: Weiser Books, 1982), pp. 206–207.
4. Ravenscroft, *The Spear of Destiny*, p. 45.
5. Cecil Roth, *A Short History of the Jewish People* (London: East West Library, 1953) p. 165–166.
6. A. J. A. Zuckerman, *A Jewish Princedom in Feudal France 768–900* (New York: Columbia University Press, 1972), p. 37.

7. Zuckerman, *A Jewish Princedom in Feudal France*, p. 49.

8. Roth, *A Short History of the Jewish People*, p. 165.

9. Haim Beinart, *Atlas of Medieval Jewish History* (New York: Robert Lafont, 1970), p. 23.

10. Zuckerman, *A Jewish Princedom in Feudal France*, p. 60.

11. Beinart, *Atlas of Medieval Jewish History*, p. 23.

12. Zuckerman, *A Jewish Princedom in Feudal France*, p. 34.

13. Zuckerman, *A Jewish Princedom in Feudal France*, p. 112.

14. Zuckerman, *A Jewish Princedom in Feudal France*, p. 165.

15. *Tractatus adversus Judaeorum inveteratam duritiem*, PL CLXXXIX,col. 560 (church document).

16. M. N. Adler, *The Itinerary of Benjamin of Tudela 459–467* (N.p.: Joseph Simon, 1983).

17. G. Saige, *Les Juifs du Languedoc* (Farnborough, UK: Gregg International, 1971), pp. 272–293; see also J. Regne, *Étude sur la Condition des Juifs de Narbonne* (Marseilles: Lafitte Reprints, 1981), pp. 127–132.

18. T. Hodgekin, *The Barbarian Invasion of the Roman Empire*, vol. 8, *The Frankish Empire*, (London: Folio Society, 2002), p. 127.

19. Edward Gibbon, *The Decline and Fall of the Roman Empire*, vol. 6, (London: Folio Society, 2001), p. 170.

20. Robert Fossier (ed.), *The Middle Ages*, (Cambridge: Cabridge University Press, 1989), p. 422.

21. Fossier, *The Middle Ages*, p. 484.

22. Fossier, *The Middle Ages*, pp. 426–427.

23. Fossier, *The Middle Ages*, p. 424.

24. Hopkins, Simmans, and Wallace-Murphy, *Rex Deus*, p. 106.

25. Wallace-Murphy, *The Templar Legacy and Masonic Inheritance*, p 25.

26. Wallace-Murphy and Hopkins, *Rosslyn: Guardian of the Secrets of the Holy Grail*, p. 199.

27. St. Clair L-A de, *Histoire Généalogique de la Famille de St. Clair* (Paris, 1905).

28. St. Clair L-A de, *Histoire Généalogique de la Famille de St. Clair*.

29. St. Clair L-A de, *Histoire Généalogique de la Famille de St. Clair*, p. 8.

30. St. Clair L-A de, *Histoire Généalogique de la Famille de St. Clair*, p. 8.

31. St. Clair L-A de, *Histoire Généalogique de la Famille de St. Clair*, p. 9.

32. Hopkins, Simmans, and Wallace-Murphy, *Rex Deus*, p. 105.

33. Hopkins, Simmans, and Wallace-Murphy, *Rex Deus*, pp. 107–108.

34. St. Clair L-A de, *Histoire Généalogique de la Famille de St. Clair*.

35. Emile Mâle, *Notre Dame de Chartres* (Paris: Flammarion, 1983), p. 9.

36. Colin Ward, *Chartres: The Making of a Miracle* (London: Folio Society, 1986), p. 7.

37. Gordon Strachan, *Chartres* (Edinburgh: Floris Books, 2003), p. 9.

38. Ward, *Chartres: The Making of a Miracle*, p. 8.

39. Ravenscroft and Wallace-Murphy, *The Mark of the Beast*, p. 75.

40. Ward, *Chartres: The Making of a Miracle*, pp. 8–9.

41. Ravenscroft and Wallace-Murphy, *The Mark of the Beast*, pp. 74–75.

42. Michel Kubler, "Une Vie par réforme l'église," *Bernard de Clairvaux* (les editions de l'Argonante).

43. Kubler, "Une Vie par reforme l'eglise."

44. St. Clair L-A de, *Histoire Généalogique de la Famille de St. Clair.*

45. Barnavi, *A Historical Atlas of the Jewish People*, p. 78.

46. Barnavi, *A Historical Atlas of the Jewish People*, pp. 98–99.

47. Wallace-Murphy, *The Templar Legacy and the Masonic Inheritance*, p. 18.

48. Michael Baigent, Richard Leigh, and Henry Lincoln, *Holy Blood, Holy Grail* (London: Jonathan Cape, 1982), p. 61.

CHAPTER 10

1. Renee Querido, *The Golden Age of Chartres* (Edinburgh: Floris Books, 1987), p. 84.

2. Hopkins, Simmans, and Wallace-Murphy, *Rex Deus*, p. 113.

3. Querido, *The Golden Age of Chartres*, 114.

4. William of Tyre, lib xii, cap 7.

5. John J. Robinson, *Dungeon, Fire and Sword* (London: Brockhampton, 1999), p. 31.

6. Charles G. Addison, *The Knights Templar* (London: Black Books, 1995), p. 5.

7. C. Knight and R. Lomas, *The Second Messiah* (London: Century, 1997), p. 73.

8. Helen Nicholson, *The Knights Templar* (Woodbridge, Suffolk: The Boydell Press, 2001), p. 22.

9. Leroy Thierry, *Hughes de Payns, Chevalier Champenois, Fondateur de L'Ordre des Templiers* (N.p.: Editions de la Maison du Boulanger, 1997), p. 34–35.

10. J. Laurent (ed.), *Cartulaire de Molésme*, pp. 214

11. Robinson, *Dungeon, Fire and Sword*, p. 36

12. Gardner, *The Bloodline of the Holy Grail*, p. 256.

13. Thierry, *Hughes de Payns*, pp. 107–108.

14. Hopkins, Simmans, and Wallace-Murphy, *Rex Deus*, p. 112.

15. Hopkins, Simmans, and Wallace-Murphy, *Rex Deus*.

16. Nicholson, *The Knights Templar*, p. 22.

17. Anon., *Secret Societies of the Middle Ages* (Whitefish, MT: Kessinger Publishing, 2003), p. 190; see also Nicholson, *The Knights Templar*, p. 26.

18. Graham Hancock, *The Sign and the Seal* (London: Sphere, 1990), pp. 94, 99; see also Ravenscroft and Wallace-Murphy, *The Mark of the Beast*, p. 52.

19. Hancock, *Sign and Seal*, pp. 49–51.

20. Ravenscroft and Wallace-Murphy, *The Mark of the Beast*, p. 52.

21. Robinson, *Dungeon, Fire and Sword*, p. 37.

22. Georges Bordonove, *La vie quotidienne des Templiers* (Paris: Hatchette, 1975), p. 29.

23. Anon., *Secret Societies of the Middle Ages*, p. 195.

24. Nicholson, *The Knights Templar*, p. 96.

25. Anon., *Secret Societies of the Middle Ages*, p. 199.

26. *liber ad milites Templi: De laude novae militiae.*

27. S. T. Bruno, *Templar Organization* (self-published), p. 65.

28. Bruno, *Templar Organization*, p. 165.

29. Peter Jay, *Road to Riches* (Weidenfeld and Nicolson, 2000), p. 118.

CHAPTER 11

1. Ean Begg, *The Cult of the Black Madonna* (London: Arkana, 1985), p. 103.
2. Tim Wallace-Murphy and Marilyn Hopkins, *Rosslyn: Guardian of the Secrets of the Holy Grail* (Shaftsbury, UK: Element Books, 1999), p. 105.
3. Wallace-Murphy and Hopkins, *Rosslyn: Guardian of the Secrets of the Holy Grail.*
4. Wallace-Murphy and Hopkins, *Rosslyn: Guardian of the Secrets of the Holy Grail*, p. 62.
5. Wallace-Murphy and Hopkins, *Rosslyn: Guardian of the Secrets of the Holy Grail*, pp. 181–182.
6. Begg, *The Cult of the Black Madonna*, (London: Bloomsbury, 1994), p. 13.
7. Malcolm Godwin, *The Holy Grail*, p. 14.
8. Godwin, *The Holy Grail*, p. 16.
9. Emile Mâle, *Notre Dame de Chartres* (Paris: Flammarion, 1983), p. 141.
10. Godwin, *The Holy Grail*, p. 12.
11. Godwin, *The Holy Grail*, p. 18.
12. Trevor Ravenscroft and Tim Wallace-Murphy, *The Mark of the Beast* (London: Sphere, 1990), p. 52.
13. Andrew Sinclair, *The Discovery of the Grail* (London: Century, 1998), p. 27.
14. Sinclair, *The Discovery of the Grail*, pp. 27–28.
15. Godwin, *The Holy Grail*, p. 6.
16. Joseph Campbell and Bill Moyers, *The Power of Myth* (New York: Doubleday, 1990), pp. 197–200.
17. Published by Weiser Books, York Beach, ME, 1995.
18. John Robinson (ed.), "The Gospel of Thomas," in *The Nag Hammadi Library* (London: HarperCollins, 1990).
19. Campbell and Moyers, *The Power of Myth*, pp. 197–200.
20. Michael Baigent, Richard Leigh, and Henry Lincoln, *Holy Blood, Holy Grail* (London: Jonathan Cape, 1982), pp. 262–268.
21. Baigent, Leigh, and Lincoln, *Holy Blood, Holy Grail*, p. 163.
22. Baigent, Leigh, and Lincoln, *Holy Blood, Holy Grail*, p. 163.
23. Cited by Fritjof Capra in *The Turning Point* (London: Flamingo, 1983), p. 410.
24. Cited by Ted Roszak in *Where the Wasteland Ends* (New York: Doubleday, 1978), p. 154.
25. Louis Charpentier, *The Mysteries of Chartres Cathedral*, (London: Rilko, 1993), p. 145.
26. Louis Charpentier, *The Mysteries of Chartres Cathedral*, p. 86.
27. Ian Dunlop, *The Cathedrals Crusade* (London: Hamish Hamilton, 1982), p. 6.
28. Information supplied by the Provencal Templar scholar, Guy Jourdan.
29. *La Régle de St Devoir de Dieu et de la Croissade* (medieval document).
30. Fred Gettings, *The Secret Zodiac* (London: Routledge & Keegan Paul, 1987).
31. J. F. Colfs, *La filiation généalogique de toutes les Écoles Gothiques* (cited by Fulcanelli in his *Le Mystère des Cathédrales*).
32. Wallace-Murphy and Hopkins, *The Templar Legacy and the Masonic Inheritance.*
33. Gordon Strachan, *Chartres* (Edinburgh: Floris Books, 2003), p. 14.
34. Idries Shah, *The Sufis* (London: Jonathan Cape, 1969), pp. 166–193.

35. Shah, *The Sufis*, p. 29.

36. P. D. Ouspensky, *A New Model of the Universe* (London: Arkana, 1931), p. 345.

37. Fulcanelli, *Le Mystère des Cathédrales* (Sudbury, England: Neville Spearman, 1977), p. 36

38. Fulcanelli, *Le Mystère des Cathédrales*, pp. 39–41.

39. Charpentier, *The Mysteries of Chartres*, p. 81.

40. Charpentier, *The Mysteries of Chartres*, p. 165.

41. Charpentier, *The Mysteries of Chartres*, p. 139.

42. Blanche Mertz, *Points of Cosmic Energy* (Chartres, France: Editions Houvert, 1965), p. 105.

43. Y. Delaporte, *Les Trois Notre Dames de Chartres* (Chartres: France: E. Houvet, n.d.), p. 11.

44. Fulcanelli, *Le Mystère des Cathédrales*, p. 123.

45. Wallace-Murphy and Hopkins, *Rosslyn: Guardian of the Secrets of the Holy Grail*, p. 176.

46. G. Quespel, "Gnosticism," *Man, Myth and Magic*, p. 40, 115.

CHAPTER 12

1. J. Regne, *Études sur la condition des Juifs de Narbonne* (Marseilles: Lafitte, 1981), pp. 3–8.

2. Regne, *Études*, pp. 27–9.

3. Regne, *Études*, pp. 90–91.

4. M. N. Adler, *The Itinerary of Benjamin Tudela* (New York: Phillip Feldheim, 1907), p. 459.

5. A. J. Zuckerman, *A Jewish Princedom in Feudal France* (New York: Columbia University Press, 1972), p. 96.

6. Michael Costen, *The Cathars and the Albigensian Crusade* (Manchester: Manchester University Press), p. 38.

7. Zoé Oldenbourg, *Massacre at Montségur* (London: Phoenix/Orion Books, 1999), pp. 24–25.

8. Costen, *The Cathars and the Albigensian Crusade*, p. 38.

9. Costen, *The Cathars and the Albigensian Crusade*, p. 37.

10. Malcolm Barber, *The Cathars* (London: Pearson Education, Ltd., 2000), p. 53.

11. Oldenbourg, *Massacre at Montségur*, p. 2.

12. Oldenbourg, *Massacre at Montségur*, pp.54–55.

13. Barber, *The Cathars*, p. 11.

14. Oldenbourg, *Massacre at Montségur*, p. 29.

15. Oldenbourg, *Massacre at Montségur*, p. 27.

16. Costen, *The Cathars and the Albigensian Crusade*, p.73.

17. Arthur Guirdham, *The Great Heresy* (Saffron Walden, UK: CW Daniel, 1993), p. 23.

18. Michele Aué, Simon Pleasance (trans.), *Cathar Country* (Vic en Bigorre, France: MSM Publishing, 1995).

19. Costen, *The Cathars and the Albigensian Crusade*, p. 65.

20. Oldenbourg, *Massacre at Montségur*, p. 69.

21. Stephen O'Shea, *The Perfect Heresy* (London: Profile Books, 2000), p. 12.

22. Oldenbourg, *Massacre at Montségur*, pp. 41–42.

23. Costen, *The Cathars and the Albigensian Crusade*, p. 59.

24. Simon De Vries, *Cathars, Country Customs and Castles* (N.p.: Comtal Press, 1993), p. 2.

25. Oldenbourg, *Massacre at Montségur*, p. 50.

26. Oldenbourg, *Massacre at Montségur*, pp. 56–57.

27. Barber, *The Cathars*, p. 96.

28. Oldenbourg, *Massacre at Montségur*, pp. 58–59.

29. Guirdham, *The Great Heresy*, p. 38.

30. See the "The Gospel of Thomas," James Robinson (ed.), in *The Nag Hammadi Library* (London: HarperCollins, 1990).

31. Guirdham, *The Great Heresy* , pp. 45–47.

32. Barber, *The Cathars*, p. 74.

33. Guirdham, *The Great Heresy*, p. 19.

34. Guirdham, *The Great Heresy*, p. 18.

35. Guirdham, *The Great Heresy*.

36. Yuri Stoyanov, *The Hidden Tradition in Europe* (London: Arkana, 1994), p. 160.

37. Aué, *Cathar Country*, p. 13.

38. Guebin and Moisoineuve, *Histoire Albigeoise de Pierre des Vaux-de-Chrnay* (Paris: Libraries Philosophique, n.d.).

39. Guirdham, *The Great Heresy*, p. 16.

40. Oldenbourg, *Massacre at Montségur*, pp. 59–60.

41. Stoyanov, *The Hidden Tradition in Europe*, p. 159.

42. Bernard's letter cited by Wakefield and Evans in *Heresies of the Middle Ages* (New York: Columbia University Press, 1991), pp. 122–124.

43. Stoyanov, *The Hidden Tradition in Europe*, p. 156.

44. Wakefield and Evans, *Heresies of the Middle Ages*, pp. 140–141.

45. Costen, *The Cathars and the Albigensian Crusade*, pp. 112–114.

46. Costen, *The Cathars and the Albigensian Crusade*, p. 114.

47. Georges Serrus, *The Land of the Cathars* (Portet-sur-Garonne, France: Editions Loubatières, 1990), p. 15.

48. Costen, *The Cathars and the Albigensian Crusade*, p. 23.

49. *Innocentii III Registrorum sive Epistolarum*, vol. 215, cols. 1354–1358

50. Aué, *Cathar Country*, p. 15.

51. Stoyanov, *The Hidden Tradition in Europe*, p. 173.

52. Raymonde Reznikov, *Cathars et Templiers* (Portet-sur-Garonne, France: Editions Loubatières, n.d.).

53. Information supplied by Nicole Dawe of the Abraxus Templar Research Group.

54. Lyn Picknett and Clive Prince, *The Templar Revelation* (London: Bantam, 1997), p. 104.

55. Guirdham, *The Great Heresy*, p. 55.

56. Costen, *The Cathars and the Albigensian Crusade*, p. 43.

57. Arnauld Aimery, *Patrologia Latina*, vol. 216, col. 139; also Caesarius of Heisterbach, vol. 2, pp. 296–298.

58. Guebin and Moisoineuve, *Histoire Albigeoise de Pierre des Vaux-de-Chrnay*.

59. Serrus, *The Land of the Cathars*, p. 20.

60. Costen, *The Cathars and the Albigensian Crusade*, p. 128.
61. Guirdham, *The Great Heresy*, p. 63.
62. Costen, *The Cathars and the Albigensian Crusade*, p. 132.
63. Costen, *The Cathars and the Albigensian Crusade*, p. 160.
64. Guirdham, *The Great Heresy*, p. 83.

CHAPTER 13

1. Peter De Rosa, *Vicars of Christ* (London: Corgi, 1989), p. 226.
2. Michael Baigent and Richard Leigh, *The Inquisition* (London: Penguin, 1991), p. 20–21.
3. Yuri Stoyanov, *The Hidden Tradition in Europe* (London: Arkana, 1996), p. 178.
4. Edward Burman, *The Inquisition: The Hammer of Heresy* (Wellingborough, UK: Aquarian Press, 1986), p. 39.
5. Papal Bull of Pope Innocent IV, *Super Extirpatione*.
6. Burman, *The Inquisition: The Hammer of Heresy*, pp. 42–43.
7. H. C. Lea, *The Inquisition of the Middle Ages* (New York, 1955).
8. Paul Johnson, *A History of Christianity* (London: Weidenfeld & Nicolson, 1978), p. 253.
9. Douglas Lockhart, *The Dark Side of God* (Shaftsbury, UK: Element Books, 1999), p. 73.
10. Papal Bulls of Innocent IV *Cum negocium* and *Licet sicut accepimus* (church document).
11. Papal Bull of Innocent IV, 1252, *Ad extirpanda* (church document).
12. Burman, *The Inquisition: The Hammer of Heresy*, p. 62.
13. Baigent and Leigh, *The Inquisition*, p. 27–28.
14. Johnson, *A History of Christianity*, p. 254.
15. Cited by Peter de Rosa in *Vicars of Christ*, (London: Corgi, 1989), p. 228.
16. Johnson, *A History of Christianity*, pp. 253–255.
17. Lea, *The Inquisition in the Middle Ages*.
18. De Rosa, *Vicars of Christ*, p. 249.
19. De Rosa, *Vicars of Christ*, p. 249.
20. Rollo Ahmed, *The Black Art* (Taiwan: Senate Books, 1994).
21. Cited in Lockhart, *The Dark Side of God*, p.75, from *Institutions of Public and Ecclesiastical Law*, by Marianus De Luca.
22. Baigent and Leigh, *The Inquisition*, p. 38.

CHAPTER 14

1. Geoffrey Regan, *Lionharts, Saladin and Richard I* (London: Constable Publishing, 1998), p. 91.
2. Malcolm Barber, *The Trial of the Templars* (Cambridge: Cambridge University Press), p. 11.
3. John J. Robinson, *Dungeon, Fire and Sword* (London: Brockhampton, 1999), p. 405.
4. Barber, *The Trial of the Templars*, p. 24.
5. L. L. Borelli De Serres, *Les Variations monétaires sous Philippe le Bel* (Paris, 1902), pp. 293–294.

6. Trevor Ravenscroft and Tim Wallace-Murphy, *The Mark of the Beast* (London: Sphere, 1990), p. 52.

7. Barber, *The Trial of the Templars*, p. 40.

8. Haim Beinart, *Atlas of Medieval Jewish History* (New York: Robert Lafont, 1970), p. 59.

9. Chris Knight and Robert Lomas, *The Second Messiah* (London: Century, 1997), pp. 127–128.

10. Knight and Lomas, *The Second Messiah*, p. 133.

11. Noel Currer-Brigs, *The Shroud and the Grail* (London: Weidenfeld & Nicolson, 1987), p. 95.

12. F.W. Bussell, *Religious Thought and Heresy in the Middle Ages* (London: Robert Scott, 1918).

13. Currer-Brigs, *The Shroud and the Grail*, p. 96.

14. Barber, *The Trial of the Templars*, p. 47.

15. Barber, *The Trial of the Templars*, p. 45.

16. Baigent, Leigh, and Lincoln, *Holy Blood, Holy Grail*, p. 46.

17. Lizerand, *Le Dossier de l'Affaire des Templiers* (Paris: Belles Lettres, 1989), p. 16.

18. Barber, *The Trial of the Templars*, p. 45.

19. Barber, *The Trial of the Templars*, p. 47.

20. Barber, *The Trial of the Templars*, pp. 47–48.

21. Barber, *The Trial of the Templars*, p. 57.

22. Papal Bull of Clement V, *Pastoralis Praeminentiae*.

23. Barber, *The Trial of the Templars*, pp. 193–195.

24. Barber, *The Trial of the Templars*, p. 200.

25. Tim Wallace-Murphy, *The Templar Legacy and the Masonic Inheritance within Rosslyn Chapel* (London: Friends of Rosslyn), p. 22.

26. Wallace-Murphy, *The Templar Legacy and the Masonic Inheritance*.

27. Peter Partner, *The Knights Templar and their Myth* (Rochester, VT: Destiny Books), p. 82.

28. Hopkins, Simmans, and Wallace-Murphy, *Rex Deus*, p. 172.

29. Partner, *The Knights Templar and their Myth*, p. 83.

30. Ravenscroft and Wallace-Murphy, *The Mark of the Beast*, p. 53.

31. Barber, *The Trial of the Templars*, pp. 178–193.

32. "Les Templiers dans les Alpes Maritimes," *Nice Historique*, Jan.-Feb. 1938.

33. Currer-Briggs, *The Shroud and the Grail*.

34. Garza-Valdez, Leonicio, *The DNA of God*.

35. Papal Bull of Clement V, *Vox in excelso*.

36. Stephen Dafoe and Alan Butler, *The Warriors and the Bankers* (Ontario: Warrior Books, 1998).

37. Wallace-Murphy Hopkins, *Rosslyn: Guardian of the Secrets of the Holy Grail*, p. 106.

38. Robinson, *Born in Blood*, pp. 164–166.

39. HRH Prince Michael of Albany, *The Forgotten Monarchy of Scotland* (Shaftsbury, UK: Element Books, 1998), pp. 65, 150.

40. Wallace-Murphy, *The Templar Legacy and the Masonic Inheritance*, p. 22.

41. Fr. Hay, *The Genealogie of the St. Clairs of Roslin* (Edinburgh: Maidement, 1865).

CHAPTER 15

1. Barber, *The Trial of the Templars* (Cambridge: Cambridge University Press, 1994), p. 46.
2. Marilyn Hopkins, G. Simmans, and Tim Wallace-Murphy, *Rex Deus* (Shaftsbury, UK: Element Books, 2000), p. 229.
3. Michael Baigent and Richard Leigh, *The Temple and the Lodge* (London: Corgi, 1992), p. 135.
4. Baigent and Leigh, *The Temple and the Lodge*, p. 148.
5. Baigent and Leigh, *The Temple and the Lodge*, p. 149.
6. Baigent and Leigh, *The Temple and the Lodge*, pp. 149–150.
7. HRH Prince Michael of Albany, *The Forgotten Monarchy of Scotland* (Shaftsbury, UK: Element Books, 1998), p. 125.
8. Baigent and Leigh, *The Temple and the Lodge*, p. 150.
9. Baigent and Leigh, *The Temple and the Lodge*, p. 152.
10. Baigent and Leigh, *The Temple and the Lodge*, p. 155.
11. Tim Wallace-Murphy and Marilyn Hopkins, *Rosslyn: Guardian of the Secrets of the Holy Grail* (Shaftsbury, UK: Element Books, 1999), p. 7.
12. Wallace-Murphy, *The Templar Legacy and the Masonic Inheritance.*
13. HRH Prince Michael of Albany, *The Forgotten Monarchy of Scotland*, p. 102.
14. Michael Foss, *Chivalry* (London: Michael Joseph, 1975), p. 189.
15. Foss, *Chivalry.*
16. Lawrence Gardner, *Genesis of the Grail Kings* (London: Bantam, 1999), p. 225.
17. Michael Baigent, Richard Leigh, and Henry Lincoln, *Holy Blood, Holy Grail* (London: Jonathan Cape, 1982), p. 106.

CHAPTER 16

1. Ian Wilson, *The Blood and the Shroud* (London: Weidenfeld & Nicolson, 1998), p. 185.
2. Wilson, *The Blood and the Shroud*, p. 8.
3. Wilson, *The Blood and the Shroud*, p. 9.
4. H. Kersten and E. R. Gruber, *The Jesus Conspiracy* (Shaftsbury, UK: Element Books, 1994).
5. Robert de Clarii, *The Conquest of Constantinople*, E. H. Neal (trans.) (Toronto: University of Toronto Press, 1997).
6. Hopkins, Simmans, and Wallace-Murphy, *Rex Deus*, p. 182.
7. Herbert Thurston, SJ (trans.), *Memorandum of P. D'Arcis* (no ascertainable information).
8. Noel Currer-Briggs, *The Shroud and the Grail* (London: Weidenfeld and Nicolson, 1987), p. 106.
9. Lyn Picknet and Clive Prince, *Turin Shroud: In Whose Image?* (London: Bloomsbury, 1994), p. 118.
10. Hopkins, Simmans, and Wallace-Murphy, *Rex Deus*, p. 182.
11. Wilson, *The Blood and the Shroud*, p. 117.
12. Pope Sixtus IV, *de Sanguine Christi.*
13. Wilson, *The Turin Shroud*, p. 190.
14. Wilson, *The Blood and the Shroud*, pp. 64–67.

15. Wilson, *The Turin Shroud*, pp. 14–15.

16. Wilson, *The Turin Shroud*, pp. 52–54.

17. Wilson, *The Turin Shroud*, pp. 60–62.

18. Wilson, *The Turin Shroud*, p. 62.

19. Wilson, *The Blood and the Shroud*, p. 105.

20. Wilson, *The Blood and the Shroud*, p. 202.

21. Tim Wallace-Murphy and Marilyn Hopkins, *Templars in America* (York Beach, ME: Weiser Books, 2004). See the chapters on the Newport Tower.

22. Wilson, *The Blood and the Shroud*, pp. 225–227.

23. Wilson, *The Turin Shroud*, p. 8.

24. L. A. Garza-Valdes, *The DNA of God* (London: Hodder & Stoughton, 1998), pp. 32–37.

25. Wilson, *The Blood and the Shroud*, p. 226.

26. Garza-Valdes, *The DNA of God*, pp. 16–19.

27. Garza-Valdes, *The DNA of God*, p. 69.

28. Garza-Valdes, *The DNA of God*, p. 26.

29. Pierluigi Bauma-Bollone, "Identification of the Group of the Traces of Blood found on the Shroud," *Shroud Spectrum International*, 6 March 1983, pp. 3–6.

30. Wilson, *The Blood and the Shroud*, p. 88.

31. Garza-Valdes, *The DNA of God*, p. 39.

32. Garza-Valdes, *The DNA of God*, p. 57.

33. Public Lecture in Paris, *The Image of Christ Visible on the Holy Shroud of Turin*, given 21 April 1902 by Professor Yves Delage.

34. David Sox, *The File on the Shroud* (London: Coronet, 1978), p. 66.

35. Wilson *The Turin Shroud*, pp. 25–26.

36. Wilson, *The Turin Shroud*, pp. 26–27.

37. Wilson, *The Turin Shroud*, p. 21.

38. Wilson, *The Turin Shroud*, p. 22.

39. Robert Wilcox, *Shroud* (London: Bantam, 1978), p. 136.

40. Wilson, *The Turin Shroud*, p. 23.

41. Wilson, *The Turin Shroud*, p. 24.

42. Wilson, *The Turin Shroud*, pp. 2–25

43. Wilson, *The Turin Shroud*, p. 29.

44. Wilson, *The Turin Shroud*, p. 30.

45. Fr. Roland de Vaux, *Fouille au Khirbet Qumran*, published in *Revue Biblique*, vol. 60 (1953), p. 102.

46. Iraneus, *Against Heresies*.

CHAPTER 17

1. Previte Orton, *Outlines of Medieval History* (Cambridge: Cambridge University Press, 1916), p. 457.

2. H. A. L. Fisher, *A History of Europe* (London: Edward Arnold & Co., 1936), p. 389.

3. Robert Fossier, *The Middle Ages*, vol. III (Cambridge: Cambridge University Press, 1989), p. 77.

4. Orton, *Outlines of Medieval History*, pp. 463–465.

5. Fisher, *A History of Europe*, p. 388.
6. Margaret Starbird, *The Tarot Trumps and the Holy Grail* (Lakewood, WA: Woven Word Press), p. x.
7. Richard Cavendish, *The Tarot* (London: Michael Joseph, 1975), p. 17.
8. Marilyn Hopkins, G. Simmans and Tim Wallace-Murphy, *Rex Deus* (Shaftsbury, UK: Element Books, 2000), p. 148.
9. Starbird, *The Tarot Trumps and the Holy Grail*, p xi.
10. Hopkins, Simmans and Wallace-Murphy, *Rex Deus*, p. 148.
11. Malcolm Godwin, *The Holy Grail* (London: Bloomsbury, 1996), p. 234.
12. Starbird, *The Tarot Trumps and the Holy Grail*, p. x.
13. Starbird, *The Tarot Trumps and the Holy Grail*, p. 3.
14. Starbird, *The Tarot Trumps and the Holy Grail*, p. 5.
15. Godwin, *The Holy Grail*, p. 236.
16. Godwin, *The Holy Grail*, p. 338.
17. Orton, *Outlines of Medieval History*, p. 467.
18. Fisher, *A History of Europe*, p. 393.
19. Esmond Wright, *Medieval and Renaissance World* (London: Hamlyn, 1979), p. 218.
20. Michael Baigent, Richard Leigh, and Henry Lincoln, *Holy Blood, Holy Grail* (London: Jonathan Cape, 1982), p. 378.
21. Eli Barnavi, *A Historical Atlas of the Jewish People* (London: Hutchinson, 1992, p. 126.
22. Haim Beinart, *Atlas of Medieval Jewish History* (New York: Robert Lafont, 1970), p. 77.
23. Barnavi, *A Historical Atlas of the Jewish People*, p. 126.
24. Barnavi, *A Historical Atlas of the Jewish People*, p. 127.
25. Baigent, Leigh, and Lincoln, *Holy Blood, Holy Grail*, p. 109.
26. Orton, *Outlines of Medieval History*, p. 469.
27. Godfrey Goodwin, *Islamic Spain* (San Francisco: Chronicle Books, 1990), p. vii.
28. Robert Fossier, *The Middle Ages*, vol. 3 (Cambridge: Cambridge University Press, 1989), p. 504.
29. Esmond Wright, *Medieval and Renaissance World* (London: Hamlyn, 1979), p. 218.
30. Fossier, *The Middle Ages*, vol. 3, pp. 504–505.
31. Fossier, *The Middle Ages*, vol. 3, p. 505.

CHAPTER 18

1. Tim Wallace-Murphy, *The Templar Legacy and the Masonic Inheritance within Rosslyn Chapel* (London: Friends of Rosslyn, 1996), p. 25.
2. L-A de St. Clair, *Histoire Généalogique de la Famille de St. Clair* (Paris, 1905).
3. Tim Wallace-Murphy, *An Illustrated Guidebook to Rosslyn Chapel* (London: Friends of Rosslyn, 1993), p. 3.
4. Wallace-Murphy, *An Illustrated Guidebook to Rosslyn Chapel*.
5. Wallace-Murphy, *An Illustrated Guidebook to Rosslyn Chapel*.
6. Ravenscoft and Wallace-Murphy, *The Mark of the Beast*, p. 64.
7. Wallace-Murphy, *An Illustrated Guidebook to Rosslyn Chapel*, p. 3.

8. Wallace-Murphy, *An Illustrated Guidebook to Rosslyn Chapel.*
9. Fr. Augustine Hay, *The Genealogy of the Saint Claires of Roslin* (Scotland: Maidement, 1865).
10. Cited by Chris Knight and Robert Lomas in *The Second Messiah* (London: Century, 1997), p. 32.
11. Wallace-Murphy, *An Illustrated Guidebook to Rosslyn Chapel*, p. 6.
12. Article in *Interiors* magazine, 1982.
13. J-A Durbec, "Les Templiers dans Les-Alpes Maritime," *Nice Historique,* Jan.-Feb: 1938, pp. 4–6.
14. Durbec: "Les Templiers dans Les Alpes Maritime."
15. Tim Wallace-Murphy and Marilyn Hopkins, *Rosslyn: Guardian of the Secrets of the Holy Grail* (Shaftsbury, UK: Element Books, 1999), p. 121.
16. Robert Graves' introduction to the first edition of *The Sufis* by Idris Shah (London: Jonathan Cape & Co., 1969).
17. Graves, introduction to the first edition of *The Sufis.*
18. Rudolph Steiner, from a lecture given in Berlin, 2 Dec. 1904, published as *Die Tempellegende und die Goldene Legende no. 93.*
19. Geddricke, 18th-century historian of Freemasonry.
20. HRH Prince Michael of Albany, *The Forgotten Monarchy*, (Shaftsbury, UK: Element Books, 1998), p. 120.
21. HRH Prince Michael, *The Forgotten Monarchy.*
22. Masonic archives in Freemasons Hall, Edinburgh.
23. Knight and Lomas, *The Second Messiah*, p. 53.
24. Wallace-Murphy, *The Templar Legacy and Masonic Inheritance*, p. 31.
25. Wallace-Murphy, *The Templar Legacy and Masonic Inheritance.*
26. J. S. M. Ward, *Freemasonry and the Ancient Gods* (London: Simkin, Marshall, Hamilton, Kent & Co., 1921).
27. Knight and Lomas, *The Second Messiah*, p. 203.
28. Knight and Lomas, *The Second Messiah*, p. 204.
29. Knight and Lomas, *The Second Messiah*, pp. 207–209.

Chapter 19

1. Fritjof Capra, *The Turning Point* (London: Flamingo, 1983), p. 326.
2. Cited by Marilyn Fergusson in *The Aquarian Conspiracy* (London: Paladin Books, 1982), p. 47.
3. F. Barnaby (ed.), *The Gaia Peace Atlas* (London: Pan Books, 1988).
4. Cited by Marilyn Fergusson, *The Aquarian Conspiracy.*
5. Cited by Matthew Fox in *Original Blessing* (Rochester, VT: Bear and Co., 1983).
6. M. C. Richards, *The Crossing Point* (Middleton, CT: Weslyan University Press, 1973).
7. Fergusson, *The Aquarian Conspiracy.*
8. Joseph Campbell, *The Hero with a Thousand Faces* (Princeton, NJ: Princeton University Press, 1972).
9. Trevor Ravenscroft and Tim Wallace-Murphy, *The Mark of the Beast* (London: Sphere: 1990), p. 188.

SELECTED BIBLIOGRAPHY

Addison, Charles G. *The History of the Knights Templars*. London: Black Books, 1995.

Ahmed, Rollo. *The Black Art*. Taiwan: Senate Books, 1971.

Akbar, S. W. Ahmed. *Discovering Islam*. New York: Routledge, 2002.

Allegro, J. M. *The Dead Sea Scrolls and the Christian Myth*. London: Abacus, 1981.

Allegro, John. *The Dead Sea Scrolls*. London: Penguin, 1964.

Allen, Grant. *The Evolution of the Idea of God*. London: Watts, 1931.

Anon. *Secret Societies of the Middle Ages*. Whitefish, MT: Kessinger Publishing, 2003.

Ambelain, Robert. *Jesus ou le Mortel Sécret des Templiers*. Paris: Robert Lafont, 1970.

Anderson, William. *The Rise of the Gothic*. London: Hutchinson, 1985.

Aristotle. *De Caelo II*. Available in most reference libraries.

Armstrong, Karen. *Muhammad*. San Francisco: HarperSanFrancisco, 1993.

———. *A History of God*. London: Mandarin, 1994.

———. *A History of Jerusalem*. London: HarperCollins, 1996.

Ashe, Geoffrey. *The Ancient Wisdom*. London: MacMillan, 1977.

Aué, Michèle. *Cathar Country*. Vic-en-Bigorre, France: MSM, 1995.

Baigent, Michael, Richard Leigh, and Henry Lincoln. *Holy Blood, Holy Grail*. London: Jonathan Cape, 1982.

Baigent, Michael and Richard Leigh. *The Dead Sea Scrolls Deception*. London: Corgi, 1992.

———. *The Inquisition*. London: Penguin, 1999.

———. *The Temple and the Lodge*. London: Corgi, 1992.

Barber, Malcolm. *The Trial of the Templars*. Cambridge: Cambridge University Press, 1994.

———. *The Cathars*. Harlow, UK: Pearson Education Ltd., 2000.

Baring, Anne and Jules Cashford. *The Myth of the Goddess*. London: Penguin, 1993.

Barnaby, Dr. Frank, ed. *The Gaia Peace Atlas*. London: Pan Books, 1988.

Barnavi, Eli. *A Historical Atlas of the Jewish People*. London: Hutchinson, 1992.

Bauval, Robert and Adrian Gilbert. *The Orion Mystery*. London: Heinmann, 1994.

Bauval, R. and G. Hancock. *Keeper of Genesis*. London: William Heineman, 1996.

Bede. *A History of the English Church and People.* London: Penguin, 1978.

Begg, Ean. *The Cult of the Black Virgin.* London: Arkana, 1985.

Beinart, Haim. *Atlas of Medieval Jewish History.* New York: Robert Lafont, 1970.

Betro, M. C. *Hieroglyphes, Les Mysteres de l'ecriture.* Paris: Flammarion, 1995.

Birks, Norman and R. A. Gilbert. *The Treasure of Montségur.* Wellingborough, UK: Aquarian Press, 1990.

Bock, Emil. *Moses.* Edinburgh: Floris Books, 1986.

Boehme, Jacob. *Signatura Rerum/* Cambridge: James Clarke, 1981.

Bordonove, Georges. *La vie quotidienne des Templiers.* Paris: Librairie Hachette, 1975.

Breasted, J. H. *Development of Religion and Thought in Ancient Egypt.* Philadelphia: University of Pennsylvania Press, 1972.

Brown, R. Allen. *The Normans.* London: Guild Publishing, 1984.

Bruno, S. T. *Templar Organization.* (Privately published.)

Burman, Edward. *The Templars: Knights of God.* Rochester, VT: Destiny Books, 1990.

———. *The Inquisition: The Hammer of Heresy.* Wellingborough, UK: Aquarian Press, 1984.

Bussell, F. W. *Religious Thought and Heresy in the Middle Ages.* London: Robert Scott, 1918.

Campbell, Joseph. *Occidental Mythology.* London: Arkana, 1991.

———. *The Hero with a Thousand Faces.* Princeton, NJ: Princeton University Press, 1972.

Campbell, Joseph and Bill Moyers. *The Power of Myth.* New York: Doubleday, 1990.

Cannon, Dolores. *Jesus and the Essenes.* Bath, UK: Gateway Books, 1992.

Cantor, N. *The Sacred Chain: A History of the Jews.* London: Fontana, 1996.

Capra, Fritjof. *The Tao of Physics.* London: Fontana, 1983.

———. *The Turning Point.* London: Flamingo, 1983.

Cavendish, Richard. *The Tarot.* London: Michael Joseph, Ltd., 1975.

Charpentier, Louis. *Les Mystères Templiers.* Paris: Lafont, 1993.

———. *The Mysteries of Chartres Cathedral.* London: RILKO, 1993.

Christie-Murray, David. *A History of Heresy.* Oxford: Oxford University Press, 1989.

Cohn-Sherbok, Dan. *A Concise Encyclopedia of Judaism.* Oxford: Oneworld, 1998.

Costen, Michael. *The Cathars and the Albigensian Crusade.* Manchester: Manchester University Press, 1997.

Cotterell, M. *The Tutenkhamun Prophecies* London: Headline, London, 1999.

Cowley, A. E. *Aramaic Papyri of the Fifth Century BC.* Oxford, 1923.

Crossan, John Dominic. *Jesus: A Revolutionary Biography.* San Francisco: HarperSanFrancisco, 1994.

Currer-Brigs, Noel. *The Shroud and the Grail.* London: Weidenfeld and Nicholson, 1987.

Dafoe, Stephen and Alan Butler. *The Warriors and the Bankers.* Ontario: Templar Books, 1998.

Davis, T. *The Tomb of Iouiya and Touiya.* London, 1907.

Dawkins, Peter. *Arcadia.* Tysoe, Warwick, UK: The Francis Bacon Research Trust, 1988.

De Chardin, Pierre Teilhard. *L'Avenir de l'Homme.* Paris: Editions de Seuil, 1959.

————. *The Phenomenon of Man.* New York: Wm Collins, 1959.

De Clari, Robert. *The Conquest of Constantinople.* E. H. Neal, trans. Toronto: University of Toronto, 1997.

Delaporte, Y. *Les Trois Notre Dames de Chartres.* Chartres, France: E. Houvet, n.d.

De Lubicz, Rene Schwaller. *Sacred Science.* Rochester, VT: Inner Traditions International, 1988.

De Rosa, Peter. *Vicars of Christ.* London: Corgi, 1989.

De Vries, Simon. *Cathars, Country, Customs and Castles.* N. p.: Comtal Press, 1993.

Denton, William. *The Soul of Things.* New York: Sterling, 1988.

Desgris, Alain. *L'Ordre de Templiers et la Chevalerie Macconique Templière.* Paris: Guy Trédaniel, 1995.

D'Olivet, A. F. *La Langue Hebraique Restitue.* Paris: L'Age d'Homme, 1991.

Doresse, Jean. *Ancient Cities and Temples of Ethiopia.* London: Elek Books, 1959.

————. *Les Livres Secrets des Gnostiques d'Egpte.* Paris: Librairie Plon, 1958.

Douglas, David C. *The Norman Achievement.* N.p.: Collins/Fontana, 1972.

Dowley, Tim, ed. *The History of Christianity.* Herts: Lion Publishing, 1977.

Dubos, Rene. *A God Within.* London: Abacus/Sphere, 1976.

Dunford, Barry. *The Holy Land of Scotland.* Aberfeldy, Perthshire, UK: Brigadoon Books, 1996.

Dunlop, Ian. *The Cathedrals Crusade.* London: Hammish Hamilton, 1982.

Edwards, I. E. S. *The Pyramids of Egypt.* London: Penguin, 1997.

Eisenman, Robert. *James the Brother of Jesus.* London: Faber and Faber, 1997.

————. *Maccabbeess, Zadokites, Christians and Qumran.* N. p.: E. J. Brill, 1983.

————. *The Dead Sea Scrolls and the First Christians.* Shaftsbury, UK: Element Books, 1996.

Eisenman, Robert and Michael Wise. *The Dead Sea Scrolls Uncovered.* Shaftsbury, UK: Element Books, 1992.

Elder, Isabel Hill. *Celt, Druid & Culdee.* London: Covenant Publishing Co. Ltd, 1994.

Ellis, Ralph. *Jesus: Last of the Pharaohs.* Dorset, UK: Edfu Books, 1999.

Elkington, David. *In the Name of the Gods.* Bath, UK: Green Man Press, 2001.

Eusabius. *Ecclesiastical History.* Available in most reference libraries.

Evans, Hilary. *Alternate States of Consciousness.* Wellingborough, UK: Aquarian Press, 1989.

Epstein, Isadore. *Judaism.* Harmondsworth, UK: SPenguin, 1964.

Faulkner, Robert. *The Ancient Egyptian Book of the Dead.* London: British Museum Press, 1972.

————. *The Ancient Egyptian Pyramid Texts.* Warminster: Aris & Philips, 1993.

Faulkner, Neil. *Apocalypse—The Great Jewish Revolt against Rome, AD 66–73.* Stroud, Gloucestershire, UK: Tempus Publishing Ltd, 2002.

Feather, R. *The Copper Scroll Decoded.* London: Thorsons, 1999.

Feild, Reshad. *The Alchemy of the Heart.* Shaftsbury, UK: Element Books, 1990.

————. *The Invisible Way.* Shaftsbury, UK: Element Books, 1992.

————. *The Last Barrier.* Great Barrington, MA: Lindisfarne Books.

Ferguson, Marilyn. *The Aquarian Conspiracy.* London: Paladin Books, 1982.

Fisher, H. A. L. *A History of Europe.* London: Edward Arnold & Co, 1936.

Fleming, Ursula, ed. *Meister Eckhart*. London: Collins, 1998.

Forbes-Leith, W. *The Scots Men-at-Arms and Life Guards in France*. Edinburgh, 1882.

Fortune, Dion. *Esoteric Orders and Their Work*. Wellingborough, UK: Aquarian Press, 1987.

Foss, Michael. *Chivalry*. London: Michael Joseph, 1975.

Fossier, Robert, ed. *The Middle Ages*, 3 vols. Cambridge: Cambridge University Press, 1989.

Fox, Mathew. *The Original Blessing*. Rochester, VT: Bear & Co., 1983.

———. *Creation Spirituality*. San Francisco: HarperSanFrancisco, 1991.

———. *The Coming of the Cosmic Christ*. San Francisco: HarperSanFrancisco, 1998.

Fox, Robin Lane. *Pagans and Christians*. London: Penguin, 1988.

———. *The Unauthorised Version: Truth and Fiction in the Bible*. London: Penguin, 1991.

Frager, Sheik Ragip. *Love Is the Wine: Talks of a Sufi Master in America*. Los Angeles: Philosophical Research Society, 1999.

Franke, Sylvia and Thomas Cawthorne. *The Tree of Life and the Holy Grail*. London: T. Lodge, 1996.

Frankfort, H. *Kingship and the Gods*. Chicago: University of Chicago Press, 1948.

Frazer, James. *The Golden Bough*. Ware, Dorset, UK: Wordsworth Editions, 1993.

Freud, Sigmund. *Moses and Monotheism*. Paris: Gallimard 1939.

Fulcanelli. *Le Mystère des Cathédrales*. Sudbury, UK: Neville Spearman, 1977.

———. *Les Demeures Philosophales*, 2 vols. Paris: Jean-Jaques Pauvert, 1964.

Gardner, Lawrence. *Bloodline of the Holy Grail*. Shaftsbury, UK: Element Books, 1995.

Gardner, Lawrence. *Genesis of the Grail Kings*. London: Bantam, 1999.

Garza-Valdes, Leonicio. *The DNA of God?* London: Hodder & Stoughton, 1998.

Gauthier, M. *Highways of the Faith*. Secaucus, NJ: Wellfleet, 1983.

Gedes Grosset. *Ancient Egypt Myth and History*. New Lanark: Geddes & Grosset Ltd., 1997.

Gettings, Fred. *The Secret Zodiac* London: Routledge, Keegan & Paul, 1987.

Gibbon, Edward. *The History of the Decline and Fall of the Roman Empire,* 8 vols. London: The Folio Society, 2001.

Gimpell, Jean. *The Cathedral Builders*. London: Cresset, 1988.

Glover, T. R. *The Conflict of Religions in the Early Roman Empire*. London: Methuen and Co., Ltd., 1909.

Godwin, Malcolm. *The Holy Grail*. London: Bloomsbury, 1994.

Golb, Norman. *Who Wrote the Dead Sea Scrolls?* New York: Simon & Schuster, 1996.

Goodwin, Godfrey. *Islamic Spain*. San Francisco: Chronicle Books, 1990.

Goyon, G. *Le Secret des Batisseurs des Grandes Pyramides: Kheops*. Paris: Pygmalion, 1991.

Graves, Robert. *The White Goddess*. London: Faber & Faber, 1961.

Graffin, Robert. *L'Art Templier des Cathédrales*. Chartres, France: Jean-Michel Garnier, 1993.

Gruber, Elmer R. and Holger Kersten. *The Original Jesus*. Shaftsbury, UK: Element Books, 1995.

Guébin & Moisoineuve. *Histoire Albigeoise de Pierre des Vaux-de-Cernay*. Paris, 1951.

Guillaume, Alfred. *Islam*. Edinburgh, UK: Penguin, 1956.

Guirdham, Arthur. *The Great Heresy*. Saffron Walden, UK: C. W. Daniel, 1993.

Halam, Elizabeth, ed. *The Chronicles of the Crusades*. Surrey, UK: Bramley Books, 1997.

Hamill, John and Gilbert. *World Freemasonry*. Wellingborough, UK: Aquarian Press, 1991.

Hamilton, B. *The Albigensian Crusade*. London: The Historical Association, 1974.

Hancock, Graham. *The Sign and the Seal*. London: Mandarin Paperbacks, 1993.

Hassnain, Fida. *A Search for the Historical Jesus*. Bath, UK: Gateway Books, 1994.

Hattstein, Marcus and Peter Delius, eds. *Islam Art & Architecture*. Cologne: Könemann, 2000.

Hay, Fr. *The Genealogie of the St. Clairs of Roslin*. Edinburgh: Maidement, 1865.

Hodgekin, T. *The Barbarian Invasion of the Roman Empire*, 3 vols. London: The Folio Society.

Holmes, George, ed. *The Oxford Illustrated History of Medieval Europe*. Oxford: Oxford University Press, n.d.

Isserlin, B. S. J. *The Israelites*. London: Thames & Hudson, 1998.

Jackson, Keith B. *Beyond the Craft*. Sheperton, Middlesex, UK: Lewis Masonic, 1982.

James, Bruno S. *St. Bernard of Clairvaux*. London: Hodder and Stoughton, 1957.

Jedin, Hubert, ed. *The History of the Church*, vol 1. Tunbridge, Well, UK: Burns and Oats, 1989.

Jennings, Hargrave. *The Rosicrucians: Their Rites and Mysteries*. London: Chatto & Windus, 1879.

Johnson, Paul. *A History of Christianity*. London: Weidenfeld and Nicolson, 1978.

———. *A History of the Jews*. London: Orion Books, 1993.

Johnson, Kenneth Rayner. *The Fulcanelli Phenomenon*. London: Neville Spearman, 1980.

Josephus. *The Antiquities of the Jews and The Wars of the Jews*. Edinburgh: Nimmo, 1869.

Kersten, H. and E. R. Gruber. *The Jesus Conspiracy*. Shaftsbury, UK: Element Books, 1994.

Koestler, Arthur. *The Sleepwalkers*. London: Hutchinson and Co., 1959.

Knight, Chris and Robert Lomas. *The Hiram Key*. London: Century, 1996.

———. *The Second Messiah*. London: Century, 1997.

Knoup, James. *The Genesis of Freemasonry*. Manchester: Manchester University Press, 1947.

Lacroix, P. *Military and Religious Life in the Middle Ages*. New York: Chapman & Hall, 1974.

Lea, Henry Charles. *The Inquisition in the Middle Ages*, 3. vols. New York, 1955.

Leroy Thierry. *Hughues de Payns, Chevalier Champenois, Fondateur de L'Ordre des Templiers*. N.p.: Editions de la Maison du Boulanger, 1997.

Levi, Eliphas. *The Key of The Mysteries*. London: Rider & Co., 1969.

Lionel, Frederic. *Mirrors of Truth*. Paris: Archedigm, 1991.

Lizerand, George. *Le Dossier de l'Affaire des Templiers*. Paris: Belles Lettres, 1989.

Lockhart, Douglas. *The Dark Side of God*. Shaftsbury, UK: Element Books, 1999.

The Lost Books of the Bible. New York: Gramercy Books, 1979.

Mack, Burton L. *The Lost Gospel*. Shaftsbury, UK: Element Books, 1993.

Macintosh, Christopher. *The Rosicrucians*. London: Crucible, Thorensons, 1987.

Mackenzie, Kenneth. *The Royal Masonic Cyclopedia*. Wellingborough, UK: Aquarian Press, 1987.

McManners, John, ed. *The Oxford History of Christianity*. Oxford: Oxford University Press, 1993.

Mâle, Émile. *Notre Dame de Chartres*. Paris: Flammarion, 1983.

Marcel, Gabriel. *The Decline of Wisdom*. N.p.: Philosophical Library, 1955.

Maspero, Gaston. *Recueil des Travaux Relatifs a la Philologie et l'Archaeologie Egyptiennes et Assyriennes, III*. Cairo: Institut d'Egypt, 1887.

Mathews, John. *The Grail Tradition*. Shaftsbury, UK: Element Books, 1990.

Matrasso, Pauline, trans. *The Quest of the Holy Grail*. London: Penguin Classics, 1977.

Mertz, Blanche. *Points of Cosmic Energy*. Saffron Walden, UK: C. W. Daniel, 1995.

H. R. H. Prince Michael of Albany. *The Forgotten Monarchy of Scotland*. Shaftsbury, UK: Element Books, 1998.

Midrash Bereshith Rabba (Genesis Rabba). Cambridge: Cambridge University Press, 1902.

Millar, Hamish and Paul Broadhurst. *The Sun and the Serpent*. Launceston, UK: Pendragon Press, 1994.

Miller, Malcolm. *Chartres Cathedral*. Andover, UK: Pitkin Pictorials, 1992.

Mitchell, Ann. *Cathedrals of Europe*. London: Hamlyn, 1996.

Mountfield, David. *Les Grandes Cathédrales*. Paris: Editions PML, 1995.

Moore, L. David. *The Christian Conspiracy*. Atlanta, GA: Pendulum Press, 1983.

Moore, R. I. *The Formation of a Persecuting Society*. Oxford: Basil Blackwell & Co., 1990.

Murphy, Roald. *Wisdom Literature*. Grand Rapids, Michigan, 1981.

Nicholson, Helen. *The Knights Templar*. Woodbridge, Suffolk, UK: The Boydell Press, 2001.

Nieuwbarn, M. C. *Church Symbolism*. London: Sands and Co., 1910.

Oldenbourg, Zoé. *Massacre at Montségur*. London: Phoenix/Orion Books, 1999.

Orton, Previte. *Outlines of Medieval History*. Cambridge: Cambridge University Press, 1916.

O'Shea, Stephen. *The Perfect Heresy*. London: Profile Books Ltd., 2000.

Osman, Ahmed. *Moses: Pharaoh of Egypt*. London: Paladin, 1991.

———. *Out of Egypt*. London: Century, 1998.

———. *Stranger in the Valley of the Kings*. London: HarperCollins, 1988.

Ouspensky, P. D. *A New Model of the Universe*. London: Arkana, 1931.

Parfitt, Will. *The Living Quaballah*. Shaftsbury, UK: Element Books, 1988.

Partner, Peter. *The Knights Templar and their Myth*. Rochester, VT: Destiny Books, 1990.

Pauwels, Louis and Jacques Bergier. *The Dawn of Magic*. London: Panther, 1963.

Petrie, F. *The Religion of Ancient Egypt*. London: Constable, 1908.

Philips, Graham. *The Moses Legacy*. London: Sidgewick & Jackson, 2002.

Picknet, Lynn and Clive Prince. *Turin Shroud: In Whose Image?* London: Bloomsbury, 1994.

———. *The Templar Revelation*. London: Bantam, 1997.

Powell, Mark Allen. *The Jesus Debate*. Oxford: Lion Publishing, 1998.

Proclus Diodachus. *Commentaries on the Timaeus*. Available at most reference libraries.

Querido, René. *The Golden Age of Chartres*. Edinburgh: Floris Books,1987.

———. *The Masters of Chartres*. Edinburgh: Floris Books, 1987.

———. *The Mystery of the Holy Grail*.Vancouver: Rudolf Steiner Publications, 1991.

Rachi. *Pentatuque selon Rachi, La Genese*. Paris: Samuel et Odette Levy, 1993.

———. *Pentatuque selon Rachi l'Exode*. Paris: Samuel et Odette Levy 1993.

Ramtha. *A Beginner's Guide to Creating Reality:An Introduction to Ramtha and His Teachings*. Yelm,WA: JZK Publishing, 2001.

Ranke-Heninemann, Ute. *Putting Away Childish Things*. San Francisco, HarperSanFrancisco, 1995.

Ravenscroft,Trevor. *The Cup of Destiny*.York Beach, ME: Samuel Weiser, 1982.

———. *The Spear of Destiny*.York Beach, ME: Samuel Weiser, 1982.

Ravenscroft,Trevor and Tim Wallace-Murphy. *The Mark of the Beast*. London: Sphere Books, 1990.

Regan, Geoffrey. *Lionharts, Saladin and Richard I*. London: Constable, 1998.

Regne, J. *Étude sur la Condition des Juifs de Narbonne*. Marseilles: Lafitte Reprints, 1981.

Reymond, E.A. E. *The Mythical Origin of the Egyptian Temple*. Manchester: Manchester University Press, 1969.

Reznikov, Raymonde. *Cathars et Templiers*. Portet-sur-Garonne, France: Editions Loubatières, 1993.

Rice, M. *Egypt's Making:The Origins of Ancient Egypt 5000–2000 BC*. London: Routledge, 1991.

Richards, Mary C. *The Crossing Point*. New Haven, CT:Wesleyan University Press, 1973.

Richardson, Peter. *Herod: King of the Jews and Friend of the Romans*. Columbia, SC: University of South Carolina Press, 1996.

Robertson, Roland. *Sociology of Religion*. London: Penguin Books, 1969.

Robinson, James M., ed. *The Nag-Hammadi Library*. London: HarperCollins, 1990.

Robinson, John J. *Born in Blood*. London:Arrow Books, 1993.

———. *Dungeon, Fire and Sword*. London: Brockhampton Press, 1999.

———. *The Priority of John* London: SCM Press, 1985.

Rohl, David M. *A Test of Time*. London: Century, 1995.

Roszak,Theodore. *The Making of a Counter-Culture*. London: Faber & Faber, 1971.

———. *Unfinished Animal -The Aquarian Frontier and the Evolution of Consciousness*. London: Faber & Faber, 1976.

———. *Where the Wasteland Ends: Politics and Transcendence in Post industrial Society*. New York: Doubleday, 1978.

Roth, Cecil. *A Short History of the Jewish People*. London: East West Library, 1953.

Runciman, Stephen. *A History of the Crusades*, 3 vols. Harmondsworth, Middlesex, UK: Pelican, 1971.

Russel, Bertrand. *The Wisdom of the West*. London: Macdonald, 1959.

Sabbah, M. and R. *Les Secrets de L'Exode*. Paris: Godefroy, 2000.

Saige, G. *Les Juifs du Languedoc*. Farnborough, UK: Gregg International, 1971.

Schonfield, Hugh. *The Essene Odyssey*. Shaftsbury, UK: Element Books, 1985.

———. *The Passover Plot*. Shaftsbury, UK: Element Books, 1985.

———. *The Pentecost Revolution*. Shaftsbury, UK: Element Books, 1985.

Serrus, Georges. *The Land of the Cathars*. Portet-sur-Garonne: Editions Loubatières, 1990.

Shah, Idries. *The Way of the Sufi* London: Penguin Books, 1982.

———. *The Sufis*. London: Jonathan Cape & Co., 1969.

Sinclair, Andrew. *The Discovery of the Grail*. London: Century, 1998.

———. *The Sword and the Grail*. New York: Crown Publishers, 1992

Sizekely, E. B. *Essene Teaching from Enoch to the Dead Sea Scrolls*. Saffron Walden, UK: C. W. Daniel,

Smith, Morton. *The Secret Gospel*. Wellingborough, UK: Aquarian Press, 1985.

Sox, David. *The File on the Shroud*. London: Coronet, 1978.

St. Clair L-A de. *Histoire Genealogique de la Famille de St Clair*. Paris, 1905.

Starbird, Margaret. *The Tarot Trumps and the Holy Grail*. Lakewood, WA: Woven Word Press, 2000.

———. *The Woman with the Alabaster Jar*. Rochester, VT: Bear & Co. 1993.

Stevenson, David. *The First Freemasons*. Aberdeen: Aberdeen University Press, 1989.

Stourm. *Notre Dame d'Amiens*. Paris: Hachette, 1960.

Stoyanov, Yuri. *The Hidden Tradition in Europe*. London: Arkana, 1994.

Strachan, Gordon *Chartres*. Edinburgh: Floris Books, 2003.

Swan, James A. *The Power of Place*. Wheaton, IL: Quest Books, 1991.

Taylor, Joan E. *The Immerser: John the Baptist in Second Temple Judaism*. Cambridge: Wm. B. Eerdmans Publishing Co, 1997.

Thiering, Barbara. *Jesus the Man*. London: Corgi, 1992.

Thurston, Herbert, trans. *Memorandum of P. D'Arcis*. No ascertainable information.

Trevor-Roper, Hugh. *The Rise of Christian Europe*. London: Thames and Hudson, 1965.

Uhlein, Gabriel. *Meditations with Hildegarde of Bingen*. Rochester, VT: Bear & Co., 1982.

Upton-Ward, J. M. *The Rule of the Templars*. Woodbridge, Suffolk, UK: Boydell Press, 1992.

Vanden Broeck, Andre. *Al-Kemi*. New York: Lindisfarne Press, 1987.

Vermes, Geza. *Jesus the Jew*. London: HarperCollins, 1973.

Waite, A. E. *The Holy Kabbalah*. London: Oracle, 1996.

Wakefield, Walter and Austin P. Evans. *Heresies of Middle Ages*. New York: Columbia University Press, 1991.

Wallace-Murphy, Tim. *An Illustrated Guidebook to Rosslyn Chapel*. London: Friends of Rosslyn, 1993.

———. *The Templar Legacy and the Masonic Inheritance within Rosslyn Chapel*. London: Friends of Rosslyn, 1994.

Wallace-Murphy, Tim and Marilyn Hopkins. *Rosslyn: Guardian of the Secrets of the Holy Grail*. Shaftsbury, UK: Element Books, 1999.

Wallace-Murphy, Tim, Marilyn Hopkins, and G. Simmans. *Rex Deus*. Shaftsbury, UK: Element Books, 2000.

Wakefield & Evans. *Heresies of the Middle Ages.* New York: Columbia University Press, 1991

Ward, Colin. *Chartres: The Making of a Miracle.* London: Folio Society, 1986.

Ward, J. S. M. *Freemasonry and the Ancient Gods.* London: Simkin, Marshall, Hamilton, Kent & Co., 1921.

Weighall, A. E. P. *The Life and Times of Akenhaten.* New York: Cooper Square Publishers, 2000.

———. *Travels in the Upper Egyptian Desert.* London, 1909.

Welburn, Andrew. *The Beginings of Chrsitianity.* Edinburgh: Floris, 1991.

West, John A. *Serpent in the Sky.* Wheaton, IL: Quest Book, 1993.

Wilcox, Robert K. *Shroud.* London: Bantam, 1978.

Wilson, A. N. *From Atlantis to the Sphinx.* London: Virgin Books, 1997.

———. *Jesus.* London: HarperCollins, 1993.

———. ed. *Men of Mystery.* London: W. H. Allen, 1977.

———. *The Occult.* London: Grafton Books, 1979.

———. *Paul, the Mind of the Apostle.* London: Pimlico, 1998.

Wilson, Ian. *The Blood on the Shroud.* London: Weidenfeld & Nicolson, 1998.

———. *The Turin Shroud.* Weidenfeld & Nicolson, 1998.

Winkler, H. *Rock Drawings of Southern Upper Egypt.* Oxford: Oxford University Press, 1938.

Woods, Richard. *Understanding Mysticism.* New York: Doubleday/Image, 1980.

Wright, Esmond. *The Medieval and Renaissance World.* London: Hamlyn, 1979.

Zuckerman, A. J. *A Jewish Princedom in Feudal France 768–900.* New York: Columbia University Press, 1972.

INDEX

ABOUT THE AUTHORS

Tim Wallace-Murphy studied medicine at University College, Dublin before going on to qualify as a psychologist. He has served his local community as a Governor of the local technical college and as a member of the Careers Advisory Service, the Totnes Town Council and, for over sixteen years, the Torbay and District Community Health Council, a body responsibile for monitoring the quality of health care throughout the district.

Tim is a lecturer and author with an international reputation and his work has been translated into many European languages. He has lectured in the United States, the United Kingdom, France, and Italy and was the driving force behind the foundation of the European Templar Heritage Research Network, which links scholars from all over the continent. He also organized the seminar "Who Was Jesus?" held at Dartington Hall near Totnes in 2003 and he acts as a tour guide around many of the major sacred sites in France. He is the author of *The Mark of the Beast* with Trevor Ravenscroft, *An Illustrated Guidebook to Rosslyn Chapel*, *The Templar Heritage and Masonic Inheritance within Rosslyn Chapel*, *Rosslyn: Guardian of the Secrets of the Holy Grail* with Marilyn Hopkins, *Rex Deus: The True Mystery of Rennes-le-Chateau* with Marilyn Hopkins and Graham Simmans, and *Templars in America* with Marilyn Hopkins.

Marilyn Hopkins has been studying ancient and medieval history and esoteric spirituality for nine years, although her interest spans the past twenty years. She has contributed to seminars, talks, and lectures on subjects that include the Knights Templar, Rennes-le-Chateau, the Rosslyn Chapel, Western esoteric spirituality, and early voyages to America. She coauthored *Rosslyn: Guardian of the Secrets of the Holy Grail* and *Templars in America* both with Tim Wallace-Murphy, and *Rex Deus: The True Mystery of Rennes-le-Chateau* with Tim Wallace-Murphy and Graham Simmans. She is a shamanic practitioner, a spiritual healer, a natural dowser, and a practitioner in Indian head massage.

TO OUR READERS

Weiser Books, an imprint of Red Wheel/Weiser, publishes books across the entire spectrum of occult and esoteric subjects. Our mission is to publish quality books that will make a difference in people's lives without advocating any one particular path or field of study. We value the integrity, originality, and depth of knowledge of our authors.

Our readers are our most important resource, and we appreciate your input, suggestions, and ideas about what you would like to see published. Please feel free to contact us, to request our latest book catalog, or to be added to our mailing list.

Red Wheel/Weiser, LLC
P.O. Box 612
York Beach, ME 03910-0612
www.redwheelweiser.com